BULGARIA

GREECE

İstanbul

Sea of Marmara

The Süleymaniye Mosque
1550-7, İstanbul

Bursa

Söğüt

Ankara

Eskişehir

Gordium

Polatlı

Seyitgazi

Sivrihisar

Aegean

Sea

TURKEY

İzmir

Ephesus

Konya

Kapikiri

Heraclia

Bodrum

Antalya

KOS
ISLAND

Alanya

Anatolia:
A Search
for a Place

Mediterranean Sea

CYPRUS

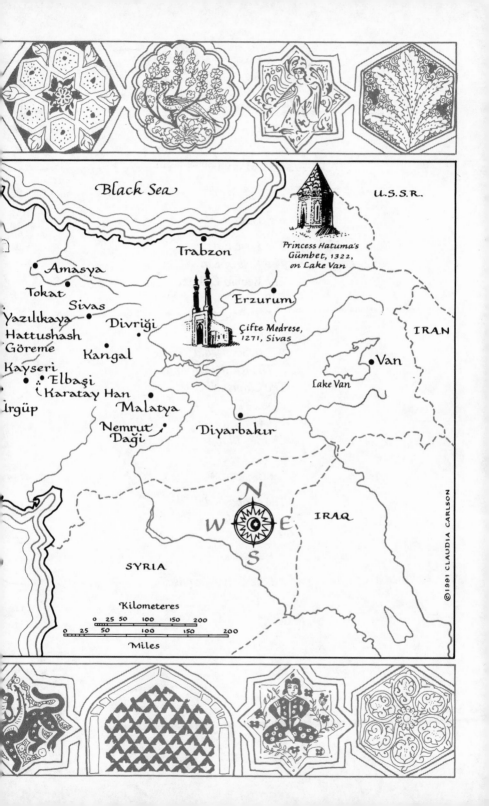

Black Sea

U.S.S.R.

Trabzon

Princess Hatuma's
Gümbet, 1322,
on Lake Van

Amasya

Tokat

Sivas

Erzurum

IRAN

Yazılıkaya

Divriği

Çifte Medrese,
1271, Sivas

Hattushash

Göreme

Kangal

Van

Kayseri

Lake Van

Elbaşi

Karatay Han

Malatya

Ürgüp

Nemrut
Dağı

Diyarbakır

IRAQ

SYRIA

© 1991 CLAUDIA CARLSON

Kilometeres

0 25 50   100   150   200

0 25   50   100   150   200

Miles

TURKISH REFLECTIONS

A BIOGRAPHY OF A PLACE

MARY LEE SETTLE

INTRODUCTION BY JAN MORRIS

A TOUCHSTONE BOOK
Published by Simon & Schuster
New York   London   Toronto   Sydney   Tokyo   Singapore

TOUCHSTONE
Simon & Schuster Building
Rockefeller Center
1230 Avenue of the Americas
New York, New York 10020

Copyright © 1991 by Mary Lee Settle
Map Copyright © 1991 by Claudia Carlson

First Touchstone Edition 1992
TOUCHSTONE and colophon are registered trademarks of
Simon & Schuster Inc.
Manufactured in the United States of America

5   7   9   10   8   6   4

Library of Congress Cataloging-in-Publication Data is
available.

ISBN: 0-671-77997-4

CONTENTS

INTRODUCTION
BY JAN MORRIS

NEITHER QUITE THIS nor altogether that, terrifically itself yet perpetually ambiguous, Turkey stands alone among the nations. For centuries it was the terror of Christianity; for generations it was the Sick Man of Europe; today it stands formidably on the edge of Asia surrounded in the universal mind, as always, by an aura of mingled respect, resentment, and fear. The assaults of tourism have not much weakened this daunting national personality. The echoes of historical quarrels, old and new, still swirl around the name of Turkey: the accusations of Greeks, the recriminations of Armenians, the clash between a secular state and a reviving Islam. One treads carefully in the Turkish presence. Turkey is no joke.

In this book Mary Lee Settle, though she certainly does not shirk these tough circumstances, brings to life the Turkey behind the reputation. She first went to the country as a refugee, and the theme of her narrative is one of communal kindnesses tempered, strengthened, and molded by an immensely long and complicated history. Searching both physically and spiritually for the roots of the Turkish identity, she finds everywhere along the way a manner of thought (rather than a manner of life), which seems to have remained immemorially constant; and this sense of human continuity makes the book far more than a travel book, giving it many of the classic qualities of the novel.

This is scarcely surprising. It was as a distinguished novelist that

INTRODUCTION

Mary Lee Settle was originally associated with Turkey—her greatly admired *Blood Tie* was set in that country—and in the 1970s she spent three years at Bodrum, on the southern coast. In a way her return to write this book is a search for the origins of the happiness she found then, a widening of her interest and intimacy from the first foothold long ago to the whole of the country and its history: to İstanbul, Trabzon, Ankara, and the troglodyte cities of Cappadocia; to the lost kingdom of Urartu; to the territories of the Seljuks and their illustrious Aladdin-Keykubad. A country, as she quotes from Nazım Hikmet in the epigraph, "Coming full gallop from far-off Asia."

It is a panoramic view of the place, yet readers may find that the book's most compelling passages deal not with kingdoms, faiths, or magnificent ruins but with immediate details and events, seen with a novelist's fructifying and serendipitous eye. A pregnant goat stands in the stern of a boat, "its horned head high." A woman observes that it had hardly been worth sleeping the night before, because her dreams bored her. A fisherman tangling his line pretends, as fishermen do the world over, that nothing has happened. Foppish men in a cafe watch soccer from a television set mounted high in a tree. A sheepdog in a spiked collar throws itself furiously upon a Mercedes. An overloaded boat sinks very slowly into Lake Van. An old man dies with perfect dignity in his seat on an airplane. Almost at the end of the book Ms. Settle finds herself high above the ancient city of Ephesus, being shown around the lonely remains of a Greek villa by a deaf mute sprung, so it seems, from the very soil itself: a sweet and silent genius of the place, living "like Caliban in a ruin."

It is demeaning, I think, to categorize this kind of art as travel writing. Ms. Settle could experience such insights anywhere, encounter such characters in her own imagination at home in Virginia, but the fact that her reflections are set against the fascination of Turkish life, against the mighty gallop of its history, is at once an intellectual enrichment and a grand artistic bonus.

PREFACE
A CIRCLE IN TIME

N 1972, I WENT to Turkey for the first time. I went because it was warm, it was cheap, and I needed a refuge. I was in the middle of writing a book, and to go there was simply an act of getting on a ferry across a little stretch of the Aegean Sea.

I knew next to nothing about it, and what I knew was not good. What I did not know then is that the country of Turkey has the worst and most ill-drawn public image of almost any country I know.

Bodrum, where I went first to visit, and stayed to live for three years, is built over the ruins of the ancient city of Halicarnassus. It was then a small town. The people there made their livings by fishing, by sponge diving, and by the influx of mostly Turkish people on their summer vacations in July and August. The rest of the time it was quiet, gentle, a dignified place of dignified people.

I found there the greatest capacity for friendship I have ever known. It was in the genes and in the past of the Turkish people, so deep and so beyond individual choice that I have wondered ever since about its sources.

This discovery was only one of the surprises—there is pride, and dignity, and honesty, and the dangerous sensitivity of essentially warm and honest people who, when they feel that their friendship has been offered and betrayed, can erupt into violence, which seems to be all that has been exported of the Turkish ethos.

PREFACE

In 1974 I left Bodrum and some of the closest friends I had ever made. I came back to a Eurocentric culture where Turkey is still an unknown country, or if it is known by those who have never been there and never known Turkish people, it is known only for its mistakes and its brutalities. The Turks I saw in *Lawrence of Arabia* and *Midnight Express* were ogrelike cartoon caricatures compared to the people I had known and lived among for three of the happiest years of my life.

Anatolia has been the home of cities and civilized states since the seventh millenium B.C., but the country of Turkey, on the same land, is one of the newer states formed after World War I. Before the First World War there was no nation of Turkey. It was part of the Ottoman Empire, which had once stretched from the Balkans to Egypt and beyond. The word *Turk* was the generic term for the majority of people who lived in that part of the Ottoman Empire that for centuries has been called Asia Minor on its coast, and Anatolia in the great high saddle of its interior.

The Ottoman Empire had been decimated by the war. It had sided with the defeated Germans, and had barely survived the invasion of the Russians and a terrible civil war on the eastern border of Anatolia. It seemed to be on its knees and ready for Allied picking by 1919.

The plan was to back and arm a Greek invasion to capture the coastal areas of Anatolia for Greece, and to divide the rest into "spheres of influence" between the French and the English, with the Italian government taking over the Dodecanese islands. After the two-year War of Independence, when a ragtag army formed in the defeated east, and led by Mustafa Kemal Atatürk, pushed the Greek army back into the Aegean Sea in 1922, Turkey was formed into a fledgling nation.

Turkey, like any adolescent nation, is still trying to find an "identity"—as our revolutionary ancestors must have tried for years after we became a nation such a short time ago.

Even the demotic language of the Anatolian Turks was not the language of the ruling and educated class, who, before the First World War, spoke an ornate mixture of Turkish, Persian, and Arabic known as Osmanlica.

İsmet İnönü, who was Atatürk's right-hand man, got up in the new Parliament after the War of Independence and made a speech in words that few could follow. At the end he said, in Osmanlica, "Gentlemen, I have been speaking Turkish, the language of your country." It was the beginning of an official language as new and as old as the land, so old that it is easier for a student to read fifteenth-century Turkish poetry than it is to read the Divan poetry of the court of the Sultans written as late as 1910.

Anatolia was also the home of some of the oldest civilizations in the world, kingdoms built on kingdoms like the strata of geological time. Noah landed on one of its highest mountains, Ararat. Çatal Höyük is a central Anatolian city eight thousand years old. The Hittite Empire predated the Greek city-states along the coast by more than a thousand years. It was the major power in the center of Anatolia when Troy was besieged by provincial tribesmen from the mainland of Greece. In the second millenium the Greeks began the colonies along the Aegean coast that would become their city-states. Alexander the Great conquered it, Persia ruled it, the Romans stabilized it for fifteen hundred years, and then lost it.

In A.D. 330, the Roman Emperor Constantine the Great moved the capital of the Roman Empire from Rome to the small seaport of Byzantium, on the Bosporus between Asia and Europe, rebuilt it, and renamed it New Rome. It was known almost at once all over the Roman world as Constantinople. His empire was not thought of by its own citizens, or by its contemporary enemies for the eight hundred years of its survival, as anything but Rome; but through the years historians, for convenience, have called it by the name we know now—the Byzantine Empire.

By the sixth century, Turkish tribes had begun to cross the mountains from the semideserts of central Asia, invited as mercenaries in the pay of the Byzantine emperor. They were nomadic tribes; even up to the time of the great invasions of the tenth century, they looked like Orientals.

When they came through the passes of the Caucasus Mountains, they were followed by their families and their flocks, and protected by their fine horsemen. Their pay as mercenaries was often land, so that when, in the eleventh century, tribe after tribe of Turkish people gushed forth into Anatolia, they found that their own people had long been there, had intermarried with the native people, and no longer looked like them. They were beginning to look like the modern Turks, a mixture of the Asian tribes and the indigenous people.

The eleventh century brought the greatest change there had been for a thousand years on the plains that rose behind the Aegean coastal mountains. Anatolia had been Christian ever since Christianity had been made the state religion by the Emperor Constantine in the fourth century. With the conquering of the Byzantine army by the Seljuks, Christianity was replaced by Islam, a new and far more tolerant religion after the schismatic and heretical wars of the Christians.

It was on "the dreadful day," as the Byzantines called it, Friday, 19 August 1071, at the battle of Manzikert that the Seljuk Turks, newly converted to Islam, broke the power of the Byzantine Empire. After Manzikert, the popes and the clergy inflamed the religious and the adventurous impulse in Europe, and, led by itinerant monks and mercenaries, the First Crusade met the Seljuks and was defeated by them. It was in the years of the Crusades, when an infidel enemy was needed to rouse Christian passions, that there began the Eurocentric misunderstanding of the Turks. They have been partly unknown ever since.

In the thirteenth century the Mongols began their slow and inexorable invasion of Anatolia, and the face of the high land changed again, and again and again, as the Seljuk kingdom broke apart under family feuds and Mongol onslaughts.

There was the Black Plague and the country nearly died, and what came out of it, in the fourteenth century, was a line of *ghazis* that ruled a broken land of quarreling emirates. One of the emirates was that of the tribe of the Osmanlı, and it grew into the Ottoman Empire, to last another six hundred years.

A *ghazi* is classically an Islamic fighter against the infidel, but it has come to mean, in Turkish, the honorable name for a hero, a survivor of war, a leader. Turkey has always been a land ruled by *ghazis, aslans,* lions, those soldiers who represented to the Turkish people what they thought and hoped they stood for themselves. To tap that archetype of the *ghazi* within them was always to gather them together, as did the Seljuks of Alp Arslan in the eleventh century, Aladdin Keykubad I in the thirteenth century, Mehmet the Conqueror in the fifteenth century, or Süleyman the Law Giver in the sixteenth. In all of them there was a mixture peculiar to Turkey of artist, artisan, administrator, and war hero.

Then in the twentieth century came the latest *ghazi* who has appeared, who was able to defeat the British and Australian forces at Gallipoli, go east almost to the Russian border, come back with an army of survivors of civil war and Ottoman neglect that had been defeated by the Allies, and force the retreat of the European-backed Greeks from central Anatolia near Ankara, all the way back to the Aegean Sea.

In many ways the last has been, maybe because we have been able to see him at work, the most astounding of Turkey's *ghazis*. The presence of Mustafa Kemal Atatürk, which means "the Father of the Turks," still permeates Turkey, long after his death in 1938.

Here is what *The Cambridge History of Islam* says about Atatürk: "He was a strong man, a ruler by the virtue of his training, but not a dictator. He detested the title and continuously stressed his allegiance to national sovereignty. Atatürk was a soldier-ruler and as such had a keen understanding of the virtues and defects of his people. Unlike the Ottoman ruling class, he used his insight for the people's own good. In so doing he did not beg for popularity, but ordered, punished, and rewarded with the habit of a soldier used to obedience. But beneath the determined appearance there was a man, the orphan who was raised in the healthy, human atmosphere of the village, and then the small Balkan town of Salonica. He preserved a freshness and spontaneity towards life even after he became the most powerful man in Turkey." That could, in essence, be a description of the *ghazi* over a thousand years.

For seventy years, the Turks have been in love with Atatürk. When he died, and his place was taken as president by the less-charismatic İsmet İnönü, a woman in İstanbul mourned, "Turkey has lost her lover and now must make do with her husband."

Atatürk had a deep understanding and love for the Turks in return. He knew their ability to survive, their patience, and, above all, their pride. There is a story that when he was entertaining the Prince of Wales at a state dinner, one of the waiters dropped soup on the royal guest. Atatürk said, "I have been able to do almost everything with the Turks but make servants out of them."

It is this deep genetic seeking for a figure who is lover, father, conqueror, *ghazi,* that modern-thinking Turks fear most, the fear that the wrong man will rise to capture the animus of the people as a lover so often does.

More than any other people I have seen, the Turks are up against the heavy weight of time. The past is so powerful that it is easy to lose yourself in it and forget the strong present that contains and defines it. The people of Turkey have in themselves, in their habits, their beliefs, and their pride, all the kingdoms that have gone before them—all the blood, the grace and the toughness, sometimes the cruelty, always the warm hospitality that touches and surprises Americans who go there for the first time. It seems to be a deeper tolerance and ecumenical quality than we have ever learned to have.

They live in a land leeched by their ancestors. Maybe this is why they value and care for gardens, and why the cutting of a tree, even on your own land, is a crime in Turkey today. A Turkish friend said to me, "We can understand a man killing a man. There can be many reasons for that. But to cut down a tree, any tree, is to cut the life of all the people." All along the roads of Turkey, I saw soldiers, the young village boys who must spend two years in the Turkish army, in the back of lorries. They were being taken to plant trees. It is one of the main jobs of the conscripts. That love of plants was a part of our kinship, what I called in a novel our blood tie.

But there was more—a daily way of looking at things, not only friendship but pride and violence. Ever since I left there I have missed the daily warmth and welcome that I experienced over and over, every day. I have missed the capacity for lapidary gossip, the language that even has a verb tense for rumor and innuendo, the whole underground anarchic way of dealing with life as if the government, whatever its political affiliation, was taken for granted as the enemy. I simply felt at home.

Most Turks, even those who live on the coast, come from a background of people who live more than a mile above sea level. They have learned, by necessity, to be fighters. It is a well-known political maxim that it is impossible to govern any people who live at an altitude above five thousand feet. The sheer harsh habits of survival and having to be self-sufficient may make this true. And, even deeper in their pride, the Ottoman Empire may have been conquered, but never the Turks.

I know now that a great part of my growing affection and sense of familiarity there is an understanding born of being a mountaineer myself, and of recognizing the kind of good manners I am used to, never servile, never calculated, the sincere hospitality of country people that is not given cynically.

It is, for me, an echo of Lord Chesterfield's idea of a gentleman: "Either be polite or knock him down." This has been called "Mandarin," in a time that decries "elitism." I think that this is false. It is the independence of people who have learned to shift for themselves. A Mandarin world needs servants, slaves, privilege to sustain it and this mountain pride is free of service or hierarchy.

Turkey is more than ruins, or armies, or even the great fawn-colored spaces of central Turkey, the mountains, the wild shades of green in the northeast. It is a cared-for plant in a window, a geranium as tall as a small tree and covered with red bloom against a white wall, the controlled tumble of a grapevine, the economics of food and shade together on a trellis above a table in a hidden courtyard, the pot of basil in the captain's cabin of a fishing boat. These, to me, tell more of Turkey, the place I knew day by day, than all the great buildings and all the history, even though these things, too, are hints of habits that seem to change without ever being rejected.

Turn off a main road, wander into a village, go to see an ancient ruin, and you are in another country, the one where people live as they have for so many thousands of years. They are not conscious of saving a culture. They are not resisting change. They are digesting it, as they always have. It is so slow that it is more like the erosive carving of rocks.

It is not that they are frozen in time, far from it. They simply have, from mother to daughter and father to son over the centuries, kept ways they have found useful. They belie our naive idea that when kingdoms replaced kingdoms, or ideas replaced ideas, they somehow wiped out the past. This did not happen—not in building and not in thought. They may have changed the old patterns, but they have not obliterated them.

I had a sense that when the new armies came, and the new conquerors rolled over Anatolia like great destructive storms, the people who had survived went on about their business as soon as the turmoil was over, and they were forgotten again. It is heart-lifting to see this among the ordinary people who live there generation after generation. It is a reminder in the twentieth century, when revolutionary and puritan governments try to blot out the past and change the symbols, that all of this has been tried before, and didn't succeed then. As each new belief, or conversion, or dynasty has come, the people who have had to live through these changes have never quite succumbed to them.

There are clues all over Turkey to this instinct for revival and survival. A street meanders where a path was. A wall is rebuilt where a house has fallen. A space is left that once was an *agora,* because it has always been an open space, not for logical reasons, but for the habit of conserving, of not crossing the unimaginable barriers of change.

The movement of a tide, of a rock, of the slowly trembling earth of this part of the world calls forth legends. Even the word *meander* comes from the winding Maeander, the river that flowed to Miletus, Priene,

Magnesia, and was fed in turn by the Marsyas River, named for the satyr Marsyas, who was flayed of his shaggy goat hide by the Amazon priestesses of Apollo for daring to compete against him in music. Change, in this countryside, is a metaphor. The legend of Marsyas may hide an ancient cult demanding human sacrifice, which may have been like the flaying of the victims of the Aztecs, and the memory of it survives under the surface of legend as the little Turkish villages stand on the ancient cities beneath them.

This is where I lived and where I was so happy. For sixteen years I did not go back.

In 1989, I returned to Turkey for the first time since I had left. I went to see how much of what I remembered with such a sense of loss was misted by nostalgia, to close the circle of so much time, both ancient and the short years of my own life.

But I went, too, to complete a circle of space as well as time. What I had known was only a little stretch of coast. I wanted to go all around the country, to question and learn and give the Turks a chance, which they have had so seldom, to speak for themselves.

I searched through tier upon tier of the past and stumbled on the present. I sought the present and fell among men of the past still so alive there that it is as if I had known them. The Assyrian Sennacherib, the King of the Universe, is still carried to war in a sedan chair, and is thirsty on a fearful mountain. Xenophon leads his hoplites across Anatolia in winter through six-foot drifts of snow. Aladdin Keykubad builds an empire and entertains his friends in a silk tent on a battlefield. Alexander moves a young army through the great plains. It is all, for me, a part of the present.

So I followed the concentric circles of a journey, first as an ignorant and pragmatic escape to an unknown country, then as a return, with a naive hope of finding what I had left behind, then in a great circle of space around Nazım Hikmet's horse's head of Anatolia.

This country shaped like the head of a mare
Coming full gallop from far-off Asia
To stretch into the Mediterranean
    This country is ours.

Bloody wrists, clenched teeth
    Bare feet,
Land like a precious silk carpet
This hell, this paradise is ours.

            —Nazım Hikmet

CHAPTER ONE

A VOYAGE ACROSS AN ANCIENT SEA

T BEGAN IN the spring, seventeen years ago, on the Greek island of Kos, one of the Dodecanese islands in the Aegean, about six miles from the Turkish coast.

I didn't go to Kos for the usual reason that romantics go to live on beautiful Greek islands. I went there because it was cheap, and it was warm, and I was writing a book about seventeenth-century England.

It seemed ideal. I had a tight budget so that I could survive there until I finished a first draft, but I had an even better reason: Writers, at least this one, want to live as far from what they are writing about as they can, so that there is a psychic distance to depend on, as a photographer will step back and back, adjust the focus, watch and wait. So I had backed away from the seventeenth to the twentieth century, from war-torn Cromwellian England to a Greek island.

Friends who lived there had written me about how beautiful Kos was. They were right. It was a spacious green island where the sea-wind blew. We walked among the ruins of the ancient city where Hippocrates was born, and sat by the ancient, gnarled tree where it was said that the Hippocratic oath had been taken by doctors through the centuries.

The mountains began their slope about two hundred yards from the side of my house, and in the morning I could hear a series of clicks that sounded like woodcutters working in the distance. When I went to find the source of the noise I found hundreds of turtles copulating in an ancient grove of olive trees, their shells clicking, and I realized that the voice of the turtle was not a mistranslation for the turtledove, but a fact of spring.

I walked the pine woods beyond the Aesculapion, the ruins of the pre-Christian Greek hospital spread out over the hillside where the patients were required to tell the doctors their dreams after they had slept their first night there. There is a fountain there that was thought to cure nervous ailments but could cause panic if you drank from it without believing in its powers. One of my friends saw a woman drink from it on a dare, and she fell into a fit on the ground.

Above the ruins was an old pine forest that had been planted so the patients could walk among the trees and be calmed by the scent of pine. I sat at the top of the hill beyond it and looked from a temple platform more primitive and older than the Aesculapion itself, all the way across to the Muslim mainland of Turkey in the distance. It seemed unreal behind the scrim of sea mist, a thousand psychic miles from Christian Kos. On clear nights we could see the shore lights of Bodrum, the nearest Turkish town on the coast six miles away, a faint hint of Asia in the dark.

I had been told about my house, which cost sixty dollars a month, and everything I had been told was true. There was indeed a small blue Greek chapel in the field behind me. I could walk for miles along the nearly dry river where the deserted Turkish houses still stood so long after the Turkish people had run from their Greek neighbors during the Turkish War of Independence in 1921–1922 when the Greeks, the French, and the British had tried to divide the mainland of Anatolia among themselves after World War I. Many Greeks in Anatolia and Turks in Greece and the islands were exchanged by treaty after the civil war, Turks who had lived for centuries on the islands, Greeks who had been on the coast of Asia Minor since the time of the city-states a thousand years B.C. The numbers are staggering, when you think in terms of human families—there were 1,377,000 Greeks, 410,000 Turks.

Those deserted houses had private courtyards where the trees had uprooted the paving stones. They were the first hint I had of the sense of privacy of the Turks. The Greeks on Kos lived close to each other along long streets that led sometimes through the Hellenistic ruins of the third century B.C. without ever having changed place or direction.

My house seemed a haven. It was white and neat and it had an indoor toilet. There was a private porch in the back where I could work, away from the constant screaming of the old Greek women.

I noticed one slightly ominous thing when I got there. There were steel shutters on the two windows and the door in the front of the house that faced the street, where only a small unroofed concrete porch had been built between the house and the dirt road.

What no one had bothered to tell me was that the two sides of the house where I did not face the mountain scene or look at the pretty Greek chapel abutted onto the worst Greek slum on Kos. It had been an Italian army barracks when the Dodecanese islands were Italian. When they had left, squatters had filled it. History, as it tends to do, was catching up with me.

We Americans go out into the rest of the world disarmed by our naiveté. How many times do we hear from our own travelers to antique lands, "They were nice to me," or "They were polite to me," said with some surprise. We do not have the Englishman's protective arrogance which would answer such a remark, "Why the devil shouldn't they be?"

So, unprotected, I walked along the roads and lanes of Kos, saying good morning in my pathetic Greek, and thinking in the spring sun that the world I had strayed into "liked" me because they smiled in the sun, and said good morning back.

Now the story becomes, as seems somehow right in that part of the world, biblical. I had made two friends. One, the friend of the Americans who had suggested I come there, was called Vangeli, which means the Evangelist. He was the physical education instructor at the *gymnasium* (the high school) and it had been Vangeli who rented the house for me from friends in Athens. He and his wife were from Athens and considered themselves exiled on Kos.

The other friend, because he spoke English with a mixed Greek and Australian accent, was Apostolos, the Apostle. He drove the taxi we used since he was the only taxi driver who spoke English.

Wild packs of adolescent boys were a menace on the island. They would run through the house of my neighbor, an old Greek widow, and pull her flowers up by the roots and throw them over the fence if she left the front door unlocked, while she stood and wailed with her black shawl over her eyes. But the boys smiled at me, and left me alone.

What I did not know was that Vangeli had told them that if they bothered the American lady he would punish them. What punishment he threatened I was never told; I only knew that they never bothered me. For nearly six weeks I lived there, working well, in blissful ignorance of whatever turmoil was below the surface of the island.

When the first ferry of spring went across the six miles of sea to Bodrum, I went to see it for the weekend. The town was a surprise and a delight. Still, disarmed by ignorance, I thought everybody liked me because they called me by my first name at once, making a rhyming pleasantry of it, "Marile, *nereye,*"—Mary Lee, where do you go to? I had not yet learned that Turks do not use their last names, and indeed they had not had them until Atatürk commanded it in 1925. They chose wonderful ones—spear, bullet, volcano, mountain, Genghis (after the Great Khan)—but mostly they were known by nicknames before their given names—Tetanus Mehmet because his parlor trick when he was drunk was to eat his glass, and once he had had to take a tetanus shot when he was cut; Harley Necdet because he drove a Harley-Davidson motorcycle; Little Mehmet who was more than six feet tall.

On the Greek Good Friday Vangeli and his wife left Kos by plane at eleven o'clock in the morning for Athens to have their little girl christened. I was walking back to my house from shopping for food in the *agora.* I had just looked at my watch and seen that it was noon, traditionally the hour when Christ was crucified, the most solemn moment for Christians in the year. I was conscious that I was nearer the Holy Land than I had ever been before. The first large stone hit me in the back. I ran to my house, with stones being thrown at me from behind, got into the door, locked it behind me. I crouched behind the steel shutters and looked out from the slits between them to see who had attacked me. It was, of course, the boy pack, having their fun because Vangeli had left the island.

I stayed crouched behind the shutter, watching them throw rocks, while the black-shawled women squatters from the army barracks stood like a row of crows, watching them.

I remember thinking, "If I stay cringing behind this shutter, something in me will cringe like this for the rest of my life." So somehow I got the courage to walk out onto the porch and face them. There is an international language of sorts. It is straight Anglo-Saxon swearing, and I did it. It stopped them, literally, so that they all seemed frozen in place, like a film that has been stopped at a frame.

I picked up the largest of several rocks that had landed on the porch, and threw it at the genitals of the lead boy, a boy of about eighteen. It missed and hit him in the stomach. Then they all ran, the women, too, and I was left there alone with tears of rage running down my face.

I walked down into the town again and found Apostolos. I told him to come and help me move out of the house and into a hotel, and that I was going back to Bodrum, Turkey.

I had decided on the way into the town that I didn't have enough money or time to move farther than the mainland, and that, like Peter Abelard, since the Christians had been nasty to me I would go and live among the infidels who called me by my first name.

I had to wait until Monday for the ferry, so I saw all of the celebration of Easter on the island, including the slitting of the throats of the lambs they had made pets of; the Saturday-night procession by the light of tall beeswax candles that flowed like a slow river of flickering light in the darkness through the town; the blessing from the church on Easter morning below my hotel window, where the boy I had hit with the rock held the cross at the head of the procession, dressed as an acolyte.

On Monday morning I took the ferry to Turkey, not from choice, not from a sense of adventure, but because some adolescent boys threw rocks at me. Turkey for me then was simply the nearest port in a storm. It was even cheaper. The people had seemed graceful and hospitable, although I was beginning not to trust my instincts about this.

Halfway across the six-mile stretch of water between Kos and the mainland, I began to be afraid. I saw myself as one of those middle-aged American women, embarrassingly gallant and alone, adrift in the Aegean. I realized that I had to throw off any naiveté that I had enjoyed, and get to the facts of life in a part of the world I hardly knew. But I did know a few things about the history of the Turks and the Greeks. I knew they hated each other, as only close family can. It gave me a clue to what I should say.

When the ferry moored at the Bodrum quay, I sprang ashore and threw my arms around the neck of the first Turk I recognized, the chief of police (there is a lot of hugging and formal kissing in Turkey).

"The Greeks were terrible to me," I said. "I have come for the protection of the Turks."

I was certain that they had not heard such a thing from a tourist for several hundred years, for the Turks have been the lords of the Aegean and they are still resented as overlords and conquerors. When what I had said got around, as I knew it would, they welcomed me as if I were their long-lost sister; called me by the honorific *abla,* elder sister; and gave me, while I lived there, one of the happiest homes I have ever had.

In the three years I lived in Bodrum I learned to know it in a way I could not have done in that first weekend and the new summer days that followed it. There was a shining surface of things that seems to have been lost under so much familiarity and memory, a sometimes erroneous buried first impression. So I will try to go back to when it was surprising for me, strange and unquestioned, as in first seeing a person who will be a lover or, even more profound a tie in Turkey, a friend.

CHAPTER
TWO

THE WILDER SHORES
OF ASIA

—WITH APOLOGIES TO LESLIE BLANCHE

REMEMBER SITTING THAT first day at the *kahve,* the outdoor cafe on the quay, surrounded by Turkish people speaking a language I knew not a word of, the sun hot then and heavy on my shoulders. I had a sudden chill of recognition that I was in Asia Minor, on the shore at last of a holy land where three great religions had helped to form me and everything I knew. It was as if energy came up through the hard, lived-over ground there, and I was afraid.

Away in the distance, around the white curve of the harbor road, I watched a slow measured procession of three camels. Their *havuts,* the huge pack-saddles, were red velvet with glittering gold embroidery. They were piled high with rugs and copper pots that caught the sun. It was a wedding party from the country, where the old ways, as they are every place in Turkey, are only a street, a few miles, a turn off the fine new roads. The camels walked slowly and sedately, catching the sun. I wondered then if the pace of a people is learned from their animals. Where the camel is the beast of burden, people walk more slowly.

Rising high behind the procession was tier upon tier of Asia. On the long curve of the harbor road white houses caught the sun. A few sleek modern yachts were moored in the yacht *limanı,* the harbor, alongside the Turkish *tirendals,* the Turkish sailing boats with their fat sterns and their fine woodwork. The boats seemed alive as they rode the breathing sea, and caught the sun on their polished brasses. Behind the harbor, on a hill that must have once been the acropolis when Halicarnassus was a Greek city-state and then a Persian satrapy, I could trace semicircles faintly marked by the sun, where the theater once used the hillside for the raking of its stone seats. Below it, on the harbor road, a slim, elegant, white minaret pierced the sky.

Off Kos, the sea had been turbulent in the early spring. On the voyage I had just taken, so tame on the sleek white diesel ferry, there were surface clues to read as clearly as a mariner would read the sea scud to foretell a rising storm. On the edges of that fought-over, envied, narrow stretch of sea, so much a battleground that its now and ancient name comes from *aegis,* a shield, the cliffs have heaved up so that their strata are at a forty-five-degree angle, the violence of earthquake frozen in their tilt.

The ferry crossed the six miles of deep dark blue, white-capped sea so far from both shores. Then it sailed into the lee of the peninsula that jutted out to our left into the Aegean. I could see primitive rock tombs, long since empty, cut into the cliffs. The color of the sea surface changed; even the surface waves changed. It became at last what has to be expected by anyone with any sense of the past: wine dark, deep purple, Homeric sea. It turned to blue and then light turquoise where the rocks thrust up near the sea ceiling, so clear that when I looked over the side, I could see underwater islands and the sea floor thirty meters below.

Those islands that had once been above the water line, where there were trees, and goats, and villas, had long since sunk to underwater ledges. The pale surface of an island three meters below the water was once a bastion, protecting the shore.

Later I would know that island as well as the islands on the surface. I would know where the ruined fragments of a house were on its surface, and I would dive down the thirty-meter-steep cliff that was its side toward the harbor. I would know where the huge octopus hid in a hole that seemed only large enough for one large, baleful, human-looking eye. I would swim after the Turkish lobsters without claws, like foot-long *langoustes* in heavy armor, scurrying along the sea floor, and the red turning to green flowers in crannies on the cliff wall, and sponges that were orange and yellow in a vertical underwater garden. But that day, I knew only that the water was pale over the hidden hazard, and that the ferry sailed between it and the left-hand shore.

In that six miles of sea change, we crossed the trade routes where for three millennia or more little ships, that could have been carried on the deck of the ferry, sailed near the shore and were drawn up onto the beaches at night, or in the early afternoon if they were going north toward Miletus or Ephesus or Smyrna, now İzmir. The afternoon wind, the *meltem,* acted as a barrier, as it still does, to small sailing ships.

On the old trade route, there were ships from Tarsus, from Egypt and Tyre and Sidon, carrying tin and bronze and gold from Ophir and murex from the Aegean islands to make the purple dye that stained the garments of royalty. They were loaded, too, with cedars of Lebanon and amphorae of wine for Troy and Hattushash and Colchis. Sometimes the ships were manned by pirates, sometimes refugees, sometimes the soldiers and the sailors of Odysseus.

On the weather side of the island of Gelidonya, where the currents crossed, the ships piled up, wrecked, and there, among the sea rack, laid down in layers of time along the ocean floor for centuries, George Bass, the underwater archaeologist, would find the earliest ship burial ever found in these waters. It was a four-thousand-year-old vessel that plied the same waters as the ships that took the Achaeans to Troy.

Later I would dive where the skeletons of ships that the sea had taken eons past left smudges the shape of boats in the sand of the sea floor, the litter of a few broken amphorae that told where they were from when the sea caught them.

As the ferry slowed down, the town began to grow in detail. There it was, Bodrum, overlaying the ancient city of Halicarnassus, where in 340 B.C. one of the seven wonders of the world stood above the harbor, the Mausoleum, where Mausolus, the king, was buried. It rose more than 140 feet high, a beacon to be seen far out to sea. His wife and sister, the second Artemesia, hired the finest sculptors in the Aegean region to carry out his orders. Now there is nothing to see but a foundation dug up in the last few years that shows its size, a hint of the megalomania of the widow of its tenant. There are hints of what it was like—fragments in the British Museum, a few marble plaques inlaid at the Bodrum castle, but for its shape, and its grace, there is a still-surviving perfect small copy in the city of Milas, a few miles inland, where the children play around it in a little park.

On the left, the ferry passed a broken stretch of beach, a trickle of a spring where there were women filling gallon olive-oil cans with water. It was once a fountain, named for the nymph, Salmakis, who fell in love with the son of Aphrodite and Hermes, and begged the gods to unite them forever. Their fusion created the Hermaphrodite. The spring is still called Salmakis fountain.

In the way that never changes, the ancient triangle of cities, Cnidus, across Gökova Bay from Halicarnassus; Kos, on the island; and Halicarnassus, vied for trade. The Carians of Halicarnassus spread the word to lure the sailors into their port that the water from Salmakis fountain would make them sexy, the Cnidians spread the word that it would make them impotent, and the people of Kos said it would give them syphilis. The temples to Hermes and Aphrodite, the parents, are long gone, downed by neglect or new belief or earthquake, all of which have left scars on these shores.

To the right, all the medieval legends, the knights-in-armor, the Crusades, the castles of childhood rose on a small mountain against the sky. It was the castle of Saint Peter, begun in 1402 by the Knights of Saint John, sometimes called the Knights Hospitalers. They came to Bodrum when they were defeated by Tamerlane and lost their castle at Smyrna. It is a stone memory dominating the sky above the town as it has for nearly six hundred years. It was only when, later in that first day, I climbed up to it, that I saw that much of it, too, was ruined and snaggled.

On either side as the ferry slid in beyond the breakwaters were the huge stone barriers built more than two thousand years ago when the town was a Carian city-state, now topped, because of sea rise, with modern concrete.

As we came into port we could see, below the water, the walls of the ancient harbor and, on the shore, a modern town, using, as they always have there, the old materials to make a new place. Nothing was wasted; the past was fused with the present in walls, on thresholds, in gardens. An old wall made to keep the animals penned in was held together by pre-Greek shards, and the street on the way to the buses, the pharmacy, the bank, crossed a sacred way paved over and forgotten.

In April the deceptively modern town of Bodrum was still Turkish; the legions of tourists had not yet invaded this place so used to invasions through the centuries. It was Friday, the day of the *pazar,* and the day for the conservative Muslim minority that went, officiously, to the mosque. There were the true faithful going past us, and there were the politically righteous, letting themselves be seen and counted.

At the *pazar,* women from the country in their head scarves and their *şalvar,* those wide comfortable Turkish trousers with that inherent sense of color the Turks have, mixed with booted, trousered women from the cities; elegant women, some so beautiful that it made me think of the seraglio and how their blood is the blood of many kingdoms, remembered in the faces of the handsome Turks, as the old kingdoms are overlaid by the new. Here you find the ice-blue eyes of the Circassian, there the tilted eyes of the Tatar.

Later, when I met some of these women, who spoke three languages easily at the dinner table, they made me feel, at first, as if I were still living in a tree with my rear end painted blue with woad. This feeling passed when I realized that in the Middle East a person could be stupid in several languages. I learned almost to read a Turk's age by the second language he or she spoke. The older Turks speak German, the middle-aged tend to speak French, and the young speak English, which tells something about the spread of influence in what are called, so mistakenly, third-world countries, as if these ancient places had sprung up like mushrooms on a vacant land after the Second World War.

The *pazar* stretched along the main square, with its tented booths to shade the vegetables, picked at dawn in the country gardens. The produce had been brought in by camel, by donkey, by the ever-present *dolmuş,* the jeep that could be stuffed so full of people that they called it by the same name as the stuffed grape leaves of the *dolma.* The Turks are natural gourmets; they pick their vegetables young so that the okra is the size of your little finger, and the tomatoes, scented by the warmth of the morning, are perfect for the day they are picked.

High wooden barrels of rice and beans, mounds of spices, orange and brown and green and astonishing red powders, spread their scents through the modern square. From the glass-fronted bank at one end of the square, past the hardware store, where plastic vied with old copper pots, at the other, the morning smelled like *The Arabian Nights Entertainments,* all warmed by the sun.

Across the main road, an open park overlay the buried remains of the palace of Mausolus. The *pazar* had spread over it—the clothes, pots and pans, all the wares of the peddlers. People from the country walked under the trees where the bougainvillea grew, between the stalls selling cheap cloth, clothes, and kitchen utensils. Above them the tamarisk trees danced, caught in the sea breeze.

After the frenetic pace of the island Greeks, the Turks were slow and stately, dignified. I sensed people of great pride. They trod on the palace grave, bargaining for head scarves and cheap sweaters and bolts of cloth and camel straps, or stood patiently at the tinsmith having heirloom copper kitchen pots retinned.

April is the month of *çiçekler,* the flowers. There are three quite classic spring storms in the Aegean, lasting, the sailors say, three days each, and they soften the hard earth left by eons of humans who have long since cut away most of the forests, or let their animals eat the hills arid. But in April the ground comes alive with color in the fields where once the forests came down to the water. Now what woods that remain are far behind the town, in the hills, in the defiles, where, as a feral hint, you can glimpse wild boars and bears still.

The hills around the town, for most of the year, had only patches of camel thorn and short hard meadow grass, except for this miraculous month, when the anemones in all their bright colors sprang up out of the dead ground, the asphodels, with a name out of poetry, waved like gray ghosts of flowers in the fields and in the hollows near water of the little creeks that would disappear later in the summer. Later, the beautiful wild pink oleanders would bloom, with their deceptive fingers of leaves and their poison sap that can kill when the foreigners who camp along the ridges use their branches by mistake to cook kebabs. But in April the campers had not come yet, and the grass grew thick around the flowers.

For the rest of the summer and into the late fall, color came from the domestic flowers and shrubs and herbs that Turkish people love and nurture: tree-size geraniums, heavily scented basil with tiny leaves that the fishermen and the captains of the charter boats put in their cabins for good luck at sea, little knowing or remembering that basil was a sacred plant belonging to the Mother Goddess.

Nothing, neither a belief nor a piece of stone nor a memory, was wasted there, and never has been. The wrack of earthquake has always been rebuilt into houses and mosques, inns and cattle byres. All along the Aegean coast, when the Roman Empire became Christian, some of the old temples were allowed to fall, some torn down in a religious passion, some made into quarries and lime pits. Their outer walls, their classic columns were incorporated into the new churches, then into mosques.

In no place is this truer than in the castle of Saint Peter, now a museum. When the Knights Hospitalers came to Bodrum, they found the wreck of the Mausoleum toppled by earthquake, lying on the ground, and they used much of it to fill the walls and decorate them in their new castle. This is where, in the nineteenth century, when the British were buying up antiquities for so little along the coasts of Turkey and in Greece, the archaeologist Sir Charles Newton found the statues and the friezes that can now be seen in the British Museum. But many fragments of the Mausoleum are left at the castle, frozen in medieval stone walls.

There is a frieze from the Mausoleum that escaped the nineteenth-century scavengers, a bas-relief of the battle with the Amazons. On a stone tower, there is a wall plaque of marble with a writhing snake. Did the European Crusaders know when they put it there that it was a sacred object, long before the serpent was made into Satan by a new monotheistic belief?

It was in a late afternoon that April, when the sun was oblique and its shadows defined the faint hillocks where there had long ago been houses or temples, that I first went up to the castle. Already in the pace of the town, I strolled, slowly, slowly, up the great wide ramp over the first fosse, once a moat, that day a long slope covered with flowers. The stone path had been built for the troops of horse of the Crusaders. Beyond it, in the closed keep, now grass-grown too, the cliff-high stone walls enclosed a perpetual deep shade, quiet and cool, and studded with stone coats of arms of the Crusaders.

In the keep itself were the monuments and statues that had not, years ago, been taken away from Turkey. They stood, still sentinels from the time of Halicarnassus, among trees that have grown tall and formal to catch the seldom sun.

I climbed the stone stairs into the first high courtyard. The walls between the courtyard and the sea far below were almost in ruins. Through them, when I found the way later, I used to climb out onto the rocks and swim in the protected pools, and lie on my back and look up at the castle walls that seemed to be mountain-high from the water.

On the higher slopes within the second line of walls, the castle rose up the natural slope of the hill, the towers rising higher and higher, some of them roofed then, some in ruins. On the wide slopes that had been courtyards at the highest level by the towers, and all the way down the hill, I counted fourteen different shades of anemones; they littered the grass like fallen shards of color.

The museum was fairly new then, but already the exhibitions were rare and wonderful—the ox-hide shaped copper ingots from the first wreck found at Gelidonya, an ancient stone anchor, fragments of amphorae, and tools and treasures brought up from that underwater exploration. There were vases and plates that were pre-Greek—one with a wonderful octopus painting on it, a symbol of the sea god. There you could see the swirls that after the early realistic pictures of the octopus became the octopus design, abstracted into concentric circles. All of this was collected and brought there from the coast, from new digs in the villages, and from under the sea—the whole past of the way people lived on these shores from 1200 B.C. on.

I climbed across the crumbled walls and up into the highest tower, where there was a ledge overlooking the town and the harbor. Behind me, where the roofs had fallen, there was a long drop. I clung close to the serrated castle wall and looked down over the whole small sea valley of Bodrum, its color, its shape.

It was two cities. A Turkish city curved around the main harbor, with stone walls around orchards and courtyards. Some of the Turkish houses were so old that they still had the ladders that could be withdrawn, in time of siege, up to entrances on the second floor. Some of the streets were wide, for easy movement in battle, or so narrow that they were easily defended. This is a shore that has, through the centuries, withstood so much siege that building for protection was second nature, whether pre-Greek or Greek or Persian or Byzantine or Seljuk or Ottoman—the courtyards hidden, the luxury of space left for palaces, the march of armies, or the villas of the powerful. Cutting across the old town, and seeming from the tower to be superimposed on it, were the convenient roads of the modern town, built for easy access instead of protection.

Down below, to the right, was the second harbor where the Cretan Turks lived, the houses close together as they are in Greek island towns. The Cretan Turks came there in one of the earliest of those heartless shifts of population when in 1898 Venizelos took the island of Crete from the Ottoman Empire. They still call the island Kriti. There the old women shrill at each other in archaic Greek. Most of them belong to one or two extended families. Like the sponge fishermen who were their ancestors, they plied the same trade they always had on the Cretan shores and in the boats. When I saw men there with the small waists of ancient Minoans, I realized once again that artists do try to paint what they see.

It was from that eagle's nest that I first noticed, away beyond the empty hill meadows, the fragments of the outer walls of Halicarnassus, and I decided that I would walk around them. They are over three miles in circumference, and to walk them is to walk through centuries.

I started early in the morning at the shipyard at the west end of the quay, where they still launched the small ships in the way they had for centuries, from a cradle of heavy wooden trestles, with the workmen pounding away the struts in rhythm to their chant until the cradle fell forward and released the keel to slide down into the water. They used wood long proven as right for masts and keel, and some of the same methods of building as they did when boats were made here for Süleyman the Magnificent when he prepared for his invasion of Rhodes in 1522.

The shipyard workmen may have worked with electric drills, and they put modern engines in the boats made there, but when I saw a boat launched in 1972, the *imam* cut the throat of a sheep on the prow, and the captain put his hand under the stream of blood and placed a red handprint on the side, to be taken by the sea, by Poseidon, although nobody said so. The sheep had a red ribbon on its horn to show that, like Esau in the Old Testament, which is as sacred to the Muslims as to Christians and Jews, it was the firstborn, and worthy of sacrifice.

Behind the shipyard, the white tomb of a Muslim saint was outlined against the sky. There were prayer rags tied there. I climbed beyond it along the wall to the top of Göktepe, the small hill that may once have been the acropolis. At the top, there was a temple floor about forty feet long. Some archaeologists say it was the temple to Ares at the time of Mausolus. From there, so early, the harbor was as smooth as a mirror, and the castle was reflected in it as if its twin had drowned beneath the water.

Behind the temple floor there was a huge spring, a deep hole in the hill where the water ran out several hundred feet below. It has never been explored. Remembering sacred wells, and the fact that new religions tended to throw the waste of old beliefs down wells, I have always thought that this would be one of the prime places to explore to find a sacred past—pre-Greek, Greek, Roman, Byzantine Christian, and perhaps even early Muslim, for all of them tended to build where land was already sacred.

But alas, the well was already lived in, they said, by hundreds of adders. After all, snakes, too, have been sacred to the Mother Goddess of Asia Minor, the great Artemis, the lady of the wild beasts and the bees.

There is a psychic tradition deep in us all to turn one man's god into another man's devil, as the snake of Artemis, Cybele, Aphrodite, and Hermes was turned by the paternal religion that replaced it into the evil serpent in the Garden of Eden and on the wall of the castle.

Behind Göktepe and further up the next hill, nearer to the fragments of the old wall, the hillside was carved deep with primitive tombs, some with paintings on the stone that look like cartoons in some ancient comic book, one of a soldier and a bull—a Roman worshiper of Mithras.

From that far away I could look down, across the crest of Göktepe, on an illusion of the ancient city, which was so large at the time of Mausolus that the houses and their fields and vineyards ran all the way up the hill to the wall. Bodrum, from there, was smaller, and it huddled along the shore, but the shape of the streets was much the same as they must have been; those, too, unchangeable by habit and use over so many centuries. The City Hall disappeared from my mind and the square white building could, from so far away, have been the palace.

I had brought with me, wrapped in a cloth, and still cool, *beyaz şarap,* the white wine of Turkey; *meyva suyu,* the wonderful fresh fruit juice; *ekmek,* the bread that is baked every night and is always fresh; and *beyaz peynir,* the white cheese from the market below. And when I sat down on the highest hill to have my picnic, I could watch, away in the distance where the sea was blue to the horizon, given shape by its green islands, Karaada, the protector of the harbor, where there were hot springs to bathe in that come from deep inside the mountain, to remind you that the shore is volcanic, and where a huge meteorite has left a round pool forty meters deep close to the shore.

Away in the distance was the faint line of Kos. The ferry nosed into port below, and in the outer harbor a large cruise ship unloaded its passengers onto a tender to bring them into port for their obsessive shopping for the day. It was all silent movement. I was so far away up the hill along the fragmented wall that I could hear nothing but the sounds of country silence, a donkey in the distance, insects in the high grass fed by the rains.

I was in an older Asia than the city below had ever been, for it is not true that the people came initially across the Aegean from the islands. They came down from the hills, from the mountains behind where I stood, gradually, over centuries, beginning to trust and then to command the shore below their natural citadels of high ground where the wild wheat grew in natural meadows, surrounded by the protecting forest.

At the east side, in the high meadow, the wall ran to the Mindos gate, the main gate of the city where they held out for so long against Alexander the Great. It was so small in the spacious air that it was hard to believe that the history of the battle has come down as one of the most famous sieges of Alexander. Now it is a pile of stones that could have been thrown there by earthquake or left as an erratic by glacier.

I walked on across the top of the hill, and below me the city turned, disappeared, reappeared. In some places the wall was high enough to climb, in others so fragmented that the stones lay along the ground and I wondered that the farmers had left them, except that the stones of that great city-state were huge and hard to move. Up along the wall there were fields, and orchards, and farmhouses with their large, fierce dogs. These dogs are almost feral and they look alarming, the size of small ponies, with iron-spiked collars to protect their throats from wolves. Later I met an American army officer who spent his leaves searching for natural gems. He tamed every dog he met by giving them Oreo cookies from the PX.

I was already deep in the Turkish countryside, far from the carryings-on of the resort shining there far below me along the shore. It seemed a different city from the one I had seen from the tower, not spacious so much as nestled in its sea valley. The river that had formed it had long since dried up. Such valleys were the sites of battles, clashes of arms as in the days of the Trojan War, all for water and, in those deep defiles, a little bit of arable bottomland, the puny skirmishes turned into great legends by the ancient poets.

The wall, as I could trace it, ran down on the right side of the city in the distance into a narrow valley of its own. The oleanders grew along a small creek; an old tree leaned down toward the water. Here was a series of caves where a farmer had put his beehives out of the wind and rain, where the bees would suck the honey of the *ilkbahar çiçekler,* the spring flowers. But the caves had been tombs or shrines. In front of one of them lay a large stone that I saw was weathered marble, still recognizable as the torso of a woman, a goddess, who would, standing, have been ten feet tall. The torso had been carved by time back almost into its basic rock; a chthonic shape, powerful and lost in the farmer's little hollow. How could he have known that he had chosen a cave for his bees in the same place that once the goddess stood who had the bee as her symbol? But then, how many of us at Easter recognize the egg as the reminder of her immortality?

The wall went along the back of the most ancient village, the hill village, where the foundations of the round stone houses were low circles of stone, all that is left of the prehistoric Lelegian people who huddled there above the shore, long forgotten but kept buried in the minds of their descendants. It was this round shape, coupled with Greek, Roman, and nomadic influences, that would rise so many centuries later as miracles of architecture, the great round domes of the Byzantine churches and of Sinan, one of the world's greatest architects.

Even on such an idyll as that spring day, there was an ominous past. I walked past a monastery that had no roof. It was as much a ruin as all the rest of the forgotten religious fragments. It had been made into a disco, and in the day, as all night places do, it looked smaller, dull, neglected, until its lights and its noise would start again at nightfall. But this ruin may have been much newer than the others. There has been war along those shores within the lifetimes of many who still live there, but it is never mentioned. So who knows if the monastery roof fell, or if it was pulled down and left during the twentieth-century Turkish War of Independence?

There had been nights of the long knives here; much of the shore was Greek; many Turks lived across the water on the islands. So the holes in the walls could be bullet holes and fairly new, and the small Byzantine church below it might not have been an old ruin, left over from the Byzantine Empire, which had not ruled this part of Turkey since the eleventh century, but only one of the casualties of the war that followed the First World War. I was reminded of the Turkish houses on Kos, with their orchards and their courtyards, still deserted after terrible nights of civil war.

Down in the town again, it was easy to forget this past, old and new. The evening was coming on, the men were gathering along the fronts of their coffeehouses, some of them without women at all, and some, near the port as they are in most port towns, full of younger Turks, officials, the educated and Western-minded, the foreigners.

At five o'clock or so, just before the sunset, as they do in most of the towns around the Mediterranean and the Aegean, the whole town came out to stroll—men, women, children, friends—a slow promenade along the streets and the landing pier. It was impossible not to join them. The walk in the evening is traditional. I soon got the sense that if I didn't join it, I would have committed some breach of community.

So we watched the sun go down behind the hill where the old wall rose up at the west end of the town, behind the Muslim graveyard and the shipyard. It seemed to get larger as it neared the water and then it seemed to plunge behind the graveyard, and it was time for the local women to wander home together. As the weather got warmer they, too, lingered, hunkered down in their *şalvar* under the trees of the harbor road like night birds, whispering to each other when more and more strangers passed as the summer came on.

In the evening, at the *lokanta,* the restaurant across from the mosque, on a moonlit night that shone outside, brighter than the dim streetlights, musicians played Turkish music on the *saz,* the stringed instrument most like our banjo, and the *davul,* the drums caressed with the palms of their hands. The music wailed to Western ears, like a battle far away, a long time ago, a lament. Everybody danced. It reminded me of a dance we did when I was growing up, where we gathered in a circle and whoever was in the center called "Shine!" to one of the dancers, and the chosen one came into the center of the circle, shoulders wiggling, hips carrying on, until his or her individual dance was over and "Shine!" was called again.

It was that way in the *lokanta.* Turkish dancing, like the dignified pace of their walking, is slower, more contained than Greek dancing. Only the men danced. Nobody refused. I thought of warlike people before battle; I thought of what I had heard of the dervishes. Nobody refused to dance. In the center of the floor, the mayor, the chief of police, sea captains and sailors, danced their slow individual dances, until they pointed to someone else sitting at one of the tables. There was no way to escape it. There were no strangers then. No one would see that later in the year when the bars and the *lokantas* were too crowded and the tourists and vacationers had taken the town and brought their own ways with them.

But in the spring the town was calm and kind in the way of ancient hospitality, slower, easier. The communal sense was everywhere still. When one of the local men made his specialty—a *çiğ köfte* of raw meat rolled and spiced, a Turkish variant of steak tartare—he took it around to the bars in the evening so that everybody could taste it. When the international soccer games were on, both of the television sets in the town were turned so that they could be seen from the street, and men brought chairs from the nearest coffeehouse and sat there solemnly in the road, as if they were at a movie.

But even later in the summer there was a way to escape to the Turkey that waited, and still waits behind the main roads, up the hillsides, along the sea in the half-hidden coves. We would sit, new and old friends by then, at the *kahve* on the quay and we would find the captain of one of the small *kayık*, load the boat with vegetables, white cheese, bread, sweet biscuits, wine and, for ten dollars a day, we would go off into Gökova Bay, a five-day trip, where we slept on deck, woke at dawn, and dived into the glass-clear water.

The first morning I went I woke at predawn, and it was like the beginning of the world, silent water, silent sky. The little dawn wind swept across the deck and the Pleiades were misty at the horizon. I waited until it was light enough to tell the black thread from the white thread, which is the way the Muslims tell the time of their first prayer of the day, and I put on snorkeling gear and dived into the pure water, down, down, deeper and deeper down, to where a copy of *Paris Match* lay spread across the ocean floor and I was jerked back into my own century again.

The days and nights cruising in the small boats in Gökova Bay come together in my memory as one idyllic voyage, where we sailed in the days and moored in the hidden coves at night, swam, or snorkeled, or in some of those times when the Turkish government allowed a compressor aboard a boat, were able to dive forty meters down into the clear water.

It was there that I first saw fish bleed green, and learned that red turns green about thirty meters down in the deceptive light below the sea ceiling. We swam in and out and around an underwater tower-scape of chalk pinnacles, monuments of ancient volcanic violence, some ten feet high or more, leeched dead white from the centuries under the water, thrust out of the sea floor forty meters down in the twilight blue, the stillness of a cemetery of towers. Then, between high cliffs, all the way up to the sea ceiling on both sides, we swam through underwater gardens.

I made my first cliff dive in water so pure that ever since I have been spoiled for diving other places. My diving instructor and I knelt first on the top of a cliff about fifteen feet under water, called white water where we could see the bottom rocks and the little ladyfish and the pink parrot fish swim up to us and the world was small and safe and brightly colored, and the pastel shell skeletons of the sea urchins lay around, frail and beautifully shaped—so frail that I used to carry one in my hand when I dived so that if I crushed it I knew I was too tense and made myself relax and breathe, deep and slow.

Kneeling there I was afraid that tears would fog my face mask, for I had never seen such an awesome sight as the cliff disappearing down, down, down into deep sea, and the huge fish that lived there were in another world from the smaller ones we had seen in the shallow water. I thought then, "Full fathom five thy father lies; Of his bones are coral made. Those are pearls that were his eyes, . . ."

We say we quote Shakespeare or the Bible at times like these, but it is all too often hindsight—what we think we should have thought—but I did it, then and there. I said the words to myself and they turned into air bubbles, Shakespeare's way of telling about the world of underwater that he would never see. Then we launched ourselves over into water so deep that the cliff ran down into darkness below us, and soared down the cliffside as slow as dream flying, into a cave where the orange and yellow sponges were bright and the red had disappeared.

At night we moored in coves, where there was nothing else but our own boat, so small it seemed lost under the great black space. We were back in the ancient world ourselves, where the stars were scattered across the darkness, deeper and deeper as we stared, star beyond star in a depth of sky. There was silence there and had been since men first plied these waters, and on the first island where we moored, in a little cove on the lee side, the birds began to moan, haunting the night, so that I could easily see how, in the minds of people who saw all creatures as a part of the gods, the sirens were born.

Sometimes at night we pulled under the shore trees in the dead quiet of English Harbor. It was the narrowest place on the north side of the isthmus, where the south side was the Mediterranean and the Greek islands. It was called English Harbor because men from the Greek islands smuggled English flyers and soldiers, the survivors of the Greek campaign and the battles on Crete, to safety in World War II. They took them across the narrow neck of land at night to waiting Turkish boats with their one-foot drafts, shallow enough to get into the harbor, which had been at some time a smuggling run that the government boats with their deeper drafts couldn't follow.

I had brought a few tapes with me to Turkey and a small tape recorder. We set it on the deck and played the tapes. The favorite for those calm and awestruck nights, when the only light was stars or moon and one small mooring light, was Milstein playing the Beethoven Violin Concerto in D. We played it over and over because one of the captains liked it, and I still hear it, its thin sound in all that space, rising and then being lost in the night sky.

It was there, too, that homesickness intruded, as it does for Americans and all expatriates from time to time, a piercing reminder that we are far from home. This time it was a tape brought by one of the divers. Once, under the vast night, Bill Monroe sang, "My son, I can't take you back to Muhlenberg County, Mr. Peabody's coal train has hauled it away." I was back in Kentucky, which I had left at six years old, and I cried for that lost place in the night, in the Aegean, alone in the dark where no one could see me, curled up in the stern of a Turkish boat.

The deep intrusive past was never far away—echoed in a ruin, a habit, a village, a sight not meant to be a reminder but there all the same. The villages along the bay could only be reached by sea, so that for months, until the boats began to bring the tourists, or the fishermen or sponge divers went out from them, they were cut off, not asleep but self-contained, in coves along the north shore.

One of our captains was the grandson of a famous woman who lived in one of them, and had been made into Turkish legend by one of their most beloved writers, Cevat Şakır Kabaağaçlı, who lived in Bodrum for years and wrote as *Halikarnas Balıkçısı*, the Fisherman of Halicarnassus. She was Blue-Eyed Ayşe, whose husband had been lost at sea when she was very young, seventeen, and who had gone mad, they said, and thought that some of the other fishermen who moored at the village for the night were her husband, returned. Without one second or glimmer of contempt, her husband's friends pretended to be him, looked after her, and gave her children. This had been long ago and the woman I saw was nearly ninety, the ice-blue Circassian eyes still as bright as a young girl's, and so lithe that when she got aboard the boat from a dinghy to go to Bodrum with us, she refused help, and sprang up over the side, higher than her head.

To give Blue-Eyed Ayşe and the rest of his family some meat for the winter, the captain had brought them a pregnant nanny goat. It rode for several days along behind us in the dinghy, surrounded by laurel branches, its horned head high above the green, and I thought of Pan and panic and the wild sea, a sacrifice dancing along behind us across the waves.

"It was not worth sleeping last night," Blue-Eyed Ayşe told us in the morning, "my dreams bored me, very dull." But what she said was, "My dreams squeezed my soul," which is the Turkish way of saying they are bored. When I looked at her in the morning, still so bright and so ironic a face, still beautiful, I wondered if for a moment she had ever been insane. Blue-Eyed Ayşe knew what happened to widows in Turkish villages, with no one to care for them and no family to grow around them. Maybe at seventeen she had been as wise inside as the old woman I saw there.

At the end of Gökova Bay, there is an island, the island of Cedrae, or it was called that two thousand years ago. When we went ashore there we found, more complete than most of the other theaters, a Roman amphitheater half covered with trees, where the stones were tangled with vines and roots. We sat there on the stone seats facing the high mountain, only a few hundred yards across the end of the bay. I saw that it was a natural backdrop, where, at the beginning of Aeschylus's *Agamemnon,* when the news of the fall of Troy and Agamemnon's return to Mycenae was flashed by relay fires, they must have been lit high on the mountain before us, a marvelous theatrical effect.

Around the east end of the island there is a small beach where the sand is like no other I have ever felt in my hands. Each grain is as round as a tiny ball bearing, smooth and white. It is said to be good for rheumatism. When we were there a young village girl had brought her grandmother and had buried her in it up to the neck. There is no other sand like it anywhere in the region and it is believed as strongly as if it were in living memory that Cleopatra had it brought by trireme, so that she and Antony could lie there together on their honeymoon. Then Cedrae was a small city, perhaps a well-known resort for Romans, as Bodrum has become for half the world since I lived there. But when I first saw it, it was remote, tree-grown, inhabited only by hundreds of wild black goats that looked ominously Pan-like.

Now, in Bodrum, the villas of the modern rich have replaced the Greek, Carian, Persian, Roman, Ottoman villas of bright marble shining in the sun. Then, in one day—a thousand years ago, a hundred, yesterday—those villas were dashed down into the receiving sea where, in the lazy afternoon, we used to snorkel over the tumbled green-grown stone of their foundations and their terraces.

One day that first summer two friends and I took a picnic to the deserted end of a beach a mile or so away to the east of Bodrum, where there was only one small house in the distance, almost out of sight. We walked the old caravan track along Gökova Bay, worn by centuries of the pads of camels and the hard strike of donkeys' hooves, and nomads and pilgrims and travelers, until it was a deep groove in the soft white stone.

The afternoon moved with the sun, easy, quiet, not a sound but the whisper of the water when someone decided to swim. Snorkeling was good there among the rocks that ended the beach. The clean stones were alive with fish and sponges and sea anemones, free of the green algae and the sea urchins that are near Aegean shores where the waste of humans has been thrown for hundreds of years.

One friend was a young German woman whose bone structure still showed a malformation from the time after the Second World War when she was born and there was not enough to eat. The other was a young Turk, a university student, one of those watched always by the secret police. (The Turkish government fears the independent mind, as civil servants always have.) I was the third, and I had over and over been charged with the accusation that my country was the aggressor in a war in Vietnam that I could only say that I was against—too timid an answer for the political contempt that had grown in Europe by 1972.

But that day I lay on the beach to dry after snorkeling, and lazed and thought, Here we are, three people from three hated nations: the Germans for the Nazis, before this girl was born; the Turks for their treatment of the Armenians, which my Turkish friend that day would have fought against; and I for what I thought was a senseless and brutal invasion of a small peasant nation so far from our own shores.

The novel I was writing, *Prisons,* based on the history and events of the Cromwellian wars in the seventeenth century in England, crept at strange times then into the present, as it did that afternoon, drying in the sun. I thought of a letter from the "agitators," the official representatives of the common soldiers in Cromwell's regiments, elected to speak for the others. Several troops of horse had refused to go with Cromwell to fight in Ireland.

"What have we to do in Ireland," the letter began, "to fight and murder a people who have done us no harm?" For that mutiny men died, some were exiled to the new colony of Virginia, thinking they had failed, and yet over the centuries, they had won, and I, a free woman from that new colony, lay that afternoon on the shore of the oldest civilized world.

The sun moved the shadows over me. Power and its crimes are remembered, the revolts against the decisions of the powerful all too easily forgotten. How little we really know about brave and unknown people in the brute face of silence, the manipulation of facts, the terrible comfort of old hatreds. I wonder, looking back now, if this book was not born then without my dreaming of it, or the need for it, all the questions and all the traveling and all the memory that would be part of it, on that afternoon in the late sun.

The last year I lived in Bodrum was 1974. All through the summer there had been rumors and waiting and hope against hope, as there is before wars break out. The Cretan Turks at the Greek end of Bodrum were picking up terrible speeches on the Greek radio, partly from Cyprus, where one Cypriot Greek right-wing madman, Nicos Sampson, editor and bully, was bragging about the hundreds of Turkish people he had killed. Mass graves dug up after the 1974 invasion of Cyprus proved that he had told the truth. The Colonels, who were in power in Greece, were backing Sampson to take over the island.

The newly elected Turkish Prime Minister, Bülent Ecevit, a rather gentle scholar who had translated T. S. Eliot into Turkish, was begging the British prime minister, and whatever other powers he could, to intervene in Cyprus to protect the Turkish minority there. All of this, combined with the saber rattling of the Colonels, was causing an attendant and terrible quietness, as in a sickroom. I only saw this from the point of view of a small town, of people listening to the radio, especially the BBC, which everyone tended to trust more than either the Turkish or the Greek broadcasts.

One weekend I went diving along the coast with a group of Belgians. On Saturday night three of us came back to Bodrum, dressed in our bathing suits and shirts, to find out what was going on. As we rounded the point where Bodrum should have appeared in a halo of lights, with its Saturday-night noise and music, there was silence and complete darkness, as if the city had disappeared.

It was total blackout. As our small boat came into dock, a hand came down to the prow. All I could see by a flashlight was the sleeve of an army uniform. He said something in Turkish. Our boat had been commandeered by the army.

All evening long we listened to the Greek radio from Kos saying that the Greeks were going to invade the next morning at dawn. I tried to make a joke of it, to convince them that no army invaded at dawn, and that besides, Kos was so near that the jet planes would fly beyond it on takeoff, and any other silliness I could whistle in the new dark to calm my Turkish friends, but they had seen too many wars, centuries of wars. The still, cold waiting was in their genes.

At 4:30 in the morning almost the whole of Bodrum heard the news from the Greek broadcast—the Greeks were invading. They announced that they were going to bomb all along the coast from airfields on Kos. I couldn't remember any airfields on Kos, but the other islands were uncomfortably near, and saber rattling or not, the threat was there. People huddled around transistor radios, their faces intent and gray, like the faces I remembered in England during World War II. The Turkish army was at the ready all along the Bodrum shore.

Down at the ancient main street along the sea front, I heard a sound like a wind in the night touching the sides of the houses. I walked to the corner of the street. The little city had gone back a thousand years.

It was time, as it always had been, to take to the bare hills. A long line of women, of children, of their animals, trudged slowly through the predawn darkness, like a shadow parade. They walked quite silently, the women dressed in *şalvar* with their heads covered, donkeys piled high with household treasures. There were no cars, no sounds of any motors. I could hear a baby cry, a sheep bleat. Otherwise, it was a silent procession of refugees from the madness they had always known. All day they sat in the hot sun on the hills where there was only camel thorn left of the great forests that had once been there. Nothing happened.

I had already planned some weeks before to leave. It was time to come back to America for my term's teaching job. Several days later, after the invasion of Cyprus had begun, I was in İzmir, three hours up the coast.

I heard a wild cheer in the street. I went to where a group of men were standing around a radio on a pushcart. The Greek Colonels had fallen. Ecevit was giving an open press conference in Turkish, English, and French, explaining to the world why Turkey had gone into Cyprus. Already the act had brought down the government of the Colonels, who had held Greece for so long in the vise of military dictatorship. It was this fact that the men around the pushcart took the most pride in. The Colonels had been a threat to the area for years, and finally someone had acted.

"Aslan!" the men whispered to each other as Ecevit spoke. "Lion." It was their highest compliment for a man whom they considered had brought down a dangerous military dictatorship in Greece, and had rescued the Cypriot Turks from the hands of Sampson.

I came back that summer to a country where people did not know what had happened or why, who condemned Turkey for an act of aggression, who had learned nothing about the Turks since the Armenian troubles, and who didn't even know the difference between an Arab and a Turk. In 1989, I returned to Turkey for the first time, to begin that circle of curiosity and questions that would lead me all over the country. I was not looking for abstract answers; I was looking for people, and past and present, and the validity of memory, which is the most obscure search of all.

CHAPTER THREE

THE LORDS AND LADIES OF BYZANTIUM

HE TURKISH THAT I speak is direct, like a child's. I call it, honoring *Casablanca*, "such much" Turkish. So this language, with its echoes of nomads and emperors, pashas and *ghazis*, sultans and riches, and country matters, with its verbs of more than forty tenses, including the very useful one for innuendo that I wish we had, its oblique politenesses, this language with its own poetry of front- and back-rhyming vowels, this old tongue that contains within it all the past of Anatolia, is, for me, a shorthand. I get along, though. Turks are very polite people.

I stood on a street corner in İstanbul and held out my hand to a Turkish traffic policeman, who was directing crowded, fast, darting, manic traffic that ignored the level crossing as if it had been a dead animal in the road.

"Korkuyorum," I said. I am scared.

He held up one imperious hand and stopped the traffic. To the music of furious horns, he took my hand and led me slowly across the street called the *Divan Yolu*—the road to the palace that followed the Roman Mese, the great central artery of old Constantinople, the Roman road that runs from the Hagia Sophia to the Theodosian walls and beyond, aimed straight at the heart of Europe. This was the road of the Janissaries, the Crusaders, the armies of Mehmet II, the Turkish conqueror of Istanbul.

We reached the other side. *"Çok teşekkür ederım,"* I give you much thanks, I said, of course.

"Bir şey değil, hanım efendi," It is nothing, ma'am, he said. The traffic waited.

"Allahaısmarladık," the Turkish good-bye that means, "We are putting ourselves in the hands of God," I said, meaning it in the İstanbul traffic.

"Güle, güle," he said, go happily.

At last the traffic moved again.

At times like these, and there are so many, İstanbul turns in pace to a country town. There are long walks there, and afternoons, like towns in the country in summer. It is a city of nearly ten million people that spreads from Europe to Asia, up the Bosporus, along the Sea of Marmara, up the Golden Horn.

I had thought of going to Turkey on my own, as I had done so long ago, with what I look back on now, knowing what I do, as somewhat comic courage. I had forgotten Turkish manners. I was met at the airport by the colleague of a friend of a friend. Already I was being handed from *arkadaş* to *arkadaş*—that word for friendship, one of the most important words in the Turkish language. It is a way of living, a self-expectation as old as the nomads, although the people who are so hospitable must have long forgotten why they do it. They just do it. It is as natural as kindness or anger. My new, solicitous friend, Ziya, whose name means "luminous," was an elegant, young, English-speaking İstanbul University graduate.

He may never have read Ibn Battuta, the fourteenth-century traveler who was handed from *akhis* to *akhis,* an old Turkish word for the generous organizations of young men who followed the standards of *futawwa*—an ideal of nobility, honesty, loyalty, and courage—but he was following, without considering anything else, the same rules of hospitality.

Ibn Battuta wrote, "We found ourselves in a fine building, carpeted with beautiful Turkish carpets and lit by a large number of chandeliers of Iraqi glass. A number of young men stood in rows in the hall, wearing long shirts and boots, and each had a knife about two cubits long attached to a girdle around his waist. On their heads were white woolen bonnets, and attached to the peak of those bonnets was a piece of stuff a cubit long and two fingers in breadth. When they took their seats, every man removed his bonnet and set it down in front of him, and kept on his head another ornamental bonnet of silk or other material. When we took our places, they served up a great banquet followed by fruits and sweetmeats, after which they began to sing and dance. We were filled with admiration and were greatly astonished by their open-handedness and generosity."

Now the word is *arkadaş,* not *akhis,* but it has the same sense to it, and although my young friend was dressed in a beautifully tailored Western suit, the same sense of care was there, the same warm concern.

I had come, as we all do when we go to cities we have heard about so much, to find an İstanbul I already thought I knew—my city of presuppositions—whispers and memories of pashas and harems and sultans and girls with almond eyes, the Orient Express of Agatha Christie, the spies of Eric Ambler, the civilized letters of Lady Mary Wortley Montagu.

My favorite travel book is *Eothen,* by Alexander Kinglake, published in 1844. I expected the "Asiatic contentment" he found there, and the naive world of his pasha, whose ecstatic vision of European locomotives he had never seen was, ". . . their horses are flaming coals!—whirr! whirr! All by wheels! Whiz! whizz! all by steam!"

I found almost at once that I had been as naive as the pasha. I had forgotten, except intellectually, that shadowed behind it all, like a huge broken monument of memory, was Constantinople, the Byzantine Empire of Constantine the Great, Justinian and Theodora, Julian the Apostate. In the fifteenth century, Mehmet the Conqueror captured it, and moved the capital of the young Ottoman Empire from Bursa and called the ancient city İstanbul.

It has one of the most familiar skylines in the world, but it is still a mystery. That is partly because of age, and partly because it is a monument to four men who changed the faces of cities and of borders, and the way the eye sees, yet who have been almost forgotten.

There they are, standing out against the sky over İstanbul. The first, nearest the confluence of the Golden Horn, the Sea of Marmara, and the Bosporus, thrusts up against the sky, one of the oldest and most magic of buildings, Hagia Sophia, built by the Emperor Justinian, who, in his long reign—from A.D. 527 to 565—built buildings that stretched all over the Byzantine Empire, and changed it forever. The second, the Mosque of Süleyman, honors two men: Süleyman the Magnificent, and Sinan, the architectural genius who captured light and changed the way both the Middle East and Europe looked at buildings. The third is the mosque that is the monument to Mehmet the Conqueror, who rode into a nearly ruined and long neglected Constantinople, repaired it, rebuilt it, and changed its name to İstanbul.

We drove past the great walls of Theodosius, then along the walls that are all that is left, except for fragments, of the first palace of the Byzantine emperors. We turned through one of the ancient gates and up the narrow road toward the Sublime Porte. We entered a maze of uphill streets, a welter of turns and horns and tombs and mosques and markets and people.

İstanbul is not the only place to have great monuments and the memory of great men, a city pulse like no other, its own sense of excitement. It has all of these but, beyond them, it has wonderful neighborhoods and streets, streets full of people, streets used as markets, with snarls of traffic beyond anything I have seen in any other city, with drivers who are incredibly polite and pedestrians who obey no laws, not even those of survival. I saw a taxi driver patiently instructing two lost country people who were walking down the middle of the street while we waited in heavy traffic and a snarl of drivers honked like furious geese.

Ziya took me to a line of pastel-painted Ottoman houses on the cobblestoned Street of the Cold Fountain. The old houses there have all been restored and combined into an inn called, appropriately, Aya Sofya Pansiyonları, since it looks out on the building built by Justinian in the sixth century as the Church of the Hagia Sophia, the Holy Wisdom, and changed by Mehmet the Conqueror in 1532 into the mosque now called Aya Sofya. The houses use the great wall of Mehmet's palace of Topkapı as their back walls.

As soon as I got to my room I called home, to Virginia. Somehow it seemed, not new, but old and right, to call the person I love most from Byzantium.

If there is a heart of the city, I found it in that little walking street between its two greatest monuments. Between the Byzantine Empire and the Ottoman, in front of my Ottoman house, I strolled at the pace of the Turks, which all the tourists seem to catch. To hurry and scrabble seemed silly and rude.

At dawn, the first call to prayer came from the Blue Mosque, and was echoed, fainter and fainter in the distance, from minarets all over the city of mosques. The gulls rose up in clouds from their perches on the roofs of Hagia Sophia and flew toward the water just beyond Topkapı, where the Sea of Marmara meets the Bosporus and the Golden Horn. They came back to roost there and flew among the minarets; their wings turned pink in the spotlights that illuminate the mosque at night.

Hagia Sophia seems to float there, on the hill that was the ancient acropolis of Byzantium, above the meeting of the three waters: the Bosporus, the Sea of Marmara, the Golden Horn.

It has been the font of three empires. Here emperors and sultans were crowned, first the Byzantine Romans, and then the terrible Latins who decimated it in the Fourth Crusade and formed the short-lived Latin Empire. Here Mehmet II, child of the Osmanlı Turks, ordered the blood of the slain washed from the marble floor, and had his name read as sultan at the first prayer in the new mosque of Aya Sofya.

Aya Sofya is a museum now, a new monument to the secular leader Atatürk, whose personal hatred of the clergy has left a void in Turkey that threatens to be filled dangerously.

More than a museum, too—I have walked many times through its great doors, and I have never heard a voice raised. The first sight of its captured space of golden light and twilight is more than breathtaking. I can only use the overused word: awe, an experience of awe.

The building covers more than four acres. It is wider than a football field is long, and yet there is not the overpowering sense of diminishment and human frailty that I find in the great dark spaces of the Gothic cathedrals. It is like walking into a field that contains the last sunset, under a dome that is a reflection of the sky, in the golden light of an early evening after a sunny day; a dome that rises to the height of a fifteen-story building and yet seems to shelter and not to intimidate. Most of the gold is gone, and the earliest mosaics were destroyed by the Iconoclasts between A.D. 729 and 843. The wall mosaics you see today were inlaid in the tenth century, some so high they seem to fly above you, some as intimate as portraits at the level of your eyes. The Holy Virgin looks down from the crown of the apse, so gentle on her gold chair that she seems just to have paused there for a little while to rest. Over the middle door of the inner narthex, called the imperial door and larger than the others, a tenth-century Christ receives obeisance from the kneeling emperor, supposedly Leo the Wise, who, according to the street joke of the time, was asking forgiveness for his many marriages.

Inlaid designs of marble veneer still make the walls into a patterned play of color from all over what was then the Roman Empire.

Dark green marble columns hold up the balconies so that they seem to soar. Some of these tall columns are said to have come from the temple of Artemis at Ephesus, and if so they would link the Hagia Sophia to the temple of the Asian Mother Goddess, all the way back to the Amazons.

But the controversy among scholars is almost as old as the story. Justinian did send out orders that marble should be brought from all over the empire for his church, and much was brought from the earthquake-broken city of Ephesus. The best explanation of how the legend rose is found in Selwyn Lloyd's *Ancient Turkey*. He says that the Artemision, one of the Seven Wonders of the ancient world, had already long been so lost to earthquake and silt and the reuse of its marble by the sixth century, that it was thought that the gymnasium, the only large building left partly standing, was the temple. The columns may well have come from there.

Maybe so, but sometimes legends are truer than facts. From a prehistoric grove on the Aegean, where the Amazons clashed their shields and sang as the women do in *The Bacchae,* to the great temple of Artemis that grew there, to the Church of Hagia Sophia, the mosque of Aya Sofya, the museum, and to the first morning I saw it, is only a step, a dream of a night in archetypal terms. To legend and to me, they are the columns that once were in the place sacred to the great Anatolian Mother Goddess, so old that for centuries she needed no name.

The walls of the church were once covered with mosaic portraits of Byzantine rulers, but few of them are left. One is the Empress Zoë who, having been a virgin until she inherited the purple in her fifties, took to marriage as if she had invented it, and when she changed consorts, only the head on the mosaic of her coruler was changed, so that her last husband looks a little like one of those pictures you can have taken at the fair, when you stick your head through a hole and become Garbo or Scarlett O'Hara or the latest pop star.

Vague bishops look down from high above the second row of columns, and on all four squinches that help hold up the great dome there are huge cherubim with their folded blue wings. They have never been covered over, not by the Iconoclasts, who in their puritan zeal destroyed so much of Byzantine imagery, nor the Muslims, who do not allow any replica of the human figure. They have been restored through the centuries. Perhaps they were too high for the early reformers to reach, and when the church was made into a mosque, the Muslims still believed in fields of angels.

Although thousands of people troop through the building day after day, believers and unbelievers, there is a quiet corner of Hagia Sophia left, a niche out of time. Up on the north balcony, gentle in the sun of one of the windows, there are fragments, faces, a part of a robe, a hand intact and lifted in blessing—a sacred icon of a tragic Christ with a mourning Virgin on one side and John the Baptist on the other.

Across from it on the floor is the tomb of the Venetian Doge, Enrico Dandolo, who, nearly ninety and blind, was the first Venetian ashore at the capture and sack of Constantinople by the Crusaders in 1204. When the Byzantines returned, after nearly sixty years, it is said they took the bones of Dandolo and threw them to the dogs in the street.

Once the colors were dazzling. Now in that vast and grand simplicity, there is the subtlety of age, a visual echo. Thousands of people from all over the world visit Aya Sofya every day, as they have done since it was built. But now, instead of the voices of Goths and Latins, and rough Galatians, and traders from Cathay, instead of the shaggy skin trousers of the Scythians, the togas of the Romans from the west, the white robes of the Arab tribes, the stiff gold-laden caftans of the Byzantines, the silk shifts of the traders from China, there are English voices, and German, and French, and Japanese, tourists dressed in clothes that seem in modern times to be all alike, a world of jeans and T-shirts, and the man-made textiles of traveling clothes in chemical colors. There is a sprinkling of women in black *yaşmaks* from the Arab countries, where ever since it was the Caliphate and the Ottoman Sultan was also the Caliph of Islam, İstanbul has been one of the centers of the Muslim world.

But there is a more surprising monument to Justinian, and it would certainly seem so to him. In 532 he ordered that columns that were still lying, unused, from the broken, abandoned pagan temples that had fallen to neglect and riot and earthquake, and the change of religion, be used to hold up the roof of an underground cistern. The columns were the flotsam of the past that littered Constantinople. It was an engineering job, part of the water system, no more. For years, since long before the Ottoman takeover of the city, the cistern was forgotten, which probably saved it from being used yet again as material for rebuilding.

There are 336 of these columns. The thousands of tons of silt that had nearly buried them have been cleared out; the long rows that are as near to being like a Roman temple as can be found anywhere are uncovered in the half darkness, and their presentation is one of the theatrical triumphs of the showing of ancient monuments. Theatrical—yes—but the light and sound captures its magic. Lights flirt and change from the distance, open vistas darken them again. It is totally romantic. I seemed to be, and I knew I was not, discovering it for myself.

The columns seem to go into an infinity of darkness. I passed one that was the twin of one I had seen up in the street where once the Forum of Augustus stood. They had been carved like tree trunks with the branches lopped; the lopped places looked like eyes. One upside down, one on her side, two sad Medusas, that had once guarded temples from the evil eye, had been underwater for centuries. They are now partially out of the water, and they are tinged with color from the long drowning. They lie there, looking out into the dark. The music is Beethoven, and it should be: Only that heroic sound could match the gaunt majesty of the marble forest that the Turks call the Underground Palace.

Within the crowded quietness of the first hill—the overwhelming mixture of Greek, Roman, Byzantine, Ottoman empires—the Sultan Ahmet Camii, called the Blue Mosque by Westerners, is directly across the park flanked by a classic courtyard. Over the hill to the left, to be hunted in the poor streets with their tumbling wooden houses is all that remains, according to ancient travelers, of the greatest imperial palace ever built on earth. It was so looted by the Christian Europeans of the Fourth Crusade that, three hundred years later, when Mehmet rode through it on his entry into Constantinople, it was already an abandoned ruin. I walked along nearly deserted streets in the sunny morning, and children with voices like doves, who know two words, "hello" and "good-bye," said them both, usually at the same time.

On the other side of the Blue Mosque there is a long park with three columns in a line down the middle. On one of them a stone emperor with a stone court watches a chariot race long gone. It is the old Hippodrome, where the great rivalries of the Blues and the Greens turned from the backing of chariot teams into politics and martyrdom, and where the Empress Theodora worked as a circus girl and whore.

This place is soaked with sanctity and blood. To go down below the end of the park is to pass by what is left of the huge Hippodrome wall, pierced with houses, and with gates that no longer go any place, with caves that once were rooms. I walked, or climbed, up the ruined wasteland of a hill, among the fragments and the gravelike mounds, and looked for ghosts of the palace of the Caesars.

It was an eerie search. Where once there were courtiers, a vagrant stared out from his shelter, an arch, nearly filled with earth, that had once been a high regal arch of the palace. Time had made it a cave for squatters. He watched from the darkness of the cave like a wild animal. It was the only time in İstanbul, in all the days and nights of walking, that I was afraid.

Some idea of what it may have been like, in color and in wit, can be found in the little Mosaic Museum, a work of the Australian archaeologists and the Australian government, who realize that these are monuments that belong to the world, and as such deserve what help foundations and scholarship can give the Turkish government to look after this rich heritage. Turkey has been looted so often through the centuries, that it is more than a disgrace if our own organizations, supposedly dedicated to their study, join in the theft and the neglect.

There are two contrasts—Hagia Sophia, one of the greatest of Byzantine Christian monuments, has so little money that sometimes the work of renovation and maintenance has to stop for months. No foundation has offered help with it. On the other hand, at the Church of Saint Saviour in Chora at the other end of the old city near the walls of Theodosius, the mosaics have been superbly restored by the American Institute of Byzantine Research and the Turkish Touring and Automobile Club, which is responsible for the saving of much of Ottoman İstanbul as well.

To walk into it is to walk into the color and zest of the late flowering of Byzantine art, when the Iconoclasts had at last been defeated and the formal mosaics of the early Byzantines had been forgotten for two hundred years. The figures seem to move, have depth, glow. The walls are a study of the time just before the final fall of the empire, a last spark of full life. They are contemporary with Giotto, and one wonders what the Renaissance, which had been partly fomented by discoveries in Anatolia, would have brought to Constantinople had it not fallen.

But it was only when I went to Italy a few months after being in İstanbul that I found sixth-century Byzantium, untouched by the Iconoclasts, and the loot from Constantinople taken away by the soldiers of Enrico Dandolo. Ravenna has today the only sixth-century Byzantine mosaics left in the world. It had been an outpost of the Byzantine Empire, and when the Iconoclast soldiers came on orders from the eighth-century puritan Emperor Leo, to destroy the church art, the city revolted. I had the rare experience of seeing the city for the first time so soon after being at the source of the Byzantine Empire, so much of which they inadvertently saved, that I felt that I had come from Byzantium instead of modern İstanbul.

High in the center of the apse of San Vitale in Ravenna, a young, unbearded Christ sits on a round blue sphere that floats in a gold sky, and the rivers of life flow from the green mosaic land below him. On either side of the apse are two of the most famous mosaic imperial portraits in the world.

There, beyond all that has been written of them, beyond the scurrilous gossip and the adulation, I found Justinian and Theodora, the emperor and the Evita Perón of her time, staid as only an actress imitating an empress could be.

Justinian's hair is red, his slight pudginess is there, a double chin, a pursed mouth, ruddy cheeks, under the heavy jewels of the imperial insignia. He looks oddly tentative. Trained to be emperor better than most of the Byzantines, the man who never slept, who lived like an anchorite, who rebuilt the city of Constantinople, who was the most perfect civil servant who ever graced the Byzantine throne, Justinian watches Theodora as he must have done in life, looking for some sign of approval in her imperious, sad face. He was in his mid-sixties when San Vitale was built, but not in this mosaic portrait.

In her portrait, Theodora is regal, beautiful, watchful. She would die three months after the mosaic was placed there. She was a woman of pride far beyond sheer vanity, and she would not have sent a portrait of herself aging and dying. Since there is so much guessing by scholars about the dates of the mosaics, I will guess too, but I will guess from human instinct and not from the age of stones. I think that she approved these portraits, and that she sent the best Byzantine royal artists to install them and surround them with the gold-backed colored glass and perhaps gems that make them up. She knew how to be an empress.

But in the church of Saint Apollinaire Nuovo, where long lines of virgins and martyrs march in procession toward Christ on one side and the Holy Mother on the other, and where the three wise men almost dance toward the Christ Child, there is another portrait of Justinian that has confounded scholars, too, since it was discovered a century ago. The church was decorated with those elegant formal mosaics only a few years after San Vitale, but Theodora was dead, and this Justinian has grown fat, his hair is white, yet the tentative look is still there. She was adored as few women have ever been worshiped, and he is alone and doesn't care whether he is old or young or that his hair is white. He is only waiting out the rest of his long, lonely reign.

When I went to the eleventh-century San Marco in Venice I found even more of the glory and color of Constantinople in hints and imitation and loot. The wild-frontier Venetians copied San Marco from the Church of the Apostles, built by Justinian in what had been their mother city, Constantinople, and to which they still looked for art, for riches. They constructed, as provincial people do, as we build Gothic spires or Georgian chapels, an instant past by copying a church already four hundred years old.

In 1204 the Venetians nearly destroyed the great Constantinople that they had envied for so long. For centuries the bronze and gold horses that they stole from the Hippodrome stood over the center doors of San Marco. They have meant Venice to the world, caught there in the sun in silent neigh and pace. Now the horses outside the church are replicas. The originals have been moved inside to the museum to protect them from the modern corrosive air.

All around me there were Byzantine gold sacred objects, silks, vestments. The treasure room was full of gold objects from Hagia Sophia that had escaped being melted down by Napoleon. The icon of the Madonna Nicopeia, the Bearer of Victory, that was carried before the Byzantine army, and that had so failed them when the Fourth Crusade took the city, stood in a chapel by the high altar. The Byzantine crucifix with its twisted body of an agonized Christ that they say bled when one of the crusading marauders stabbed it with his sword, was two feet from me at mass, and I could have touched it.

The mosaic floor that heaves like frozen waves; the incense from the East; the darkened shadows in the corners of the church's cruciform shape, covered to its domes with late Byzantine mosaics; all the gold-backed and jewel-colored glass catching the candlelight; the great altar where they say the body of Saint Mark himself, stolen from Alexandria, still rests; and even the altar floor, said to be the rock where the Christ stood to preach the Beatitudes; all these treasures surrounded me in this pirates' church, glittering with ancient loot.

The shapes are in İstanbul, the great stone edifices, but the color, the jewels, the curious intimacy, the personalities of Justinian and Theodora, the glorious fragments from grand imperial worship, are there in Italy, a hint and a memory of the city that was called, in the sixth century, the richest city in Christendom.

On the first evening that I was in İstanbul I walked out into the park between the Aya Sofya and the Blue Mosque, which stands on the ground where the Imperial Palace once stood. I found a man with two fawns, as delicate as Persian paintings. He was letting them crop the grass. The people from the crowded, poor neighborhoods of wooden houses, tilted with age over the hill amid the ruins of the Imperial Palace of the Caesars, had flocked, whole families, to the spacious walks and gardens. By evening, the tourists were mostly gone. İstanbul had become Turkish again.

The Turks were using the city as they would have used the villages that many of them came from: as outdoor living rooms where they visited, strolled, or sat and watched the *son et lumière* at the Blue Mosque and listened to Turkish poetry being read in tragic lilting voices into a microphone, not because they especially cared about poetry, but because it was there and they are a polite people and it was evening and the poets were trying and it is a tradition all the way back to Nasrettin Hoca to listen to storytellers, declaiming their stories in the *miş* tense, *bir var miş, bir yok miş,* maybe it happened, maybe it didn't.

On the following morning, after the quiet people and the poetry I could not understand—only the lilt and passion of it—after the most awe-inspiring building I had ever seen, I sat with a heavy-minded civil servant who had offered me tea because I was a foreign writer. He sat there explaining the obvious, when an old man, threadbare, proud, came by selling his poetry. It was printed on thin pink paper, and it had in it the images of the old Ottoman court or Divan poetry, grown as thin as the paper, half starved and discounted. He must have been eighty years old, the poet, and it was a love poem, about the almond eyes of *houris,* and about long black hair, and windows and veils of morning and hidden faces. I bought the thin little broadsheet, and we smiled at each other like friends. He reminded me of the people that I had found in the work of Sait Faik, whose stories about the streets and the people of İstanbul are the finest prose I know in modern Turkey. He is Turkey's Chekhov. Alas, too few have been translated, and so Sait Faik must wait for a translator to release his İstanbul for Western readers.

The old poet would have talked with me but when he saw a man who so obviously represented government, he looked down and thanked me politely and went away. Turks don't like government, whatever it is. They have, at least the poor, a residue of ancient fear. When I gave him the equivalent of fifty cents, the civil servant said it was too much, that he was a beggar who had too much pride to beg, so he sold the broadsheets. I said, *"Yok,"* the magnificent final negative of the Turks, "he is a poet." I did not tell him that I had more in common with the threadbare writer than I did with him, but I too had caught, from my hungry friend, a little of his fear.

But he, and the Ottoman love poem, had drawn me out of the deep past, and made me ready to walk into the İstanbul of Mehmet the Conqueror. Cities have levels of time, and I find myself, like a mushroom hunter in a field who doesn't see anything after a while but mushrooms, able to concentrate my vision on a period of time, and keep it there until I walk out again into the present. At least I thought it was so until I walked in İstanbul, and kept stumbling over a present as pulsing with life as any past there has ever been.

I went to nearby Topkapı, a vast intimacy of stone tents with walls of bright tile and veins of gold—pavilions and gardens, retreats and follies and space. Its jeweled pavilions are sparsely furnished, as if the Ottoman sultans remembered in their souls that they had been nomads and must be ready to move along. I saw this over and over later in Ottoman houses: not poverty—far from that—but cupboards that could be emptied quickly, beds that could be rolled away. An echo of tent living in wonderful, wood-carved rooms.

Oh, all that I expected of Ottoman excess was there at Topkapı, and more—the jewels as big as hens' eggs, the aigrettes made of feathers and diamonds, the fine chinaware that had been encrusted with precious stones as if it had caught a disease of riches, the jeweled hasps of daggers, the gold boxes, the walls of tile and gold in the cozy, one-roomed pavilions.

The Ottoman reputation for intrigue and for murder is there, too, in the Harem, a clutched warren of rooms, baths, and courtyards. But no romantic horror story can convey the claustrophobia and the beauty of the place. It is a huge, ornate prison for women, and for many of the sultans, who hid there in fear of their lives, victims of the irony of absolute rule. There is, in all that rich imperial polyglot, no place to be alone.

I set out to find a clue to what life in the Harem must have been like, for nothing is dead in İstanbul. Yesterday and today are intertwined every place. There are two seventeenth-century Turkish baths, *hamams,* where guidebooks written by men promise marble floors and steam-misted tiled rooms with ancient columns. In both of the historic *hamams,* I had only a glimpse of the imposing entrance to the main baths, all for men. The women's section is entered through a very unassuming side door.

I expected to be brought Turkish coffee, and to be wrapped in thick, warm Turkish towels. Instead I was shoved into a cold, dirty cubicle, given a thin towel, and told to undress. The attendant pointed to a door with her cigarette.

Inside, the room was domed and vaguely warm. In the center there was a raised platform. Around the sides were basins with very hot running water, but instead of the brass bowls I had expected, there were plastic dog bowls.

At one of the basins an enormously fat naked old woman, with arms of iron, was sitting washing her underwear. She was the attendant, a eunuch figure, pendulous and mighty. They are an ancient guild, those masseuses, and for the first time I had a sense that I was in a room that might have been like the reality instead of the romance of the Harem.

She lumbered over to me, forced me down onto the low ledge and, without a word, began to scrub me with a loofah, harder than I have ever been scrubbed in my life. Dirt came off in rolls of black. She then washed my hair and poured basin after basin of very hot water over me, hair, head, body, and all. I could not be anything but passive. It was like being bathed as a small child by an angry mother. She grabbed an arm and held it high while she soaped my armpit. She grabbed a leg and scrubbed it as if she were taking barnacles off a keel.

Then she motioned me to the raised massage platform of stone, and proceeded to beat me up. It wasn't fat on her arms, it was muscles. Finally I was able to escape. She waddled after me with a towel around her middle, looking like a wrestler on television, and demanded *bahşiş,* a tip, the only time I ever heard the word in the nine weeks I was in Turkey.

I got out of the place as fast as I could. I walked down the steep ancient street called Fish Street, where the music shops are clustered in the Turkish way of having all the same kinds of shops together, and then to the Galata Tower. I suddenly realized that I was more relaxed than I could ever remember. Across the Galata Bridge and then along the Roman walls at the Sea of Marmara, I wandered in a stream of people.

When I want comfort, cosseting, I will not go to a *hamam,* but I still suspect that I was nearer to the atmosphere and the treatment in the Harem than I will ever be again. There may be singing and dancing and gossip in the *hamam*—the guidebooks say so—but not in that place and not that day, even though I was told that it was the most famous *hamam* in İstanbul, and that Florence Nightingale had been beaten up there, too.

The Ottomans did not destroy Constantinople; they rebuilt it as İstanbul. Mehmet II repaired its bridges, its water supplies, turned its churches into mosques, and what we see today of the Byzantine culture is there because of the protection of the Ottomans who came later.

I was guided through much of this by one of the finest guidebooks I have ever seen of any city except Kyoto. It is called *Strolling Through İstanbul,* written by two teachers at the local Robert College, Hilary Sumner-Boyd and John Freely. They share in it their years of discovering İstanbul. I used it in my own way, taking the book, following it for a little while, getting lost in the labyrinthine streets, and discovering for myself, as they had done. I still read it, knowing where it leads, and I am back in İstanbul, wandering through that intimate, imperial, small, huge city.

Then, as they had done, over and over, I stumbled on treasures, tumbles of old buildings, antheaps of people working as they always had, here in an abandoned basilica, there in a *han,* a pious foundation for travelers founded by the Valide Sultan, the mother of one of the sultans in the seventeenth century, now full of the noise and smell of printing and tanning. Shiite Muslims from Iran, who have been there for centuries, looked up with blackened faces from their work, stripped to the waist in the heat, and greeted me as politely as if it were still a *han,* instead of a conglomerate of factories and shops.

On the low wall, which is all that is left of one of the Byzantine mansions, a young man sat beside a professional letter writer, who had placed his typewriter where the round atrium had once been. He was pouring out his inarticulate heart, so that the letter writer would translate it into the suitable, flowery prose of an ardent love letter.

Sometimes, early in the morning when the streets were still almost deserted, I would say good morning to the shopkeepers setting up their shops, the peddlers with their wonderfully colored vegetable and fruit carts, the children with their hello–good-byes. Some of them, a little bolder, would ask if I was German or French or English, and when I got tired of that, I told them I had come from the moon the night before—but I told them in the *miş* tense for fairy tales and possibilities.

In all the early morning walks I saw only one person who had slept out of doors. No matter how poor Turkish people are, they look after their own. To do anything else would bring shame to their extended families. He was a young man with a fine, new Harley-Davidson motorcycle. He slept on a bench near the wall below the Palace of the Caesars. His motorcycle was chained to his leg.

Later, I struggled through the crowds along Divan Yolu in Sultanahmet, which leads to Beyazit Square, where the fifteenth-century mosque of Sultan Beyazit II towers over the Grand Bazaar, started in the sixteenth, now grown over acre after acre of Beyazit, until today you must push through an international crowd of drifters and shoppers under several miles of domed and vaulted ceilings.

There it is, the essence of mercantile İstanbul, more than four thousand shops and thousands of merchants. I think of it as the lungs and not the heart of the city. It is, and always has been, a huge commercial mart since it was started as a warehouse, probably for the old palace, built there by Mehmet when he found the imperial palace of the Caesars in ruins. He soon left it to the merchants and the retainers, and built Topkapı, on the hill overlooking the three waters that come together below it.

Under the high vaulted ceilings, in a maze of turns and secret places, there is covered street after covered street of glory and kitsch, gold and brass, transistors and hookahs, copper and plastic, silk and shoddy, and outside, in one of the astonishing quiet corners between the bazaar and the mosque, I found a print of a painting of Süleyman the Law Giver, careening his horse under the arches of one of the same cobbled streets I had just come from. Among the crowds of students in blue jeans and T-shirts from the university that stands where Mehmet's first palace stood, a beggar from the *Arabian Nights* huddled at one of the many bazaar doors, saying, "Alms for the love of Allah."

Here, as in every place I went in Turkey, I walked into the past, and into a kind of peace that must have been there for so long when there was a sense of sacredness around the mosques. Beyond the wall that shuts a courtyard of the mosque from the street, there was not a voice raised, not a single frantic, "Please madam, buy leather!" Away from the noise and frantic buying and selling, grabbing and coaxing, of the street, there are tables set up under old trees, and when I walked through the gate I walked into an oasis of calm.

There old men were selling rings and knives and jewelry from what I suspect was their own family's poor inheritance, goods that we call ethnic for lack of a more complimentary term. It was a pool of honesty and quiet bargaining.

Small boys brought chained brass trays of tea to the sellers, and old men left over from revolution and Ottoman manners walked hand in hand with friends they had had since childhood, meticulous men, with their cracked shoes kept polished and their clean shirts, living too long on too little, walking together under the trees. There is a lot of physical contact between men in Turkey. They hold hands. They kiss. They walk with their arms entwined. It is somehow more masculine, more quietly dignified, than our habits of physical avoidance, as if we were afraid to touch.

This is a part of the sense of intimacy I miss and always will; they made me part of it. Even after nine weeks back in Turkey, when I returned to Washington and a clerk was rude to me in a hotel, I had become so used to that easy politeness that I started to cry from shock.

Beyond the mosque, there is a seventeenth-century abandoned *hamam,* where the old had made what was once the new, and remnants of a frieze of Roman soldiers are a part of the wall, some of them upside down.

But when I turned away from the crowds in the main streets, there were the secret spaces: chickens wandering the grounds of mosques, vegetable gardens, flowers and dogs, and always the children who said hello–good-bye. I stopped for a smiling crowd of children in a crocodile, going to school. There are still, as there always have been, hundreds of neighborhoods that are like villages, with the same politeness, the same quietness, that I found farther east in Anatolia.

Because of these areas of simplicity, İstanbul has another quality that very few large cities have. It has afternoons, long lazy ones like when I was a child. On an afternoon like that I walked with a friend along the wall of Theodosius at the extreme eastern end of the old city.

The only reminder of frantic İstanbul was the line of fast cars coming through Edirne Kapi, the Adrianople Gate that Mehmet the Conqueror rode through on 29 May 1453, in royal turban and sky-blue boots, some say with a rose in his hand, some say the sword of Mohammed, at the head of a Muslim army shouting, "Halt not conquerors! God be praised! We are the conquerors of Constantinople!"

A beautiful chestnut horse was tethered in a small open meadow below the wall, its owner unaware that it grazed where the Emperor's horses were once kept. Children played on the swings of a playground over a part of what is left of the last palace of the Caesars, and their mothers gossiped and smiled where once Byzantine women did, looking out over the Golden Horn.

There was a small part of the last palace complex of the Caesars, the Blachernae; its snaggled towers and some of its walls with windows that are open gaps are all that still stand, but beside them, surviving, is a pure reminder of Byzantium, a small palace, its Byzantine brick outer walls with their bicolored designs almost intact. It is without a floor, but its walls, its arches, and its courtyard have survived. It is Tekfur Serayı, the Palace of the Sovereign. It has been a warehouse, a factory, a zoo, and now it stands, an empty shell.

It is kept by a woman who also keeps goats, and who welcomed us as if the palace, not the small hut she lived in, were her home. At the top of the wall that made a closed meadow for her in front of the last fine facade, we could see all the way to the Sea of Marmara, along that great skyline of Mehmet and Süleyman and Sinan and Justinian.

Ottoman İstanbul is honored and reflected by that one great soldier turned architect, Sinan, who lived from 1491 to 1588. He was a member of the Janissary Corps, the elite body of soldiers taken from Christian families as small children and raised in the imperial court as Muslims and guards of the sovereign, who became in time the most feared soldiers in the empire. The Muslim children, captured or bought in the same way by the Crusaders and raised as Christians, were known as the Turkopolier. Sinan was a military engineer until his fifties when Süleyman tapped him to be his official architect, an act of patronage like the Pope demanding Michelangelo's presence in Rome.

Any city that has such an architect has its own immortality. There are forty-one of his buildings still standing. The Haseki Hürrem Hamamı, built for Süleyman in honor of his wife, the Frenchwoman known in the

West as Roxelana, is across the paved yard-cum-street in front of Hagia Sophia. It is now a museum and salesroom for Turkish carpets, and is beautifully restored in all its Ottoman whiteness.

Within the outer walls of Hagia Sophia is one of the saddest and most beautiful of Sinan's buildings. It is the tomb that he built for Sultan Selim II in 1577. It is covered with delicate, multicolored İznik tiles, used as mosaic pieces to make large patterns of trees, plants, abstract designs. It is now being restored after the nineteenth-century thievery by an İstanbul dentist, who stole one of the superb wall plaques on its facade and sold it to the West. His fake replacement is already faded, but on the other side of the door, the original tiles of Sinan seem to have been put there yesterday.

The interior is full of that strange diffused glow from window-pierced walls that Sinan created in all his buildings, made not to see out of, but to let in light. There, in tiny catafalques the size of children's beds, are thirty-two children of Selim, murdered in the royal way inherited from the Seljuks, with the silken bowstring, to insure the succession of Murat, the eldest son. It was Ottoman custom, to keep civil war from breaking out at the death of a monarch, but afterward there was such grief that the silken bowstring was replaced in time by lifetime imprisonment among the women of the Harem, of princes who might revolt and claim the sultanate.

It was on that afternoon at the walls of Theodosius that I found what to me was the jewel of that genius of an architect, the Mosque of Mihrimah, the daughter of Süleyman, on the hill near Edirne Kapi.

Sinan and Mihrimah—I think of walls that are stone strong and let the light in like lace, of space within that has the same quality as that of Hagia Sophia, even more light because the interiors are so simple and the clear walls so pierced with windows and so high. He created gentle spaces, sheltering without diminishing, soaring without losing a sense of the human, and alive with color, always color, refined and glowing, and filled with quietness. Here, in the Mosque of Mihrimah, is the simplicity of Islam that in other hands can turn to boredom, but not with Sinan, not with his genius for capturing light and space and letting them both soar upward.

In the great Mosque of Süleyman, the men go on praying in the magnificent space, undaunted by the thousands of tourists, some of whom sit in a circle in the entry, being lectured in several languages by their guides about Sinan, whose name means spearhead, one of the great architects of the world, about whom they have probably never heard.

It is all İstanbul, as polite and friendly as a country village, as noisy and clotted with people as any city in the world, old, and sleepy, and busy. I felt, not welcomed, but taken for granted there. They are used to so many strangers. For more than fifteen hundred years of empire, İstanbul has welcomed an international horde from whatever the known world was and is.

Crowded, dirty İstanbul; blowsy, insouciant. I thought of Simone Signoret in *Ship of Fools,* more exciting, beautiful, fascinating than a younger woman without her wise seductiveness could ever be.

CHAPTER FOUR

A LAST, LOST ROME

ON A MONDAY afternoon in August, when the sun was low behind the skyline of İstanbul, making the domes and the minarets black against the light, I left for the last capital of the Roman Empire. I had made for myself a strange navigational chart to follow, of times and spaces and kingdoms. It seemed right, after leaving the greatest Eastern capital of the Roman Empire, to go to the last, forgotten one.

It is a small seaport on the Black Sea, the ancient Greek city of Trapezus, the fifteenth-century kingdom of Trebizond. For eight years after the fall of Constantinople to the Ottoman Turks, the tiny kingdom of Trebizond, which considered itself the heir to Rome, held out against Mehmet the Conqueror. All I knew about it was that Rose Macauley said there were towers there, and I loved the name—Trebizond. I saw it as a lost and haunted kingdom.

The sea route lay north through the Bosporus, and then east close to the coast of the Black Sea. It had been the path of Jason and the Argonauts when the land at the eastern end of the sea at the foot of the Caucasus was called Colchis. Now it is the way the car ferry of Turkish Maritime Lines sails to the Turkish city of Trabzon. It has had this name for seventy years, but it is indicative of how little we know of Turkey that the *New York Times* still insists on calling it Trebizond, and Mehmet the Conqueror, Mohammed.

The ship left in the late afternoon from the dock across the highway from the Roman city wall. Topkapı looked deceptively small above us, half hidden among the trees. The dock was crowded with Turkish families from the Black Sea towns, backpacking students, automobiles, trailers, vans. The cars were loaded with a lot of noise and derisive comments from the men lined along the upper decks, entertained by the errors of others. On the dock ahead of us a lone fisherman cast his line with some care and snagged the guy rope of the ferry. He didn't show that he cared. He simply stood there, dignified and alone.

We finally got off when the last large vacation van, pulling a trailer and plastered with religious slogans in German, was trundled aboard. Across the water where the Golden Horn, the Bosporus, and the Sea of Marmara meet, we looked out on Asia, at the suburb of Scutari where Florence Nightingale had cared for the soldiers from the Crimea.

Turkish fathers held up children and pointed out the sights. Students from Europe stood three or four deep at the prow, trying to take it all in. Behind those of us who were trying a little too hard to see, including myself, Turkish country people sat in long rows along the decks, silent and watchful, not showing that they were curious about the great city we were passing, but missing nothing. The men wore dark European trousers, but many of the women were in *şalvar,* with their heads covered with bright shawls.

We sailed north from İstanbul into history and legend and twilight. We passed Rumeli Hisar, the citadel on the European side of the Bosporus that Mehmet the Conqueror built in the sixteenth century in four months for the siege of Constantinople. The huge towers loomed up against the evening sky, opposite the fortress his father had built across the water in Asia. A chain of boats between them cut off one of the escape routes from the Byzantine city, soon to be conquered and renamed.

I wondered then if there had not always been a watery trap there. I was already finding that legends are founded on facts in this part of the world. The Argo of Jason had to run a gauntlet on the Bosporus that was called the Clashing Rocks. They parted and then clanged together again, crushing the boats that tried to sail between them. The Argonauts were told that beyond the hazard was the shore where the river Acheron flowed out of Hades into the unknown sea.

As for us, just after we passed the two fortresses, we sailed under the newest of the modern bridges that connect Asia and Europe, not as a barrier, but as a right of passage. Already, we could see the lines of light from the cars high above us.

Sunset darkened toward night. The wind rose and people left the foredeck. I turned to follow them, and I saw that all along the decks, under the lifeboats, around the tiny swimming pool, everywhere they could find room, students had spread sleeping bags and staked their claim on places for the trip.

Some of them had already done their laundry in the public wash-rooms, and it hung on ropes, chains, stanchions, and railings, moving a little in the new night wind, scores of waving socks and underwear like little flags. Circles of students made picnics, drank wine and mineral water from the bottles they had brought. Their voices were low and sweet; once in a while I heard laughter, but it was soft. The silence of the sea and the night and the space had muted them.

The little lights in the most outlying suburbs of İstanbul fell behind us, and beyond them we were in darkness. Even as large and full of people as the ferry was, I thought that from above it—bird high—it would look as frail as the Argo as it left the Bosporus and sailed into the Black Sea.

Inside the "Pullman" section there were seats like those on a plane. Turkish women and their children had already made their dinner from the food they had brought aboard and were going to bed, while the men stayed on deck and their cigarettes glowed in the dark.

Those of us who had cabins had bought food vouchers in a compli-cated method of paying that required lining up at the purser's office and complaining. We sat at long mess tables in the dining room. There was no menu, but the Turkish hors d'oeuvres called *meze;* the inevitable lamb; the vegetables, which in Turkey are better than they are almost anywhere else I have ever been; the crusty Turkish bread, were delicious. People, including myself, began to make friends with others who spoke the same language. I even tried to speak enough Turkish to make myself under-stood to a businessman from Samsun across the table. We didn't get very far. So many people there speak a little English, and want to practice, that it is hard to get anyone to speak Turkish with you.

We stopped on Tuesday at Sinop, named for the clever Amazon queen who asked for one wish when she was in danger of being seduced by Zeus. He gave his word; she wished for perpetual virginity. There, too, is where the Argonauts found the friends of Hercules, who joined the crew of the Argo. It was the main seaport for the Hittite Empire in the second millenium B.C., and at one time the kingdom of Trebizond reached beyond it to the west. It was at this port, in 1853, that the Imperial Russian fleet destroyed the Turkish navy, an attack that helped foment the Crimean War.

By Wednesday morning we had reached the lovely little town of Giresun. The first cherry trees are said to have come from here to Europe, brought by the Romans. The name, Giresun, comes from the same source as cerise and cherry. There are miles of cherry groves along the narrow coastal space between the mountains and the sea. Rivers rush down the gorges and make this one of the most fertile stretches of land in Turkey. From the boat, the Byzantine fort loomed high above the town.

In the sea off Giresun, there is the island that local people tell you was first settled by the Amazons. There is certainly enough evidence, in legend, in names, surviving habits—women fighters in the Turkish War of Independence just after World War I, sturdy women farmers—that the Amazons really did exist along these shores. The Laz women, descendants of the indigenous seafaring tribes of the Black Sea coast, who have the reputation of being the most industrious, intelligent, belligerent people in Anatolia, have been more independent traditionally than most Muslim women in the past.

On Wednesday afternoon we sailed into the port of Trabzon. The city is set across two deep ravines where the water rushes in torrents down from the mountains that shut it away from the great plains of Anatolia. Nestled below the high barrier of trees, it looks like a lush garden. On the narrow green shore, the tea plantations scent the air all the way out to sea.

It was from the mountains that we could see looming behind the city that the men of Xenophon's Ten Thousand called out *thalassa, thalassa*—the sea, the sea. At the end of their terrible crossing of Anatolia in winter, they crowded the heights (they will tell you still in Trabzon where they stood) and "the soldiers with tears in their eyes embraced each other and their generals and captains."

Nearer the shore we could see the mixture of modern concrete apartments that are the visual bane of Turkey; the ancient walls, first built by Hadrian; and, on the hillside, someone pointed out a large villa, built to house the Czar of Russia for one day while he reviewed the Russian troops who were occupying it during the First World War. The Russian army retreated before he ever used it, and it was bought by a

Greek family who come back to see it, year after year. It is now a school. It stands above the port, a symbol of the sheer useless expense of despotism. This shore has suffered through the centuries, more than the rest of Turkey, because of its unfortunate position as a corridor between imperial Russian and Ottoman Turkish autocratic conceit.

Arkadaş to *arkadaş*—it was happening again. I saw him from the rail, standing on the dock and looking carefully at the passengers as they walked down the shaky, steep gangway ladder. He was, of course, a friend of friends, a professor from Ankara who had been born in Giresun, and who took it upon himself to be my host in his own country of the Pontus.

Ihsan, whose name means "kindness," is a Laz, one of those descendants of the wild tribes from the Black Sea, whose fierce dedication to their part of the world and mountain pride has made them a feared minority for centuries. It was Laz men who formed Atatürk's dramatic bodyguard, dressed in their black, traditional clothes. They are the butt of ethnic jokes in other parts of Turkey, but no one tells them in front of a Laz. It is said of them that they speak with their pistols.

There was another, closer reason why he had decided to come himself when my friends wrote him and asked who could show me Trabzon, one that bound us together as soon as we began to talk. Ihsan had been a graduate student at West Virginia University, and he was seeing to it that I was being welcomed in Anatolia as he had been welcomed in my own mountains. His wife is Toni Cross, whom he met there, and who was later to show me old Ankara as if it were her own house. Ihsan had driven several hundred miles from Ankara to stand on the dock and repay a hospitality he didn't owe to a stranger.

Ihsan may have been a far cry in looks from the pistol-packing Laz, but he had the same pride in his place, the same sense that no one could show me that part of the world but a Laz. He, instead, looked like what he was, an economics professor from Ankara, if there is a way that economics professors look—handsome, Turkish, and slightly round.

He was also, as I hope I am, a lover of good food, and for the next week, we sat for long hours over good food and good talk and I was at home again.

He drove me to the Roman square of Trabzon, up and up the steep streets to where the city nestled below the mountain. This was one of the three places where, when the Crusaders occupied Constantinople in

1204, Byzantine royal families set up refugee kingdoms. The Comnene family went to Trebizond, where they were hereditary rulers.

They had been the last great rulers of the late Byzantine Empire that they and their enemies still called Rome, and they saw themselves still as the heirs of the Caesars—the pomp, the language, the style. They claimed descent from Constantine the Great, who had founded Constantinople, and, according to a sixteenth-century traveler, "had an income worthy of a king."

The city we drove through so slowly, away from the busy port, across one of the ravines, was, instead, a narrow patch of ground, port for the trade from Asia. Its prosperity through the centuries has depended on wars and rumors of wars, and, in peacetime, the arrival of caravans from Asia. In the ebbs and flows of greatness, from the Roman traders to the late nineteenth century, when it had consulates from most of the European countries, it was the port that brought riches of India and China out of Asia to be shipped to Europe.

Its latest boom has been during the long war between Iran and Iraq. War materials for both sides were shipped into the port and taken overland down the eastern borders of Turkey below the Caucasus Mountains, on much the same route that Xenophon took to rescue his soldiers from their defeat in Persia, now Iran. It flourished as a much safer alternative to the much-bombed sea route of the Persian Gulf.

Yes, there are towers of Trebizond, and they stand along the protecting wall that was built first by the earlier Romans, and then by the Byzantine Comnenes; they are regal and now useless, but they define the old city. The new city, the inevitable concrete of postwar Turkish building, has seeped out beyond them.

In the evening, from one of the primitive log follies of a wonderful outdoor restaurant spread over the hill behind the city, Ihsan and I watched the sunset until the twilight deepened and the night came down, and talked about Turkey and about West Virginia, and about mountains: how they bred the same kinds of people in any country, and how it was not borders but altitude that people had in common.

We ate a *meze* of *humus* and olives and *taramasalata,* which is an hors d'oeuvre made of carp caviar; *dolma,* the tightly rolled stuffed vine leaves; and then a soup made from the day's catch of fish of the Black Sea. I wondered if country ham, red-eye gravy, sweet potatoes, and biscuits had been as exotic food to him when he went to my mountains.

We drank a smooth, dry Turkish white wine until the great towers of Trebizond disappeared, the Black Sea disappeared, the lights of the city were flung along the shore and defined the ravines below us. A wild mountain cat crept closer and closer, and Ihsan began to pet it, and give it bits of white cheese. It was so quiet that we were surrounded by the sound of the cat's purr.

The next morning I sat on a stone wall as high as an eagle's nest where once there had been a palace. There was a bare stone window frame for the sky. Nestled against the ruins, perhaps palace rooms in their time, little houses with their gardens had used a bit of Rome as a sturdy fourth wall, and as protection from the winter wind.

I looked down at the long stretch of the fortress that bordered one of the ravines far below me. Watchtowers at intervals along the walls reached toward the sea. To see the towers and the walls from above, and to find the ruins of the palace, you have to ask the children and climb unafraid as a child climbs, follow them through a labyrinthine children's way, behind the houses, around the little vegetable gardens, over piles of ancient stone that once were part of the building and now have gone back to the earth they came from.

Once the palace was described by the fifteenth-century Bishop Bessarian as "a long and beautiful building, entirely paved in white marble, while its ceiling shines with blooms of painting, with gold and various colors. The entire dome gleams with shining stars in imitation of the heavens." The screens of marble, the statues, the columns around the imperial hall, the church within the palace, all the color, the pomp, the ceremony of empire, are gone.

But it is not right to say that the magnificence is gone. The aerie of the emperor still commands the heights. From there I could watch the modern ships as they came into port, and the dark blue sea beyond. For a minute, I saw as the emperor saw, his world, however small, but at his feet.

While I crawled and climbed among the ruins, Ihsan found shade and an old man who had fought for Atatürk, and by the time I came down again, they had found, of course, that they were distant kin.

The women of Trebizond were rumored to be the most beautiful in the whole of the East. You see why when you go to Trabzon today. I went to find the church of Saint Eugenios, the first Byzantine church built by the Comnenes when they came to Trebizond, made into a mosque after the city was finally taken by Mehmet the Conqueror in the fifteenth century. Three girls of twelve or thirteen stood in the street in front of it, giggling as girls do everywhere. They were so beautiful that they made me stop and stare. They had the almond-shaped eyes, the delicate features, of icons. When I mentioned this to Ihsan, he said that their beauty was still famous, and that the sultan's men used to raid the coast to buy women for the Harem at Topkapı.

Hagia Sophia, the Byzantine monastery church that was once outside the town, is now nearly surrounded by modern apartments where the city has grown out to it, although the view of the sea is protected and makes a local park where children play, and where, on the eve of the feast day of Saint Eugenios, the patron saint of Trebizond, the people of modern Trabzon go swimming. It was the ancient ceremony of preparation for the Saint's Day. They have long since forgotten why they swim on 23 June; they simply say that it is an old custom of the city.

In the garden and along the wall, there are stones dug up in and around the town: Ottoman tombs, Byzantine headstones, Roman carved stelae, and, against the porch, the large head of a bull, looking older than all the rest, although nobody can tell you where it came from.

There is still a reminder of what the palace may have looked like in the bright religious murals painted inside the church, some of them so wild in design that they reminded me of the paintings of Oskar Kokoschka. They date from the short, lively renaissance of Byzantine painting in the fourteenth century, just before the Turkish conquest. The murals have been restored and cleaned by the Russell Foundation and the University of Edinburgh.

There are mural pictures of biblical stories, portraits of heroes, saints, soldiers, members of the Comnene family—from ceiling to floor, provincial painted imitations of the mosaics of semiprecious stones and gold that are on the walls and ceiling of the Church of Saint Saviour at Chora. In them you can read the past of the city, its color, its courage as a tiny kingdom that had lasted for two hundred years after the recovery of Constantinople by the Byzantines, and eight years after the fall of Constantinople to the Ottoman Turks. It was in those eight years that it was the only city that could call itself the heir to imperial Rome.

For more than 250 years it had protected itself, partly by its position across the two ravines that acted as moats, and partly by judicious marriages: to the royal family of the kingdom of Georgia, to Seljuk

Turkish emirs, to the Ottoman Turks, and to the heads of the powerful Muslim tribes that lived in the mountains and the high plains, the tribes of the White Sheep and the Black Sheep. Legend never dies, and the aristocratic titles, as in the time of the Golden Fleece, had to do with nomads and their flocks.

The kingdom extended for miles beyond the city. We drove into the mountains where, three thousand feet up a cliff in front of a huge cave, the ruins of the monastery of Sümela seem to cling to an almost perpendicular mountain wall as miraculously as the great trees that surround it. It was here that the first Emperor of Trebizond was crowned.

In the fourth century, two monks built a church and the beginnings of a monastery there, in what was probably already a cave sacred to the Mother Goddess. It was said that they brought an icon of the Virgin painted by Saint Luke, but the icon has long since gone from Sümela. Nobody knows where it is, but in the church of San Zanipolo in Venice there is an icon of the Holy Virgin, said to have been painted by Saint Luke, which tradition says was brought across the Danube by a monk (whether he walked or swam I don't know) who was fleeing ahead of the Turks. I suspect that it is one of the many pieces of loot brought out of Constantinople by Dandolo.

Puritanical Muslims, fearing the "evil eye," have carefully obliterated the huge Byzantine eyes of the saints and holy figures on the bright frescoes that are still in the cave church and along the cliff walls.

Ihsan and I seemed to teeter on the edge of a vast nothing, nearly a mile high, looking over the miles of black forest below us, still so thick there with its strong, ancient trees so close together that the description of it in one of the oldest books of Turkish heroic tales, *Dede Korkut*, is still true. *Dede Korkut* is a collection of the earliest Turkish legends, from the heroic age of the Turks when they first came to Anatolia. There are the black forests, the women warriors, the nomadic pride and riches.

Sacred places do not lose their power, no matter how many times religions change, and no matter how many tourists climb the frightening heights today to see the place. The baptistery, the sacred well in front of the pre-Christian sacred cave where the monks made the first church, is still a place of pilgrimage for the local Muslim people. They bring sick children there for blessing and when they have recovered they bring them again to touch their foreheads with the holy water.

Of all the places in what was once the kingdom of Trebizond,

Sümela retains the essence of the early Christian world of the Byzantine saints, who in their zeal seemed to want to fly nearer to God in those wild retreats. Partly that was to protect them from the waves of Asians that for centuries crossed the mountains into a greener world from their deserts, bringing their flocks and their people, their own fighting legends, their wild elegance, their magnificent fearsome horsemen.

It is as if what we call the Byzantine world is still there to be found in and around Trabzon in miniature, in the echoes of their love of color at Hagia Sophia and in the fragments left of the frescoes at Sümela, in the Byzantine churches saved by being turned into mosques, and in the lush narrow fields that the mountain tribes looked on with longing, and all too often invaded.

Ottoman Turkey is there in the mosques, on the back streets in the center of the city, where lost *hans,* inns that once welcomed travelers and their camel caravans from far Tatary, are now used as factories for hammering the local copper pans and ornaments, the ancient walls taken for granted by the men who work there.

The central square of the city was once the Roman forum. In the late nineteenth century, Abdül Hamid II, known along this coast as Abdul the Damned, sent the Turkish army to put down an Armenian revolt that existed mostly in his own paranoid mind. He was the last of the absolute monarchs. He sent his army to foment murder and looting. It was cold-bloodedly done, with a bugle call to start the massacres, and one to end them in the evening. English sailors from a ship in Trebizond harbor told of Armenians being pursued as they tried to swim to safety and drowned by fanatical Turkish Muslims and soldiers.

It was in this square that one of the worst massacres of the Armenians took place. One of the officers had Armenian men trussed and sacrificed them like sheep while he quoted from the Koran.

All of this was the product of the half-insane mind of Abdül Hamid, and it was murder without excuse, unlike the civil wars during the First World War that came later, and from which a half-million Armenians and two million Turkish people are said to have died. I have wondered why this earlier massacre is not pointed out by modern Armenians as the main crime against them instead of the excesses of the civil war. Perhaps they would rather blame the government of modern Turkey, which had nothing to do with either of them, than they would a long-dead regime. It is like blaming the modern Russians for the Czarist pogroms, or the modern Lithuanians for their zealous anti-Semitism when they were occupied by the German army during World War II. The Armenians who still live there, and there are many, live in a touch-and-go amity with their neighbors under the government of modern Turkey.

It is as well to talk about the Armenian troubles here, in the east of Turkey where much of it happened. More often than not, in any country, history is invented by old hates, by passion, and by shame. No two people have shown this more clearly than the Turks and the Armenians in remembering the dreadful events of 1915 on the eastern front.

The Ottoman Empire was fighting on the side of the Germans in a brutal war against Czarist Russia along the borders of the Caucasus, where civilians and much of the Turkish army were destroyed between the hammer of Russian attack, which for years had included fomenting the local Armenians to revolt and then abandoning them, and the anvil of Ottoman neglect of the army in the field.

The front disintegrated into one of the most tragic civil wars of modern times. It is still being fought, in the press, in propaganda on both sides; the Turks burying shame and hurt by what they consider foreign misunderstanding; the Armenians drawing strength from ancient hate, and their refusal to admit that they tried to secede from the Ottoman Empire in the middle of a war and set up a Russian-backed Republic of Armenia with its capital in Van.

Both the modern Turkish government and the Armenians have hired public relations firms in Washington to plead their cause. What they need to do instead is to hire good historians who can read both the Cyrillic of imperial Russian records of backing the Armenians as a separate state, which the Turks considered to be treason in wartime, and the old Ottoman Arabic script where the orders and the dates for the Armenian population shift are hidden, to find out once and for all what happened in that black and evil time.

Anatolia is older than these quarrels, older almost than history, but never older than legend and the deep historic communal memory of its people. In Lord Kinross's history, *The Ottoman Centuries,* he says of the eleventh century, "There was a joint way of life and culture, common to conquerors and conquered, including Anatolians and Armenians," and then he quotes Paul Wittek's book, *The Rise of the Ottoman Empire:* "It was really only the Byzantine varnish which vanished, to be replaced later by an Islamic one. The local substratum survived." I think this is true not only of the Byzantine-Turkish change but of all the changes that had gone before: There is, deeper than all the rest, survival.

The massacre at Trabzon was one of the few times in Turkish history that Turkish soldiers, who still have the reputation as the most disciplined troops in the world, refused to obey orders. There were so many that they were not shot, but were jailed. Ihsan told me that his great-uncle was one of the soldiers who refused to obey orders. He said that people along the coast there still remember what families the soldiers in the mutiny came from and they will tell you with pride about a cousin, a great-grandfather, who refused to take part in the obscene massacre.

When we sat in the square in the evening drinking coffee after dinner at one of the small outdoor tables, it was crowded with quiet, elegant-looking men, almost foppishly dressed, drinking tiny cups of thick Turkish coffee and watching a soccer match on a television high in the trees.

I saw only two other women. No matter how civilized and worldly Trabzon may be as a seaport, it is in eastern Turkey and there are few women in public. But this is the country of the Amazons, and no matter how mild they may look casting eyes down when men pass them in the street, Black Sea women are descendants of women who were not allowed to marry until after they had killed a man. This is witch country, too. It was along this coast that Medea, the priestess of Colchis, called forth the obedient winds, and murdered and dismembered her brother to help her lover, Jason. No wonder then that for centuries the men kept the women in harems, at home.

Ihsan told me that in his own lifetime life there had gone from medieval to modern times. He said he remembered his father at home in the evening only two times in his life, and that was when he was too ill to join his men friends at the cafe. This is changing rapidly. I saw families with their children in a restaurant on the seashore where the waves lapped a few feet beyond the tables and the fairy lights were reflected in the water.

Things do not change and are never the same there. After Alexander Pushkin went from Russia to eastern Turkey as a young officer, he wrote, "I know of no expression more nonsensical than the words: Asian luxury . . . you cannot buy for any money what you can find in a general store in any district town of Pskov Province."

We drove the few miles from Trabzon to the Russian border, and as we got nearer the valley that had made Trabzon lush and green was only a pass between sea and mountains. The tea fields, the bright colored houses, the flowers, the vines, disappeared. The mountains came down so close to the sea that there was only room in places for the road itself.

It seemed a haunted land. I thought of witches, of the kingdom of Medea. As we drove along the coast toward the Russian border, the feeling grew stronger and stronger. Forests of dark pines made the mountains black; a faint, ghostly, secret mist hung down them almost to the water.

I had expected, as a much-vaunted NATO border, that it would be fortified. There was only the small road, and a sign in English that warned that foreigners were not allowed at the border. We drove on. Nobody seemed to care. When I asked Ihsan to turn around, he smiled and said, "Don't you want an incident to write about? All journalists want incidents." I said no, that I didn't feel like a journalist, whatever that is, and I did not want an incident, I wanted peace and happy days, and he looked as if he didn't believe me.

We got to the border. There was only a small barrier across the road, and from time to time it was lifted by a laconic Turkish customs officer, to let Russian tour buses through. On the Russian side there was a small watchtower. I saw no soldiers at all. I'm sure they must have been there, the few that there were room for, inside the tower.

But on the Turkish side the local peasants had set up a *pazar*. There were great bright piles of tomatoes and apples, nuts, spices, vegetables, hanging carcasses of lambs. Turkish *pazars* are luxurious with color. The Russians were crowded around the stalls, buying food, hardly looking at the embroidery and the small rugs that had been brought there for sale.

When we turned inland, leaving the coast of the Black Sea, we climbed higher and higher, through mile after mile of virgin forest, toward the bare plains of eastern Turkey. At the top of the pass, there was a last glimpse of *thalassa*, the sea, that had meant the way home at last to the lost soldiers of Xenophon.

It seemed right, if I was following any plan at all, to go from the last of Rome to the first kingdom of Turkey, across the high plateau, and enter Anatolia from the direction that the slowly moving tribes of Asia had come, and see as they saw. But I was beginning to doubt any plan in the ease of the summer days. I was fast succumbing to a pace that I had almost forgotten. The words, *"Yok problem,"* *"Sorma geç,"* don't bother, were coming back to me.

We drove up the mountains behind Trabzon; along the sickening passes without guardrails; looking down on the perpendicular sides of the mountains, lush with a green that was nearly black; and came out into the high meadows where the *yaylas* were, where the people from the seacoast go in summer for picnics and summer holidays, where for centuries they have stayed in beautiful wooden chalets. The trees spread there in the high meadows, and the fields are like they were when the Turkish tribes coming from the steppes of central Asia first saw them, miracles of green with water so clear that the people who come there in summer can tell the difference in the sweetness of the various springs.

They are still following the tradition of the tribes who moved the valuable flocks that were their riches to the high fields of summer. It was one of the habits and surprises that the Turkish nomads have left in the everyday life of people today, and from them I could see that discovery, in the conservative world of eastern Turkey, is a matter of the senses—eyes, ears, a watchfulness of gesture, old ways.

Most people in any culture are not aware of these reflections. The young polite Turkish boy bows to the older man, kisses his hand, and touches his own forehead with it because his parents have taught him to honor age, not because he is consciously following the manners of tribal Islam. The indigenous politeness, the courtly manners, the pride and the always incipient flashes of violence, the dignity, what they take pride in, what they love, are all there, more in the poor than in the rich who tend to follow our less formal Western manners.

We drove through the gorge of the Çoruh River. Magnificent, brutal sandstone cliffs almost met over the road that ran between them, often in deep shadow, while a thousand feet over our heads, we could see the sun flashing on the rocks. Sometimes there was only road and river, water carving and the scars of earth heave, for this is earthquake country, its nervous changeable surfaces eons slow.

Sometimes there were lush green fields along the river bottom, and olive groves that belonged far to the south. There is miraculous weather in the Çoruh gorge. Above it, the plains are under six feet of snow in winter, but there where the rock walls hold heat there is no snow, and where it is wide enough, they grow the crops of the south. Once the

Çoruh, when it was torrential, as the snows high above it melted, drowned its heroes, nomad soldiers, the soldiers of Süleyman; now it is the most famous white-water river in Turkey, and canoers come from all over Europe to challenge it.

There across the Çoruh was the first clue to the kingdom I searched for, the almost forgotten kingdom of the Seljuk Turks. It was a graceful, slim, highly arched bridge across the river, gently flowing in August, as if it had forgotten that it was ever the wildest river in Turkey.

CHAPTER
FIVE

THE KINGDOM
OF ALADDIN

Y NAVIGATIONAL CHART of the next weeks would form a great crescent from the Black Sea through the center of Anatolia, down to the Mediterranean. It would be called the Seljuk Kingdom of Rum. It would look like one of those seventeenth-century charts that had the warning "Here be Dragons," but instead of dragons there would be merchants and sultans and crusaders and mercenaries—centuries of them—and fields and buildings and roads so long traveled that they sink beneath the surface of the inland sea of the high plains.

There would be legends too, for this is a world where we have to go to legend to get the clues to facts. Unlike so many of the more familiar empires that have gone before them, the Seljuks have been a shadow.

The kingdom of Rum was one of the most short-lived in Anatolia, where several of the empires on the same land have survived for more than a thousand years. It began in 1071 and was destroyed by the thirteenth-century Mongol invasions, yet it has left a greater legacy in stone, in color, in lasting tradition, than any of the other Turkish tribes that spilled, raided, fought, or followed the grazing of their animals across the mountains into the great fertile saddleback of Anatolia. All across eastern and central Turkey, sometimes isolated in the great flat fields, sometimes tucked in back streets, in house walls, there are the unmistakable signs of their building.

To enter the heart of the kingdom of Rum, I wanted to follow the path of the thirteenth-century sultan who, more than any other Seljuk ruler, has engraved the Seljuk kingdom on Anatolia. Even his name reverberates with legend, Aladdin Keykubad—Aladdin, whose name meant "glory of the faith," a tale told at night of princesses and djinns and wonderful lamps.

He is nearly forgotten. All that is known about him is that he was "great." I wanted to find out why he was "great." Was he part of the past of manners or of might? *Aslan*—lion—the still-used name for a brave man, a "lawgiver" like the much later Süleyman, or a *ghazi,* a warrior who has survived, a great leader? He was a legend and a mystery. I asked a Seljuk scholar before I left and the answer was, "If you find him, tell me."

There we were, rolling along as safely as Turkish traffic allows in the twentieth century, following the route that, for a little while in a wild time, Aladdin had made safe by sponsoring a series of *hans* a day's journey apart by camel caravan, so that merchants could, after two hundred years of peril, travel without fear from the Mediterranean in the south, north through the Seljuk crescent, all the way to the Black Sea.

The kingdom of Rum is almost unknown in the West. It was the Seljuks who defeated the Byzantine Empire on "the dreadful day" at Manzikert in 1097. It was one of the most important battles in our Western history, but one that has been blotted from our memory.

Many of the Turkish tribes had been invited long since by the Byzantine emperors to protect the borders from the Persians, then, as now, traditional enemies. They had been in Anatolia from as early as the sixth century as mercenaries when Alp Arslan, the Seljuk leader in the eleventh century, made yet another attempt to break through at one of the defensive forts on the eastern borders of the Byzantine Empire.

The forts are still there in ruins of stone on the heights of the mountains over the eastern passes. We drove past the snaggled shapes of old castles where the watchmen are gone and the castle stones seem to have become part of the natural cliff-tops again.

Alp Arslan decided to invade once again at the fortress of Manzikert. The city had defied him before. At one siege the people of Manzikert threw a pig over the wall into the Seljuk camp—a deadly insult to Muslims—with a sign, "Marry this pig and we will give you Manzikert as a dowry."

The Byzantine army that met them was made up mostly of Turkish tribesmen and of Norman mercenaries under Roussel of Bailleul, who had ambitions of his own to set up a kingdom in Anatolia. On the fatal day, Friday, 19 August 1071, known ever after as "that dreadful day" by the Byzantines, Turkish tribes deserted and joined their own, and the Franks refused to fight. In one day the Byzantine army was destroyed. For the first time a Roman emperor fell into the hands of an enemy. The Seljuks called the new kingdom that began to grow that day the kingdom of Rum because they considered that they had conquered Rome, and they had.

The repercussions of that battle, when the floodgates broke open to the settlement of the whole of Anatolia by Turkish tribes, are still felt today. The traditional Eurocentric attitude toward the Turks began then, when the Pope called for the First Crusade to protect the Christian Byzantine Empire when it was already too late. It was then that the name Turk became a pejorative term meaning infidel, savage. I like especially the definition that comes from the Persian, "a beautiful youth, a barbarian, a robber."

So what little that is known of the Seljuks has come down to us from their enemies—wild tribesmen, barbarians, "the unspeakable Turk."

To the nomads who poured through the passes in the years after the battle, Anatolia was a heaven of grass. It is said they came slowly. Of course they did. Their animals grazed their way across, protected by fast armed outriders, who, like the American Plains Indians, could shoot their arrows with their deep curved bows from a galloping horse.

With the absence of forethought of the later Byzantines, Anatolia was awaiting them. There had been, long since, vast removals of the indigenous people, like the enclosures of Scotland, where the local villagers had been moved to make way for what had been Byzantine big business—vast herds of sheep—so that the land in the east was almost empty—a land that had, three thousand forgotten years before, sustained old empires of its own.

Of all the Turkish tribes that spilled over the mountains to Anatolia, the Seljuks of Rum had that rare quality that only a few nations have. They had an eye for what was good. Across the endless steppe kingdoms, from Armenia, from Persia, they took what they saw and liked and welded it into a style that is still so individual that it cannot be mistaken. They took from the people they conquered the local architects, builders, sculptors for their buildings, but with it all, they evolved a clear vision of their own. Scholars trace their derivations too easily, and too often miss what they have done.

Seljuk mosques are still in use in the cities of Amasya, Erzurum, Ankara, Kayseri, Konya, Sivrihisar, and Malatya. Their *medreses,* the colleges for studying the Koran, have been renovated and turned into museums in Tokat, Kayseri, Konya. Their *gümbets,* those stone tents for the dead with their conical roofs, are in the open fields, the corners of *medreses,* and mosques. In Tokat, one holds up a house. Near Lake Van, a perfect *gümbet,* like a little temple, shelters a long-dead Seljuk princess in an open field.

What they evolved, in the short time they held power in Anatolia, was all of their derivations and none of them. To miss this is to miss what they have still to offer. It is as if all Georgian architecture or Jeffersonian Revival were recognized only as derivative of Greek and Roman buildings and trim, with no recognizable quality of its own. True and not true. And like Georgian architecture, which is still being built two hundred years later, the Seljuk style survived long after the fall of their Anatolian empire. So to speak of a Seljuk building, a Seljuk facade, is to speak of a style. It was not an historic period so much as a way of seeing.

They found, when they arrived in Anatolia, a perfect marriage of local talent, raw material, their own taste, the facts of the weather, and stone. The mosques they built could not imitate the Arabian mosques, with their open courts, that they had seen. It was simply too cold in the winter. They used stone, as it had been used for centuries in Anatolia, because the local artists knew how, because it was there and rife and good to use after the frailer plaster of the Arab and Persian buildings.

What makes it transcend the sources they used—Persian, Arabic, Armenian, even Chinese? Most of all, it is their sense of life. The Seljuks were new converts to Islam when they came to Anatolia. Their religion, up until they began to move westward, had been local and animistic. Their priests were shamans. As inland sailors, they steered by the stars, and worshiped what they saw and were affected by sun and moon change and drought and flood and the stories of heroes.

They had a new religion but they still had the eyes, the habits, and the metaphors of people who had worshiped nature for centuries. Representational art, whether animal or human, is strictly forbidden by the

Koran. This is what makes Seljuk art and design so different from the more conventional Muslim design that came later to Anatolia.

There are Seljuk lions, those wonderful formal beasts, often with their tails ending with a dragon or serpent head, so that they form a fantastic orobus; the double eagle of the Seljuks; the pictures on tiles of fabulous animals and birds; the calm Mongolian faces of their tile portraits—the men, women, and angels with their long braids flying; the graceful undulating horses; the birds; the fish; and all of the astrological signs peeping out from behind leaves, in stone riots of carved flowers, snakes, and stars.

Their elegant and virile sense of form, their mixture of dignity and grace, the passions they brought and the choices they made are everywhere to be found—a fragment of a brocade in a French museum, with the name of Aladdin embroidered on it; a superb sense of color in the tiled *mihrabs,* the arched niches in mosques that show the direction of Mecca, so that the faithful can face it for prayer. In Anatolia the *mihrab* points south.

They brought the technique of making tile with them from the borders of China—the commonly used word for tile in Turkish is still *çini.* They founded an art of glazing that was the most beautiful in the Near East. The bright-colored tiles of a technique of double painting and firing, called *minai,* are still as bright as when they were fired—fragmented hints on the walls of the Muslim colleges and the hospitals in Konya, in Kayseri, in Tokat, in Sivas, in Erzurum. In the ethnographic museums all over the country, and still in some of the mosques, there are the carved wooden *mimbars,* those steep pulpits used for the Friday sermon.

They must have seen in the blue-green waters of Lake Van the color known as turquoise, Turkish blue. They used Armenian sculptors and stone masons. At the tenth-century Armenian Church of the Holy Cross on its island in Lake Van, there are walls of bas-reliefs, stories from the Bible, lively tendrils of vine, comic animals. There are reminders of this church at Divriği, and in a bas-relief in a museum in İstanbul where the Seljuk soldiers stand like the David and Goliath on the Akdamar church wall, and the dragons writhe like Armenian dragons under pointed tent-shaped roofs and stalactite carved doors.

Ihsan and I drove south along the high backbone of Anatolia. In the distance, we passed the foothills and then the shadow line of the Caucasus where the tribes had crossed, around the Caspian Sea and Mount Ararat, from the Asian steppes, the cold deserts. As far as the horizon was an inland sea of grass, stubble fields, wheat fields, a patchwork in places of sunflowers.

The villages seemed tiny under the heavy sun of August. They were so isolated, so private, that I sensed that I was intruding on their stillness even to try to know them. I watched them, passing clues to the living, as they were to the old kingdoms—that was all. We passed it all so quickly—the hint of winter to come in the neatly piled hayricks on top of the houses, shaped like high mansard roofs. Some of them looked about fifteen feet high.

They act as insulation, and slowly, slowly through the winter, they are used to feed the beasts that live in the room next to the families, each keeping the other warm in the deep snow that is combed and furrowed by the wind from the steppes that blows through the eastern passes. The villagers, with that ever-present sense of style that Turkish people have, make neat symmetrical towers of dung as high as the houses, for their winter fuel, their sides piled carefully in geometric patterns.

We passed the turnoff in the road that led to Sarıkamış, where 80,000 Turkish soldiers froze to death during the First World War, when a terrible winter blizzard came early and buried them in snow. They had only been issued summer uniforms.

We passed the abandoned field of Manzikert on the way to the nearest city that had been occupied after the battle—Erzurum. Cities have their own personalities in this part of the world, where they have been isolated for so many centuries and the great spaces between them have so often been battlefields.

Erzurum is surrounded by a grid of modern streets that were almost deserted when we drove into town. A cow walked down the middle of one of the wide boulevards built by Atatürk, who wanted to make Erzurum an eastern cultural center as well as a frontier post. He put a university there. Soldiers walk slowly around the streets, like soldiers far from home any place, unthreatening. We had passed some of them on the road, coming back to their barracks in a convoy of vans. They had been planting trees on those bare wind-sculpted hills toward the horizon.

We came into the suburbs at evening. Erzurum seemed dead until we drove into the Centrum—still called that in every city in Turkey so many centuries after the Romans have gone. As far as its life is concerned, it is still, as it always was, a vital, solemn place, with its throngs gathered around the center of the old town where the Byzantine citadel looks down on the city. Behind the citadel there is a beehive of old wooden Ottoman houses, which may be traditionally descended from Seljuk housing— wrecked, clean, hospitable, and teeming with people.

It is a conservative center like much of eastern Turkey. This does not mean that the people are Shiites, as foreigners suppose when they hear about conservative Muslims. It is conservative Sunni Islam. The men walk slowly, with that threadbare dignity that suddenly makes me want to cry; the tattered clothes, the pride, the vulnerability, which from time to time can break out into violence. They do not stare. That would be beneath them, and they answer with great courtesy when you say good morning.

Ihsan bowed and said *"Selamünaleyküm"* to an old man he passed who was sitting against the wall of the hilltop citadel, and when I asked him why he did not say it in Turkish, he said, "We are in eastern Turkey and the man is old. He has never accepted Atatürk's prohibition of the use of Arabic." He spoke of a prohibition that was announced in 1926, when Atatürk broke, for a long time, the power of the mullahs.

One of the first mosques the Seljuks built is in Erzurum. The Ulu Camii, the Friday mosque, is like a stone forest, mysterious and full of shadows, as if a grove had been enclosed and protected and made into a space for prayer. Its light, as in a forest, comes from above, from domes. It seemed to me to echo those ancient forest groves used by people in Anatolia long before the Christians or the Turkish tribes. The *mimbar,* the tall carved pulpit where the *imam* preached on Friday, is contemporary Seljuk, unchanged through the centuries, its geometric carvings aged into the color and texture of blackened stone.

The facade of the Çifte Medrese, next to the Ulu Camii but two centuries later, is a reflection not only of Seljuk tendrils of old beliefs but of that extraordinary resilience that these eastern cities showed during the most devastating of invasions. Except for the mosque, Erzurum was flattened, or supposed to have been, by the Mongols in 1243, yet the accepted date for this magnificent building, with its twin towers, is only ten years later, in 1253, while the city was being ruled by emirs subservient to the Mongols.

The Çifte Medrese has the openness and the magnificent scale and space that I would see in later buildings all the way across what is left of the kingdom of Rum. The old *medreses* were more than simple religious institutes. Some of them were scientific schools, some teaching hospitals. Except for the few that were covered, the traditional shape didn't change much—the open courtyard for contemplation, often with a fountain in the center, and sometimes used for outdoor lectures; the student rooms all around under a colonnade; and the *iwan,* an open arched, domed lecture hall. Sometimes there were several of these between the student rooms. The passion for education among the newly urbanized nomadic tribes showed in the great spurt of new *medreses* that were built as part of the mosque complexes, along with soup kitchens for the poor.

In the back of the *medrese* the children played in a field, in and out among three Seljuk *gümbets,* those conical tombs with their pointed tentlike roofs. They gathered around Ihsan, like they would a *dayı,* an uncle, asking questions. I could see why he would be a fine teacher. In a few minutes he had them laughing, the smaller ones nestling against his body.

There, that morning, was the dilemma of Turkey today. One small boy had been dressed and made so neat by his mother that he walked slowly like a grown man. He wore blue jeans, sneakers, and a lace *takke,* the skull cap that showed that he was going to the *hoca,* the religious teacher, for instruction. A little girl was in the *bakkal,* the kind of small family store that sells everything from rope to onions to bread. We had gone there to get a key for the gate to the *gümbets,* although the children had simply climbed over the fence. She was buying eight loaves of bread, and she was so small that the loaves almost covered her face.

"There are ten of them in that family," the *bakkal* owner told us, "and that is all they will have to eat today."

Hunger and religion—they are not mutually independent, for much of the religious revival is a mixture of the conservatism of the old, and a bad combination of the bitter and dispossessed and the new rich. We had already counted fifteen mosques being built in villages on the way to Erzurum. They were modern, ugly imitations of the traditional tiled mosques, looking, one after another, like public bathrooms, with their gleaming factory-produced tiles. They are being built as pious gifts when schools and hospitals, and something useful and attractive for people to do for pleasure, are what is needed.

Liberals in Turkey fear and decry this. They would like to see more money spent on secular education, on roads and health—and it is certainly needed. But the mosques are not built by the state. They are built by the conservative rich men of the community as monuments to themselves, and named after them, as they have been ever since the first mosques were built by the Seljuks.

There has been no attempt to replace the communal center that the mosque represents by any other community center or even much entertainment from outside. I talked to a young actress who worked in İstanbul and she said that a theatrical troupe had taken an English farce, of all plays, to Erzurum, that the performances were packed every night, and that the people of Erzurum begged them to come back. I thought of a Turkish "peace corps" of actors, jugglers, musicians, and poets, who are needed in the east almost as much as schools and hospitals. The profound boredom of being neglected is a dangerous illness, too.

It was hard to ignore the combination when we walked along the narrow Ottoman streets and the children poured out and the mothers smiled from the doorways. I thought of hidden hunger and pride and how it festers, and wondered if ignoring it was a part of conservative policy in Turkey, as a pot is left on the stove until it boils.

On Sunday, when we went to look at Seljuk buildings, the air was suddenly rent with the noise of horns from a procession of cars. We were in the East, where the rites of Islam are celebrated with noise and solemn gaiety. On Sunday, in Erzurum and all the way west—I saw the last of the processions in Bursa—and south to the Mediterranean, Sunday is Circumcision Day for boys from seven to twelve years old, and when it is done, and the boy has been blessed at the mosque, his family and their friends drive through the streets honking their horns, as they do at weddings.

I had no shame about asking Turkish men about their circumcisions—maybe I got away with it because I was a *gavur,* but I think it was because they had always wanted to tell about how awful it was, and they didn't dare complain to another Turk.

One had climbed a tree and refused to come down until he was promised a bicycle. When I asked if the bicycle was worth it, he said, "No."

Another had his mouth stuffed with chocolate so nobody would hear him cry. In Turkey, no matter what a man does later in life—fame, riches, politics—the old women in his town will remember forever if he cried at his circumcision.

Sunday instead of Friday as a rest day has reached eastern Turkey, too. Men, and even a few women, stroll in the evening, and as darkness came we went to a restaurant two floors above the street where we could see, shadowed by evening, the Yakutiye Medresesi, the fourteenth-century Sufi convent, with a Tree of Life and carved Seljuk lions, and one of the most beautiful minarets in Turkey; its red bricks, interlaced with turquoise tiles, leeched by darkness; the park around it deserted, its tidy shoeshine boys gone over the hill to the poor Ottoman houses where the *ağas* and the merchants once lived.

The proprietor of the restaurant apologized for not being able to seat us in the main dining room, and pointed out with some pride at the same time that there was to be the celebration of an important wedding, and that if we wished we could see the decorations before the bridal party arrived.

In the large room with its low ceiling a bandstand had been set up, and tables covered with white cloths were set to seat at least two hundred people. The ceiling was hung with swags of Christmas-tree ornaments that had been used often before. They were thin and a little tarnished in the dim light. In the center of each table there were bottles of water and Coca-Cola.

He explained that we would have to sit in the men's section, and Ihsan said that was all right, that I was a foreigner—a *gavur*. It was not the first time I had to pretend that I did not understand.

In the men's dining room the television was going with the inevitable soccer match, as in every place I went where men gathered, and they ate and drank while they watched. That is another Turkish habit, tradition, and pleasure that is unlike other Muslim countries. For millenia they have made wine in Anatolia—Xenophon talked about how good it was—and they like to drink that or *rakı,* the lethal Turkish anise drink that can be the downfall of innocent foreigners.

A meticulously dressed old man, his shoes polished but worn, his shirt freshly laundered, sat at a table near us. He was quietly drunk. When a gaggle of bully boys came in, the leader, a man who looked like he might cut your throat, not even out of malice but just because he took a mind to, went up and bowed to the old man, kissed his hand and lifted it to his forehead. Was that gesture by a bully to a drunk because he was older, because he had been his teacher, his *dayı*—the word for an uncle on the mother's side that has become a synonym for a respected or influential friend?

Maybe it was not riches or power but simply some unwritten law of politeness that made a bully boy become, for a minute, the descendant of an aristocracy of manners. As far as I could tell, none of them even glanced in my direction, even though I was the only woman in the room. I simply did not exist. I was a *gavur*.

As we left, we heard the haunting minor key of the music from the wedding. The father of the bride and the proprietor stopped us on the stairs, and ushered us into seats inside the door. There the wedding celebration was in full swing. The room was packed—all ages, all sexes, young children in blue jeans, mothers in print dresses, grandmothers with their heads covered. But there were no *şalvar*, none of the cotton finery of the local country people. This was a bourgeois wedding.

The bride sat with her new and very young husband beside the bandstand. Tradition demanded that she look very sad—a village or generation away and she would have had her hands hennaed still, been totally enveloped in a veil and red velvet wedding garment with gold embroidery, probably drugged, and been "kidnapped" by the groom's party as part of the old ceremony.

Here the bride was in a white Western wedding dress and veil. At first, all that seemed to be left of Eastern tradition was the sadness that would be remarked on by her mother's friends. I thought she looked profoundly bored.

The music, though, was pure eastern Turkish, plucked in a plaintive minor key on the stringed *saz*, and caressed on the *davul*, the drum. But the West had entered there, too. The *saz* was connected to an electric amplifier. The music was the formal lament of old Turkey, and in the center of the dance floor, a line of young men of Erzurum danced the wedding dance.

They were dressed in the traditional clothes of their region, the black tight shirts and trousers, the silver belts where once the family's best dagger would have been slipped into a scabbard and worn as a jewel. They wore silver chains around their necks with long-chained lavalieres tucked into their belts.

The dance was slow, measured, and dignified. The guests were completely silent—the Coca-Cola, the amplifiers, the Western jeans, the

Christmas ornaments, the Western wedding dress forgotten. The music told us where we were: in eastern Turkey near the Caucasus, in the city that was old when the Seljuks came. I had never been in such a silent audience. When the young men—all of whom were friends of the groom—had finished, there was a storm of applause, and then the next entertainment for the wedding came out.

He was the professional town poet and public reader. He wore a white dinner jacket and a red tie. He bowed to the bride and groom and began to declaim. His voice sobbed. He gestured. He shouted at some point when the poem he said had long escaped me. He clutched his chest. Ihsan told me that the poem had been written by a friend of the groom's who was working in Germany. He had hired the professional poetry reader. The gist of it was that he was homesick for his native land, that he was alone and friendless in a great foreign city, that he longed to be at the wedding where he could honor his friend whom he loved since they were children, and that it was a love "passing the love of women." It was the modern Turkish version of the lament of David and Jonathan. It was a time for tears from the old women with their head covers, but not as we cry so formally at weddings. They were tears for time and great space and the black clothes of night and the dancers, and the boy lost in Germany.

All of this was accepted as part of the ceremony, and when the declaimer had finished there was another storm of applause and people ran up and pinned thousand lira notes to his lapels. He went out bowing and smiling. The bride's expression had not changed at all.

Then, to the *saz* and the *davul,* and to brighter, gayer music, the wedding guests danced, women together, men together, children in and out among them. All of it was Turkish dancing and some of it was beautiful, the flung hips, the clicked fingers, hands held high above their heads, weaving the air, the undulations of blue jeans.

There was not one second of the easy sentimentality that we would expect at a Western wedding, no blushing, no romantic music—frankly, no permeation of the idea of romantic love. The bride may have been in a Western dress, but this wedding was as Eastern and as conservative in spirit as any village wedding, and the same attitude toward her future would be expected of the bride.

Marriage in Turkey is the essential woman's work. Even the emancipated doctors, teachers, lawyers, judges talk about "five o'clock emancipation," when, her profession over for the day, the woman is expected to turn into a traditional Turkish wife again. The main occupation and focus of the wife for centuries has been service to her mother-in-law, who is the head of the house. This bride, in her Western wedding dress, might not live with her in-laws as she would have done in the past, but she would live near them and be at her mother-in-law's beck and call until the mother dies, her own sons grow up, and she is in control of her own daughters-in-law. When she has a marriageable son, all too often she will choose whom he marries. It seems only fair, since the mother and daughter-in-law will be nearer to each other, day in day out, than either of them are to the men of the family. No wonder the bride was expected to look sad.

Her family would also have been paid the modern equivalent of a "bride-price." It is the opposite of the idea of a Western dowry, where the bride's family has, traditionally in Europe, provided money for the new couple. Instead, the Turkish bride is, traditionally, sold by her father.

If this seems alien to the West, it is well to remember that one of the most precious quotes from the Old Testament about love is, "Whither thou goest I will go, where thou lodgest I will lodge, thy people shall be my people, and thy God my God." It was said by Ruth, not to her husband but to her mother-in-law, Naomi. And when she married Moab, her mother-in-law, Naomi, sold her—in effect, took the expected bride-price.

When I considered this, sitting there in the near dark, it seemed less strange and, in some ways, far more pragmatic than our Western ideas of legalized sexual and romantic love. I thought of a pleasing attitude, too, toward marriage in Turkey. There are two times when a woman is considered to be half-insane and in need of care—the first month of her marriage and the first month of her widowhood. At both times she is waited on hand and foot by family and neighbors until she recovers her sanity.

When we left, the father of the bride bewailed his humble party and said in better times there would have been a real celebration. We said good-bye in the right ways we could, the strangers at the wedding.

Ihsan, the economist, said the father mourned because inflation had wiped out the middle class. But I, as a romantic, and as one whose first book read alone had been *The Arabian Nights Entertainments,* was certain that the dance had gone on for centuries, that he bemoaned his humble dwelling as formally as if it had been a tent in the desert beyond the Caucasus, or an Ottoman mansion in İstanbul, instead of a public restaurant in Erzurum in the late twentieth century, with Coca-Cola on the tables. Manners are manners and have deep roots, even the manners of apology. Since the Atatürk revolution, many Turks had forgotten how Turkish they are, but manners are unconscious, and they have inherited their courtesy from the nomads and their sense of ceremony from the Byzantines.

CHAPTER
SIX

THE EDUCATION
OF PRINCES

F I WERE GOING to introduce a Westerner to central Turkey, and had to pick a place to start, I would pick Amasya. There are people you meet whom you know you will see again, and there are cities that you know you will go back to. There is something deeper there than welcome to a stranger, and both more casual and more profound than its beauty. I know this about Amasya, and I am not the first by some two thousand years. For that long it has been its own center with its own sense of being; so graceful a place, so protected by its fortress mountains, that it was chosen for centuries as the city where Ottoman princes were sent to be educated in the arts of government.

We found it—it is a hidden city—by turning northwest, off the arterial highway across the high plains into a river valley. The mountains rose, sharp, protective, around us. We were entering another world, a green world of forests and orchards; another kingdom, the capital of the kingdom of Pontus.

On the steep mountain that forms one side of the gorge behind Amasya, the palace and the tombs of the kings who ruled Pontus are carved out of the rock above the last houses of the town. This is where the wild, cruel, almost legendary king of Pontus, Mithridates, raided and claimed an ephemeral kingdom far beyond boundaries he had inherited in 110 B.C., when he promptly murdered his mother and his brother to secure his power. He held out longer against the Romans than any other ruler in Anatolia. The Roman commander was Pompey, who finally destroyed what was left of Mithridates' kingdom in 65 B.C.

The present seemed to become the past in a few miles, and one kingdom became another, and sometimes another and another, as Amasya grew through the Pontic, Roman, Seljuk, and Ottoman centuries to the beautiful, quiet city it is today.

It lies in a deep gorge beyond a confluence of two rivers that flow north to the Black Sea. Their classic names were the Halys and the Thermadon, the river that Jason was told came from Hades. They form the Yeşilirmak, which pours through the gorge and then, miraculously, seems to be entirely still and form the central street of Amasya, with its row of Ottoman houses mirrored in the water, and its Roman-Seljuk-Ottoman bridges, whose reflections made circles in the river.

I went to Amasya following the trail of the Seljuks but I found the essence of a Turkish city—a distillation of past and present, more dramatic than in anyplace else I found in Turkey because it is all alive, all used. Nothing is set aside as "monument." It is all monument and it is all present. It honors a series of kingdoms that took a pride in it that still is such an important part of the city.

I sensed, when I walked there under the trees, along the river street, that I was visiting someone's fine house—maybe fallen a little into less affluent times than when it was the capital of the kingdom of Pontus and when later the Ottoman heirs were sent to learn the art of governing. That is unmentioned, and perhaps unthought of, in the atmosphere of hospitable pride.

As if it wanted to state this and include a near past that has helped to make it what it is now, the recognition of the duties and pleasures of a more enlightened present, the ever-present statue of Mustafa Kemal Atatürk is the finest I saw in Turkey. When the first statues were put up in the inland cities in the twenties and thirties, most of the people had just been jogged awake from a thousand years of medieval sleep by circumstance and Mustafa Kemal. Most of them had never in their lives seen a statue, as the Koran forbids the representation of humans.

It stands on a crag of rock in the middle of the Centrum. Baroque, elegant, and in some ways a dangerously inept memory of him, Atatürk sits on a wonderful Delacroix horse; he is a *ghazi*, a warrior hero. There is no sense here of his reforms, his modern views, his dandyism, his intelligence, but, like the heroes all the way back to Mithridates, he is a fighter, surrounded by heroic figures from the army that he created out of almost nothing at the end of the First World War. There are the wounded, the women, the lines of his generals who look out across the river at the tombs of the Pontic kings.

It was in Amasya where Atatürk found a force of mountain volunteers already formed to fight against the Greek partisans who had armed themselves to take part in the carving up of Anatolia by the Allies at the end of the First World War. Amasya was to be the capital of a revived Pontic kingdom.

The mountain volunteers were to form a nucleus of his ragtag army. At that point, when he arrived there, there was little organized resistance to the carve up of Turkey. It was there that he and four friends sat at a table and planned a new country to rise out of the defeated and dishonored Ottoman Empire. I like to think of them, sitting in the restaurant by the river, drinking some *rakı,* all young men, all afire with what was only an idea, and a wild, impossible one at that.

He made his first public speech announcing the resistance in Amasya, where so many kingdoms had been protected by its natural setting.

"Citizens of Amasya," he called to them, "What are you waiting for? . . . If the enemy tries to land at Samsun, we must pull on our peasant shoes, we must withdraw to the mountains, we must defend the country to the last rock. If it is the will of God that we be defeated, we must set fire to all our homes, to all our property; we must lay the country in ruins and leave it an empty desert. Citizens of Amasya, let us all together swear an oath that we shall do this."

On the first evening that we went there, Ihsan and I were sitting on the balcony of the restaurant by the river—inexpensive, familiar, an obvious gathering place for the men and the women, who seem more free there to go out in public. We looked over the black night water, with its snakelike images of the lights on the opposite bank. The shadowed statue of Atatürk loomed in the central square on the hill rise across the river.

Ihsan was telling a story about the last time he had been in the restaurant, when he and his wife had waited until late at night for a friend to arrive. The friend was driving back—a ten-hour trip—from the south coast of the Mediterranean to get there because the next day he was to receive an award for paying the most taxes of anyone in the city.

The rest of the story faded from my hearing. I thought of the batteries of lawyers and accountants who make their very good livings by keeping us from paying any more tax than we have to, and how alien the idea of pride in one's civic duty of paying taxes would be to us. I thought of the night we sat so peacefully by the river, and how long Amasya had been there, and of the people I had read about who had found haven there and their special sense of being in that quiet city, invaded over and over through the centuries, but always, as after river rise and storm, going back to its basic quietness as the river would do.

Amasya is where the rebel Norman, Guiscard, decided that he, too, would have himself a kingdom. He had been a mercenary hired by the Byzantine emperor to protect the center of Anatolia against the Turks, at a time when it was as impossible as stopping the flow of a river with a single rock. The people of Amasya thought he was so attractive and his governing so just for the city that they only stopped trying to get him back, after his capture, when they thought he had been blinded, which tended to be the mildest punishment meted out to traitors. But it had not been done; he was able to persuade the emperor to hire him, yet again.

Behind the wall of the castle, now lit at night so that it and the nearby tombs of the Pontic kings, which are cut into the mountain, cast a romantic glow across the steep mountainside, there is only the formal garden of evergreen trees, a small *hamam,* and a well-cared-for space of grass, to help you remember that it is called, locally, the Castle of the Maidens, for the harems that were there when the Ottoman princes were Amasya's governors.

I went out early in the morning to see the Seljuk mental hospital, built in 1308, and in use until the mid-nineteenth century. As early as the fourteenth century the treatment of mental patients was astonishingly modern. They were not chained or beaten as in Europe. Instead they were talked to, given exercises, sedated by warm-water baths, and made calm by music and dancing and sometimes hypnosis.

It was 6:30, the sun was new, and the facade of the hospital was a perfection of Seljuk carving: the florets, the twining vines, and a kneeling figure on the keystone of the door. Was it the slave of the local sultan who had had it built in honor of his ruler? I thought that nobody was there and then—I had not even heard him—a smiling boy-man was standing beside me, awkward and helpful, treating the hospital as if it were his own home, an attitude I would find over and over with volunteer guides.

He was a natural. They are not isolated in Turkey, but are cared for by their families. Inside the hospital, built in the traditional *medrese* style, with an *iwan*—the open lecture hall—on either side and another at the far end, and the patients' rooms in long colonnades, he took me to room after room, some full of rubble, all empty and forgotten, except, I think, by him, who had made it a second home. His brother, or father—I never knew—saw that we had become friends when we came out of the great door; he sent tea and those huge round sesame-covered rolls, called *simit,* over to us, and we sat together on the sill of the Seljuk carved window in front of the hospital in the sun and ate our breakfast together. When I tried to pay for it, they both refused. But the boy insisted that I take his picture in front of the Seljuk facade.

One of the most fascinating buildings I saw in all of central Anatolia is in Amasya. It is the Kapı Ağası Medresesi, built in 1488 by the "white eunuch" who was the head of the harem and an important government official, even though he was an imperial slave, as a tribute to Beyazit II, who, as one of the Ottoman princes, governed in Amasya when he was young.

It is octagonal. Its large paved courtyard that morning was full of adolescent boys playing football, not in any organized way, but simply kicking the ball back and forth in the sun. They played like boys who don't know each other very well. Some of them seemed just to have arrived—they still carried cloth duffel bags and suitcases. There were piles of luggage at the door—still, as late as 1488, in the Seljuk style. In the entrance, with its stalactite carving and its pointed arch, a table had been set up and some of the boys were registering.

I took for granted that it was an army recruiting station; it certainly was officially used and cared for, clean, repaired, painted. Then I saw the sign over the facade of the door—it was a school for *imams* and *hocas,* or Koran readers, like a seminary in Europe or America, the building still used for the function it was built for, not, as in so much of post-Atatürk Turkey, turned into a museum, a relic. Since they were school-age boys, the instruction period may have been only in the summer.

Here it was in the morning, boys playing football, and the sign, the reason unchanged from when the *medrese* was built five hundred years ago—both the strength and the dilemma of modern Turkey. These were not backwoods peasant boys. Most of them were fairly well dressed, lively, contemporary.

So on one side of the river the statue of Atatürk, and on the other, in the white eunuch's *medrese,* the boys there to learn to be Muslim priests and readers, and between them river run, the quietness of buildings and people, the years.

I stayed at a restored Ottoman house, where the courtyard was like a little museum of its own: the outdoor oven, the carved wooden stalls, the paving that was scrubbed every morning like an outdoor room, and the central hall that was so clean that I remembered to "take my shoes from off my feet" in the polite Turkish way.

The ceiling of my room was carved wood, the wall cupboard finely paneled. All along the front of the room, where the windows let in filtered sun through hand-embroidered curtains onto the carpets and the pillows, there was a seat built against the wall. I had again the nomad sense there that after long genetic training in being prepared, even the most settled of Ottoman houses was designed to be deserted in an hour. The only movable furniture was the two low beds, and those were a concession to visitors. In the time the house was first used there would have been mattresses to sleep on, rolled into a corner in the daytime.

In the morning we sat at breakfast, and a small dog wandered over to be petted. A cat sat on the whitewashed wall, and one of those huge pillows, covered with carpeting, had been laid on a low platform against the house for the *ağa* who was no longer there to sit in the sun.

I had asked for a car and driver to pick me up in Amasya for the next part of my Seljuk search. I had been specific. I wanted, I told them, a mature, English-speaking driver, an uncle to protect me, a *dayı.*

Now I am well aware that the classic way for the intrepid literary traveler to go through the wilds of Turkey is by donkey, or ancient Jeep, or even, if novels count, by white camel. However, I asked for a Mercedes. The roads in Turkey are dangerous. Turks are wonderful drivers. If they weren't, they would all be dead. They take hair-raising chances, on hills, on curves—"Whirr! whirr! All by wheels! Whizz!," as the Pasha said to Kinglake. It is a game, a macho test. It was on these roads that I was planning to go south, and then west, in central Turkey where the traffic is heavier and much faster than it is across the great plains of the east.

After breakfast, the day before he was to hand me over to Avis, Ihsan had a long impassioned telephone conversation, in Turkish far too fast for me to follow, with the driver in Trabzon who was to pick me up. When he finished he said, "There is no problem. He is a Laz, like me. He has a good Laz accent. I told him exactly what to do, how fast to drive and no more, and where to take you to dinner." Once again, I was being handed like something fragile and cared for, from *arkadaş* to *arkadaş*, for even though they had only met on the telephone they were kinsmen of the same belligerent tribe.

My driver arrived. Avis had carried out their promises to the letter. He was mature—twenty-two—and a student at the University of Trabzon. He spoke English as I spoke Turkish, at survival level. We simply started out by putting a Turkish-English dictionary between us, and off down the road we went, first to the buildings in Amasya that I had missed and wanted to see before I left.

I think the miracle of friendship that I would find over and over began then. Yusuf had known little about the Seljuks, so instead of lingering, slightly bored beside the car while I crawled among the ruins and photographed the florets, stars, tendrils, and animals of the Seljuks, unnoticed to the contemporary young Turks, who have a passion only for the future, he came with me.

He had a passion, too, a passion to find out about Turkey. He had been brought up in Holland and had only come back to Turkey, to Trabzon, when he was an adolescent, and he knew far less of his own country than he knew of Europe. This is what Yusuf had missed, and now he was finding his own place, a place where he should not have been a half-stranger, but was.

This is not unusual in Turkey. In a country where there are few jobs, Turks tend to go to Europe and stay there, sometimes for several generations, to work. In every place but Germany, where they are treated appallingly, their ability to work, their pride, their ease of life is honored. Only in Germany are there terrible street jokes, like the riddle, "Why does the train from Frankfurt full of Turks arrive empty in İstanbul?" The answer: "The train stops at Auschwitz."

The surprise of the morning was always Yusuf, who began to develop an eye for hints and fragments, especially Seljuk. The best part of Amasya, and of the other cities we visited, was the discovery, the hints and fragments, the possibilities of conjuring whole buildings from a half-buried cave that had been an *iwan,* from a bit of imperial Roman carving sunk into a wall. It was Yusuf who pointed out a Seljuk *han,* an inn still used for merchants, only now the merchants are the hardware store, where wheelbarrows are piled high against the carved entry, and a builder next door who has left a pile of lumber propped against the wall that reaches to the roof. There are empty oil cans, a *bakkal,* and, in the middle, a pharmacy where they sell the oil of flowers.

CHAPTER SEVEN

SAINTS, SELJUKS, AND WILD DOGS

S O YUSUF AND I set out to trace the paths of Aladdin, who, more than any other Seljuk ruler, engraved the kingdom of Rum forever on the Anatolian land. We drove south toward Tokat with the dictionary between us. There was a rare politeness about this part of the journey. Far from the ubiquitous dragomans of English travel books, who are either cheating Englishmen or saving their lives from bandits in an ecstasy of the already expected, Yusuf was an educated, well-dressed, extremely polite young Turk—with all that that phrase implies—and so I realized that I must not embarrass him. So we made a pact that he would do all the paying, food, hotel, tickets, everything, as if he were my escort, and I would pay him back at the end of each day, so that he would not be humiliated. Only of course that word was never used. Neither of us even knew the word in the other language anyway!

Tokat is in none of the guidebooks I found. It is purely and simply Turkish, with no concession—and some of the concessions are embarrassingly awkward—to an industry they call tourism, at which the Turks are new and tentative. So its pace, its people, and what happened to us there was unguided, and so a treasure.

The first Seljuk tomb that we saw, on the main street of Tokat, had been partly used to make a house, as if the house had been built against it and over it for some kind of protection. A small sign in front of it read

Sümbül Paşa 1288. Cars were parked in front of the perfect pointed stone arch of a Seljuk doorway.

Farther on we came to the museum, in Tokat's finest Seljuk building—the Gök Medrese, built in 1270. Its doorway, made of what looked like darkened stone inlaid with red marble, shone in the noon sun. A garden had been planted in front of it and was well cared for. Boys played in front of it. The museum was closed for lunch.

As we turned away a boy of about twelve came up to us and said, very seriously, in English, "If you will please wait, I will see what I can do for you." He came back in a few minutes and motioned us inside.

It was as alive within as it had ever been when it was first used. A fountain with a spout made of several portrait heads in the Oriental Seljuk style still played there, and the water in the fountain was turquoise and so were fragments of tile on the walls beside the *iwan* at the end of the garden, a contrast of eggplant purple and turquoise that I could see had once completely covered the wall. Even the fragments dazzled, shining in the sun.

In the front, inside the door, four attendants and museum workmen were having lunch, surrounded by several patient cats. They were obviously used to our young entrepreneur. They waved us all past.

The *medrese* was built around an open courtyard and the cells had been made into display rooms, so that there, beyond any other place I saw, we were able to see how a *medrese* had been used, the open doorways, the rooms intact.

Our small guide had become a curator. He explained that we were to use no flash. "This is not," he said, "allowed in the bigger Turkish museums," of which, he implied, this was one.

The first room we saw was Hittite—we were, in Tokat, nearly at the center of the Hittite Empire of the second millenium B.C. Our guide informed us that the Hittites had lived a long time ago, in the nineteenth century. We went into the Seljuk cell, where there were the curved bows, the tile fragments, then into the Ottoman rooms, all of which, he said, were nineteenth century. I listened while I looked at sixteenth-century maces, jewelry, and the Seljuk curve of twelfth-century bows.

We came to what he called the Christian room. There, in a glass casket, was a beautifully dressed young girl, a skeleton with a face made of wax, whose wax throat was cut. Wax blood fell onto her real, chestnut-colored hair. Her dress was a rich blue embroidered with gold thread over an underdress of gold. She lay on a red silk cover with gold embroidery. Our curator said that she was a saint of the Christians.

On either side of her were what were obviously nearly modern statues of Christ, and a Holy Virgin. On the walls were large gold-backed medieval icons of the head of Saint John held by an angel, a wonderful Saint George, a bearded patriarch. These were old, how old I couldn't guess, and I hesitated to ask where they had come from and when, for Tokat was in the vanguard of the War of Independence, when there were huge movements of population between Turkey and Greece, and many deaths and lootings on both sides.

Our guide added, "Nineteenth century." When I asked if I could photograph just the saint—whom they called Christina—he said no and then he said yes, and then, "If you would like I will tell you a story." And there was a sense of settling down, Yusuf, me, and the boy, who now had turned into an old, wise, quiet storyteller, and his voice lowered for the new part.

"Christina was the daughter of a very strict Christian father," he told us. "She fell in love with a handsome and rich Turkish boy. When she tried to run away with him on a white horse across the mountains, her father found out and cut her throat. So there she is. She is now a saint."

It was a classic story all the way back to *Dede Korkut,* where nomad Turkish warriors loved and won Christian princesses who rode and fought like Amazons. The same story is told about Seyit Gazi, the eighth-century Arab Muslim hero, and his Christian princess. It was the story that reflected so long ago the romantic side of intermarriages between Turks and Christians, as the Western story of Cinderella reflects the Western conventional hope of marrying royalty or riches. As told by our storyteller, it was *The Arabian Nights,* its iconography all wrong, all right, all in the story, and all, of course, nineteenth century.

All the time, all the miles, I was getting nearer to the hope that I could find something of Aladdin. I found the first hint, the first shadow of him, in Sivas.

There are dour cities and Sivas is one of them. It turns its back on you. Few tourists go there. I suspected that very few visitors of any kind went there, yet it seemed a city where there was a lot of industry. A sign hung above the traffic on the main street offering tickets to a lottery where the prize was lessons in English, a sad sign that must bite deep into the pride of such a withdrawn place.

The Ulu Camii, the Friday mosque, is so old that its twelfth-century floor is sunk below the modern street. It has all the mystery and shadow of the early Seljuks: the heavy columns like the trunks of trees, the cavelike corridors between them, the pure, empty spaces. When we went there in the morning, there was, all through the mosque, a sound of chanting like doves churtling.

Beside the door was the shelf for shoes. Muslims do not go into the mosque with shoes on. The phrase for the vilest kind of thief is, "He would steal shoes from a mosque." The shelf was full of the same kind of sneakers you would find at any playground in America or Europe. All throughout the building, near column after column, little boys in *takkes* and blue jeans sat on their heels at low triangular wooden Koran tables, chanting Arabic from the Koran in words that none of them could understand, and swaying back and forth in time to their chanting.

When we left Yusuf said, "I wish you hadn't seen that," as if it were a shame to his country. It is easy for Westerners, or has been in the past, to discount the danger of a fundamentalist revival in the Middle East. It should not be anymore. There is an ominous connection between little boys chanting in their lovely soft voices, and the guns of the right-wing hired death squads that murdered Metin Emeç, one of Turkey's most prominent columnists, in 1989.

Emeç had, again and again, accused Turkey's fundamentalists of a rising wave of terrorism that was responsible, among other death-squad hits, for the murder of the head of the Ankara Bar Association, Muammer Aksoy, an outspoken critic of the right-wing government-backed court-ship of the fundamentalists.

The incipient bitterness and a violence that can be tapped by the cynical is deep in the Turkish soul. Nobody has tried to include the poor and uneducated in their talk of reform, not even the liberals whose eyes are dazzled by the West. They accuse the Motherland Party of fomenting anti-Atatürk prejudice and driving the country back into Islamic rule. They fear that religious authority could replace democracy only fifty years after the death of Atatürk, and I think they are right to fear it. But they do nothing about the lack of understanding between themselves and the poor that I saw in eastern Turkey—with their neatness, their politeness, their pride, their poverty—from whom they could learn something of an identity and a source of pride, too. The Western-leaning liberals of Turkey stay too much in the cities, let anti-intellectual prejudice grow in a fertile soil, and do little about bridging the gap. Atatürk's deep, bitter prejudice against religion may have gone too far in trying to stamp it out, and his actions have left a deep wound in the Turkish people that needs to be healed and not used cynically.

We were following Aladdin but we were also on the road of Atatürk, going from east to west in the triumphal direction of the great *ghazis*. It is ironic that one of the modern buildings that the people of Sivas take most pride in is the one where Atatürk called the first congress of the new Turkey in September of 1919, to begin consolidation of resistance to the Allied occupation and those plans to carve up the country among themselves that were a hangover from nineteenth-century arrogant diplomacy.

It was from Sivas that he, and İsmet İnönü and the thousands of half-starved Easterners, who had suffered so under the Russian occupation and in the civil war with the incipient Republic of Armenia that had been backed and armed by the Russians, began the march that would end, two years later, at İzmir and the sea, with a Turkey behind them freed of the danger of partition by the Western powers.

It is in Sivas that we found two of the most famous Seljuk buildings in Turkey. They stand facing each other across an ancient, narrow street so that the shadow of one falls perpetually on the other as time circles the sunny days. On one side is the Çifte Medrese with its twin minarets that call to mind the twin towers of medieval churches, with the carved vines reaching, as the Muslims of the time would have said, to heaven, and that do seem to be growing toward it. There is only, now, a facade with its beautifully carved doorway. Behind it, against the wall, are traces of floors and rooms so that we could see that it was once a two-story college, and the foundations, exposed by archaeological digging, reach deep into the park behind it. It is a perfect example of the fact that building went on in the Seljuk style even after the fall of the Seljuk empire.

This, as well as two of the other Seljuk buildings in Sivas, was built during the rule of a Mongol vizier in 1271. The Mongols, like the Seljuks, have been misinterpreted too often in European history. They did destroy much of Persia, but, except for a few cities where resistance was strong, and they had to lay siege too long, they destroyed little in Anatolia, and they built a lot—not Mongol but Seljuk, and not shaman, which was their own religion, but Muslim.

On the other side of the narrow cobbled street is the hospital built by Sultan Izzeddin Keykarus I in 1219. He was a sensitive poet who died young of tuberculosis. The epitaph on the front of his tomb says, "My wealth was of no use to me. My Sultanate is finished. The day of my journey from this transitory world to the next was the 4th Shawwal 617" (A.D. 1219). He is buried in a *gümbet* in one of the walls, with a pointed, decorated dome that rises over the roof of the hospital. I was getting nearer to the mystery of Aladdin. The poet Izzeddin was Aladdin's older brother, and it was his viziers who, against Izzeddin's will, kept Aladdin imprisoned through most of his reign.

Now the hospital of Izzeddin is hung with beautiful rugs from all the villages around Sivas. Twenty years ago it was a roofless ruin. Now the *iwans* are roofed over again. There are tables to sit out in the garden for tea or coffee. The lion's head fountain that no longer spits water is in the center of the courtyard. Two sassy small Seljuk lions that have the humor of a couple of feist dogs, medallions of the sun and the moon, and the stones from unknown graves are set around the courtyard, some against the walls, some littering the grass. The wall of the tomb itself is lacy with fine blue faience tile interspersed with brick, in the old way of the Great Seljuks of Persia.

A young man made friends with us and offered, if we liked, in the best *akhis* tradition, to get us mounts to go hunting with him for wolves, wild cats, and what he called "beer" in the near hills. He also sold rugs. He seemed lonely there in a city where he had obviously been all his life. I thought of a young man, a hunter, a dreaming *ghazi* with the historic memory of Turkey, the banners whipping the wind, in one of the great buildings of the Seljuks, hospitable and sad, hoping I would buy a rug or at least a pair of Phrygian socks. These are heavy knitted socks the weight of boots, with the ancient traditional designs, for sale in the *iwans,* and in the garden in the center. Somehow the rugs do not seem out of place there on the stone walls. There must have been color, and the sound of a fountain, and merchants going back and forth when the hospital was used for the sick. They, too, as in Amasya, were treated with music and hypnosis, in an atmosphere of peace.

At night the rugs stay on the walls. Nobody thinks of moving them.

But this is still eastern Turkey and thievery is little known and summarily punished (not by cutting a hand off, as many Westerners still believe about Turkey, but by isolation and shame to the family).

One day we drove a hundred miles from Sivas to find another lost place. In the distance, on the crests of hills on the horizon, we saw tent cities that seemed flattened by the brute sun of August. They were refugees from yet another of those heartless population resettlements, this time from the Communist regime in Bulgaria. Turkey is full of refugees that the rest of the world has not given them credit for receiving—not only ethnic Turks from Bulgaria but also Kurds from Iraq after the Iraqi government used poison gas to decimate whole Kurdish villages.

For the first few miles the highway was alive with the new Turkey, changed so radically since I lived there sixteen years ago. There were Mercedes buses, huge trucks, Turkish cars driven as if they were trying to escape the wind, and slowly, solemnly, stopping all the hurry and attempted bustle of the traffic, a tractor with the whole family or village in a cart behind it, being driven to market, drawn along at ten miles an hour.

Then we turned off the main road. We went over and around mountains so spacious, so desolate, so bare of vegetation that it seemed a landscape of the moon. Veins of iron and of some green mineral streaked the mountainsides. The road was empty and travel was easy between the fields; shepherds were watching flocks on the horizon.

Türkmen nomads had set up their wide-winged black goat-hair tents in the sun and children played around them, while the women sat in the tent shade, bright in their striped clothes and their head scarves. It was bucolic, unthreatening, timeless.

I realized what inured ought to mean—humans honed and shaped as much as the mountains and the endless fields by wind and rain and an indifferent sun. It has made Turkish country people, under their harshness, almost naively gentle.

The road was a semipaved path across this endless deceptive wasteland. Below the fields we could see the lines of cypress trees that made the formal green oases of villages. Finally, in the distance, from a mountain, we came down into a valley, about five miles long and a mile wide, that hid a little kingdom. I remembered the Cornish town of Lostwithiel, which means lost within the hills. It was like that. It seemed at first cut off from any contact with an outside world, except the few cars that came, like we did, to find a past there.

The road seemed to end at the small town of Divriği. Along the mountain ridge above and in front of us, the huge wall of the fortress castle still stretched over the contours of the hill. I thought of the nomad emir who said, "I must be a king. I've built a town."

We crossed a small stream and on either side of us were well-built, well-roofed modern houses. Downhill from the castle, and almost nestled on the slope, was the combined mosque and hospital that makes Divriği famous. It was built by the Danishmends, a tribe within the new Seljuk sultanate, but it, more than any other Seljuk monument, is completely individual. It dates from early in Aladdin's reign.

The passion of scholars for tracing sources is up, literally, against a stone wall there. They tend to leave out the element of play, and the north door of the mosque is nothing but play, as if the carvers had woven an embroidered tapestry and turned it into stone cat's cradles of designs, vines, an exuberance of flowers. Eight-pointed stars seem to roll across the top of the door. Baroque leaves curl; swirls of stone arabesques burst their bounds and are flung across the facade from one staid line of carvings to another. The stone was soft, the carver was left alone, and the monument is a work of joy, the color of a deer pelt in the sun.

The hospital, within the same walls but behind the mosque, has a calm, graceful interior. The columns are individual—there is little sense of their being "matched," any more than the trees they imitate. Stairs go up into the second-story rooms and we looked down on the fine floor, the *iwan* entry, and up at the lantern dome.

From above, we could look down on the tomb whose pointed conical roof rises above the roofline of the complex. The lady founder, her husband who founded the mosque, and some of their family are interred in stone caskets, set at floor level. They still lie there, after eight hundred years, undisturbed by invasion and time and neglect, well cared for with their silk and embroidered coverings over the carved stone. There is little organization about this. I wondered if it were local pride or the *imam* or the government archaeologists that has kept the thirteenth-century tombs in that isolated place so newly covered, and so neat.

We ate lunch with the old men in their *takkes* and their beards, and with a gaggle of tidy, well-dressed young men who looked like they might have come from some government office buildings, who walked together across the bridge to the restaurant. The food was some of the best I ate in Turkey. The flies and the men gathered around the huge round flat baking dishes of *börek*, a meat or vegetable pie, and lamb stew, or piled high with the salad that is a part of every Turkish meal. There was a scent of spices and newly baked bread. Yet I thought that few Westerners would have dared eat there, with our passion for the trappings of cleanliness. I know that Turkish people are very clean, and very food-minded, so I chose from the great dishes, and Yusuf and I ate together, with nobody watching us, or at least seeming to.

But I was beginning to have a suspicion that there was more to the hidden town of Divriği—the well-dressed young men, the new houses—than the thirteenth-century monuments.

Across the river we saw the roofs of the old town, the Ottoman houses, and we went along the dirt roads where the carved wooden-and-lathe balconies were built out over the unpaved paths. As in Erzurum, some of the once-rich Ottoman houses had been left to fall, and some of them were full of families, women leaning out of the windows, children playing in the lanes between them.

We stopped at one of the most impressive, obviously an *ağa's* house. Part of the roof had sagged, and the wall around its courtyard had been patched. I was photographing it when the woman who lived there came out, and invited us to come in for coffee.

She was barefooted, dressed in *şalvar,* her head covered, her palms orange with henna stain, still a sign of beauty among country people. We went up the narrow stairs to the second floor, her living room, and we took off our shoes at her door. She took my hand, kissed it, and lifted it to her forehead. Her daughter was dressed in Western clothes, but her hands were hennaed, too. The mother took us into what had been an Ottoman living room. The ceiling, where it had not sagged and been repaired, was finely carved wood. A bench ran all the way along the wall, covered with carpeted and embroidered pillows. There was a worn, beautiful old rug on the floor in the rich colors of gems and spotlessly clean. In the corner stood a large television.

While she went to make coffee in the hallway that they used for a kitchen her daughter, a bright young girl, told us that the young man whose portrait was on the wall in uniform, was the son of the house, that her father had been killed in the mine, and that her mother was a widow.

The mother was young, very hospitable, and smiling to have company when she came back with the thick Turkish coffee in tiny old cups. She explained that she didn't know who owned the house she lived in, that she only paid the rent to somebody who came from the city—which city she didn't say. She was condemned to be a widow for the rest of her life, and widows can have a hard time in Turkey unless there is an extended family to help them, and even then they tend to be unpaid servants.

She was proudly independent. She lived in the single room with her daughter. Her son—she was vague about him—was someplace else. She had a good job, and when we asked what it was she said she worked in the iron mine across the mountain pass where most of the people of Divriği worked.

I asked what her job was, and she said she was a miner, but that she didn't do the heaviest work, that was for the men. She asked why we had come to Divriği and when we said we had come to see the Seljuk mosque and the hospital, which were about half a mile away on the opposite hill, she laughed. "I have only been there once in my life," she said, "but I have been once to Kayseri, too."

I knew who the well-dressed men who looked like government employees were. It accounted for the well-built small new houses, the television set, the absent landlord she didn't know. We were in one of Turkey's iron-mining towns, and that was, to them, the center of things, not the useless ruins.

When we left she kissed my hand again and touched her forehead, far from industry and iron-mining, as she would have done had she been there in the thirteenth century. Her manners and her hospitality and her hennaed hands were medieval, but when work time came she worked as a miner in the iron mines, and in the evening she and her daughter would watch state television until some young man's family found the bride-price, so her daughter would marry.

We had gone through the town of Kangal, where the most famous sheep dogs in Turkey come from, the Kangal dogs, who stand as tall as Irish wolfhounds, and who wear iron collars with spikes six inches long that you can buy in country hardware stores. It is to protect them from the wolves that they are bred to attack on sight. They are half feral and completely loyal to the shepherds who train them.

As we were driving back toward Sivas, we saw ahead a large flock of sheep crossing the road, slowly, as sheep do, anthropomorphically arrogant and lackadaisical. There seemed to be hundreds of them. A Kangal dog sat in the road on either side of the flock to guard it from cars. We stopped. The dog in front of us sat quite quietly, between the Mercedes and the flock, hardly seeming to see us. She glanced once or twice at us, but mostly she stared at the flock, without moving, so strong that her spiked iron collar did not even make her hang her head.

We waited. Far in the distance beyond the flock another car waited. It was a time of all around patience. Nobody seemed to mind the interruption. The sheep and the shepherd had the right of way. Then I found out why.

When almost the last of the sheep had ambled across the road—two or three were still on the pavement—Yusuf started the engine to get ready to move. When the dog heard the engine start, she attacked the car. She leapt up over the hood at the windshield, her teeth bared. Yusuf turned off the engine again. The shepherd called her, and she slid off the hood and quite calmly she went back to her post until the last foot of the last sheep had crossed.

The shepherd leaned into the window of the car and apologized to Yusuf. We told him we thought his dog was beautifully trained. He laughed and said, "If you want her, open the door to the back seat and you can have her." She was the size of a small pony. When the last sheep was finally away into the field, the dog went after the flock, without noise; she herded by pointing like a bird dog if a sheep strayed at all. Then dogs, shepherd, and flock went out across the fields and we were allowed to move again.

CHAPTER EIGHT

ALADDIN WITH MUSIC

FROM SIVAS, ALL the way to the Mediterranean, we were led by a series of monuments to Aladdin that stretch across Anatolia, north to south, from Sinop on the Black Sea to Antalya and Alanya, the Mediterranean resort and port that still carries his name. We could see them as we drove, some away across the fields, isolated in the distance, some so ruined that they seem to be half-natural stone hillocks, some almost intact. They are what survives of a series of *hans,* huge country inns a day's march apart by camel caravan, a distance that we were covering in the Mercedes in about half an hour.

They were Aladdin's solution to a problem that had dogged Anatolia for centuries. Long before Manzikert, and for a hundred years after it, the high, tumbled plateau of Anatolia, all the way east to the mountains, had been a battlefield of marauding Turks, of Byzantine rebels, of mercenaries who sold themselves and their small armies first to one side and then to the other—rebels, emirs, emperors, Crusaders.

What had been an ancient commercial route to Europe, east to west, north to south, part of the road that Xenophon took and that was the caravan route to the Mediterranean and the Black Sea, had long been abandoned. Merchants from the East had to go around both Crusader and Türkmen, and the armies of the Byzantine emperors, to get to Europe.

There was hunger along the route, too. All too often, what land had been under the plow was left neglected, and returned to pasture or wilderness. Villagers moved into the few walled cities that had not been destroyed, or literally went underground, as they did in the subterranean towns of Cappadocia, which was a huge crossroad for the armies.

Wild Türkmen tribes marched with their families and their flocks. They had evolved a way of life that could be set up and fortified overnight. They carried long staves and set them up around their camps with their shields against them, much as wagons were circled in the Old West.

They came quite silently. In the evening outside the city walls, there would have been open fields and meadowland all the way to the edge of twilight. In the morning, as far as they could see, the round tents of the tribesmen who had moved in in the night, their element. The townsmen who had stayed behind the stone walls, found, as often as not, that their refuge-fortress had become a prison and they were starved out.

Near our own time, the Suez Canal was an attempt to control the route. So was the ever-present longing of Russia to take the Bosporus and the Dardanelles—to say nothing of Churchill's mistake at Gallipoli. The discovery of America was the result of another commercial attempt to go around the Middle East to get to India. It was this lost route that Aladdin reopened with his series of royal inns, or *hans*.

The *hans* provided music, armed protection, a doctor, a veterinarian, sometimes a poet, always a bath, food and sleeping quarters for men and beasts, and, most important of all, news and gossip. These imperial connections married cities of the center of Anatolia that had been isolated from each other for centuries.

You could stay in the *han* for three days with free food, care, prayer, and entertainment. On the fourth day, if you wanted to stay on, you had to help with the work.

It was the twelfth-century *hans* of Aladdin, as much as the new safety of the cities under the rule of the Seljuks, that brought the talented masons, architects, poets, religious leaders, all the marks of civilization from across the mountains, through Armenia, along the northern seacoast. They were swept before the slow-moving hordes of Genghis Khan, and, for a little while, made the Seljuk Kingdom of Rum the most civilized empire in the Middle East. Artists, masons, holy men, pilgrims came, safe at last from the tattered armies of the Crusaders on one side and the wild tribesmen on the other.

There is a word that defines a civilized empire, and has done so from the Aegean Greek city-states, to the early Byzantines, to the little kingdom of Trebizond, then to the Seljuks. The word is *welcome*. Talent goes where it can work. So an international group of wandering artisans carved the *hans,* the *masjids,* those small mosques in the center of the *han* courtyards with the always-present double eagles and Seljuk lions on the walls.

Facades were carved with exuberant gaiety that refused to be confined to scrollwork and calligraphy: rosettes on either side of interlaced marble entries; an animal calendar of the old Turks with fish, a man, a horse, a lion, and birds intertwined in a rolling circle; palmette leaves and an eared eagle; vine tendrils with birds looking out.

Over the arched gate might be carved a chicken, the symbol for the local emir, or a calm slightly Oriental face, peeping from behind the stone vines that meant safety to the caravans that passed slowly through the great imperial doorways in the evening after a day's march.

The first of these that we stopped to see was the Sultan Han, called that after Aladdin, on the Sivas–Kayseri road. In many ways this was the most beautiful of all, and the most typical of Seljuk grandeur modified by a dignity of taste that was their mark. Through the fine archway into the center of the courtyard is the *mescid,* a small mosque with twining serpents along its open arches, another ancient animist Seljuk trademark.

The courtyard is huge. On either side are the open arched porches where, in summer, the animals could be tethered and fed. At the back of the courtyard on one side, the bath, on the other the entry to living quarters, and through a second fine door in the center of the back courtyard wall, the winter quarters of the animals and their keepers.

Light comes obliquely from a great dome above open rooms divided by arched corridors that must be twenty feet high. They are a hint of the scale and height of Seljuk palaces long disappeared. I thought that the hexagonal pointed dome above them was a Seljuk tomb of a founder, but it was not; it just let in light, much like the domes of the tenth-century Armenian churches.

I kept crashing against the fact that Yusuf was an excited twenty-two-year-old, finding his country for the first time. He bounded up steep stone steps, over roofs, around the towers, up ramps, over piles of stones, and then looked back innocently to see if I was following. The inevitable,

"Come! Is no problem," usually seduced me into climbing too, out of a mixture of curiosity, bravado, and shame. The Sultan Han was no exception.

I struggled after him up steps, each about a foot and a half high, onto the stone roof of the winter quarters. A long, vaulted roof ran down the center, with a flat roof on either side. Only one other person was there, a German guide who was inspecting it to see if he should bring tourists to see it. He pointed to a lion's head drainage spout below and said with some disgust, "It is not original."

I didn't bother to point out that had it been there would have been no stone roof for us to stand on, and, as in pictures of it thirty years before, only an overgrown courtyard, desolate broken columns, sheep wandering inside the open doorway, and that he could see twenty or thirty like that if he preferred.

Almost all of this *han* has been reconstructed, and so it is possible to see how it worked. For myself I liked the reconstructions. From the roof, where the guardian soldiers stood sentry, we could see as they saw, open land all the way to the horizon, where they could pick up a distant cloud of dust that could be a caravan to be protected, or marauders. This comfortable and civilized *han* was so well-built that it once withstood a siege of an army of twenty thousand Mongols for two months.

In the lane as we walked to the car, a mad dog, only a puppy, ran sideways down the center of the road, frothing at the mouth, and we got into the car to get away from it. Nobody, including the children, paid any attention to it.

Two boys passed us in a high-sided cart, like the haymow in the painting by Constable. They drove it like a chariot and waved at us.

We went off the main road, through a small village called Elbaşı (foreigner's head!), and along the fields where the harvest was going on, to the *han* that was the next surviving one on the way to Kayseri. We could see it in the distance, rising over a little village where the hay had already been mansard-stacked on the rooftops.

Across the fields there were people gleaning the last of the harvest. A young boy looked up, startled and dirty with chaff, as we passed.

A few minutes later we were at the door of the Karatay Han, this one built by the tutor to Aladdin's children. Many of them were built locally on orders from the sultan, with his model as their own.

The main facade is one of the most famous of all the Seljuk doorways. A cock was carved in a small circle on one side of the decorated doorway, and a slightly drunken lion on the other. We found another lion with a snake in its mouth, human heads, and a wilderness of leafed borders. The modern metal gate was locked.

We waited for one of the children, who had gathered, and always did when we stopped, to go to find either the schoolmaster or the *müdür,* the mayor, to bring the key. This inn was so off the beaten tourist-cum-scholar track that they were unprepared for visitors. Finally, after about fifteen minutes, I was able to go into the courtyard.

Yusuf had opened the hood of the car and was inspecting the engine. The children and the schoolmaster watched, fascinated. I felt for the first time that I was not the center of their polite curiosity. They would never have been caught *looking* at me. That would have been rude, but I could sense their inspections. Not this time. I wandered around the interior alone.

When I came out I looked at the crowd. There behind them was the boy we had passed in the field. He was washed, dressed in a clean cotton shirt and trousers. He had run home to clean himself up for visitors to his village, whom he would never speak to.

I saw other *hans,* other caravanseries, but they were nearer to what I came to call the tourist border, which seems at this point to be somewhere on a line that we were traveling, west of us a few miles into Cappadocia, and the coast of the Aegean and the Mediterranean. On the way to Konya from the east, it was still quiet, fairly undisturbed by the modern caravan, the tour bus. We were leaving a rare fine past and a simpler present than I would see until I went back later to eastern Turkey.

CHAPTER NINE

THE CITY OF ALADDIN

ONYA IS STILL permeated with Aladdin's life, his taste, his vision, his pleasures. It was an ancient city when the Seljuks made it their capital. The Hittites called it Kawania, the Romans Iconium, but they say in Konya that it was the first city built after Noah's Ark landed on Ararat (or perhaps another mountain; nobody is sure). It has grown in rings of time like an old tree, from a huge Phrygian burial mound that had been a pre-Phrygian sacred hill out to the modern, dusty concrete suburbs.

I like to walk in cities; to ask the way; to find what I want to find by getting lost in the back streets, across the wastelands where the gardens are, and the shops and the bazaar stalls; to flow with a throng of people at lunch hour, then find an empty street and go slowly. To be shunted or herded from one "historic sight" to another is, for me, to make them seem dead, and not a part of the city life around them.

In Konya, I set out alone, early in the morning, to go to the tomb and monastery of Celâleddin Rumi, the great Turkish religious mystic and poet, known by the Muslims as the Mevlana, the Lord. *Rumi* means that he was a citizen of Rum, or Rome—the name that the Seljuks called their kingdom. He has been called "the Shakespeare of Islam." He was an ecstatic poet and mystic, and in his long life in Konya, he was a beloved mixture of holy man and dancing fool of God.

Konya has been a holy place ever since the Mevlana's funeral. He was followed not only by Muslims but by the Christians, Jews, and Zoroastrians he welcomed equally in his message of universal love. He said, "If you count the courtyards of all the buildings on which the sun shines there are hundreds of houses, but if you remove the walls all these pieces of light are one and the same."

Because his poetry was written down in Persian, the court language of the time, he is remembered as a Persian poet. But he said of himself, "Though I may write in Persian, my race is Turkish."

I thought, innocently, that if I got there early enough, I might be alone for a few minutes. It is the illusion of early risers in foreign cities.

In a circular city how can you be lost? I had a map and I could read it. I knew where I was going. At least I thought I could read the somewhat impressionist tourist map, and I thought I knew where I was going. After all, I had studied. I was as blinded by knowledge as by the blinkers you put on a horse so it can look neither to the left nor to the right.

Instead, I got lost. I walked through the concrete suburbs that could have been anyplace. Only the sight of a horse-drawn cart, the ever-present climbing flowers on any piece of ground where they could be planted, the geraniums like small trees rising out of olive-oil cans up beyond the windows of ground-floor apartments, reminded me that I was in a Turkish city.

I found my way through the fine, green modern park, still deserted so early in the morning. The lake, where there would be boats all day long, was mirror-still. The Ferris wheel was halted in the dawn sky. The grass was wet with dew.

But the city of the greatest and most joyful mystic who ever lived would not let me alone. I was seduced into one wrong street after another, and I caught the pleasure of it. So I succumbed to wandering, and let the city lead me, a plan of which the Mevlana would have approved.

In a back street I stumbled onto the Sirçali Medrese, which had been built at the time of the last Seljuk sultans, while the shadow of the Mongols hung over the whole of the east of Anatolia. There was the courtyard shape, the entry with its Seljuk arch of carved stalactites pointing downward, the pious marble calligraphy over the door, formal and graceful at the same time. Above me, once I had squeezed through the wooden entry built inside the great gate when I followed one of the workmen who were repairing the *medrese,* was the high vault of the entry hall, with fragments of tile that, so early in the morning, made it a sunstruck prism of color.

Along the *iwan* at the opposite end of the rubble- and marble-filled courtyard were the glazed Sufic words of the Koran, like a vine down the wall, Turkish blue and the deep rich color of eggplant, graceful against the stone of the walls that were left.

I finally stumbled into the main street that connects Aladdin's Seljuk center, built on and around the Phrygian hill, and the wide paved space of the Mevlana monastery and the Ottoman mosque. I could see, far ahead, the tiled fluted tower that hovered over the city, with its pointed shape of the Seljuks, covered with the green tile of the Ottomans, nearly a hundred feet high above the Mevlana's tomb.

It was still so early that I wandered in the cemetery opposite the tomb. Its long shaded walks are quiet between the graves of thousands of Muslims who have been buried near the Mevlana, since one of the beliefs of Islam is that to be buried near a saint is to be nearer to Paradise. There were turbans at the headstones of the men's tombs, simple carved flowers at the women's. Some of the headstones seemed as old as the Mevlana's tomb itself, some twentieth century, but they are all of the same pattern. There is little innovation in the marble turbans, only the wearing by weather and time of the stones show their age. Innovation is a cardinal sin of conservative Islam, which has made it one of the purest and also one of the most backward of religions.

By the time I had walked back to the square, there were already several hundred people, all of them Turkish, waiting for the monastery to open. It is now officially a museum, since Atatürk thought he had broken the power of the dervishes whose center this had been since the thirteenth century.

In 1925, Atatürk dissolved the *tekkes,* the dervish centers, with much the same zeal and ruthlessness that Henry VIII dissolved the religious foundations of England. He hated their noise, what he saw as their craziness, their ignorance, their superstition, the hold that the mystics had on the ordinary people of Turkey. But most of all, I think that as a Turk who had grown up in one of the most Western of the then Ottoman cities, Salonika in Macedonia, they embarrassed him. There were whirling dervishes and whispering dervishes and shouting dervishes. Derisively, they were called the *delibaşı,* the mad heads, by modern-thinking Turks.

In the huge square, which was so quiet as I waited that morning, there had been desperate riots of the dervishes when the *tekkes* were taken over. Some were killed; nobody knows how many.

They had protected Turkey's poets ever since Yunus Emre, Turkey's most beloved folk poet, had wandered into one of their *tekkes* in the fifteenth century and had stayed. The dervishes had inherited not only the traditions of the old *futawwas* of hospitality that Ibn Battuta found in Anatolia in the thirteenth century, but of the hospitality of the *hans*.

Atatürk made few mistakes about the Turkish people. He knew and loved them and he cajoled and pushed them into the twentieth century. But he was blindly antireligious, and he was too ruthless. He forced their religion underground, and much that I saw in the east was a resurgence of this from the grandchildren of the same people who had formed his rabble army in the War of Independence.

A little, street-tough boy insisted I buy a *simit,* a round sesame-covered roll, and he gave it to me with a hand that had been dirty since the last time his mother had caught him and made him wash. So I visited the tomb of a great poet with a *simit* in my hand, a gesture that he, who was one of the most down-to-earth and humorous of mystic poets, would have understood.

A man from the country and his wife came up to me when they saw the camera around my neck. She wore the neat dark blue country clothes and the closely wrapped dark blue head scarf of a conservative Muslim woman. She had allowed herself a pretty border to the head scarf. She carried a Western handbag. She led a little girl by the hand. The little girl was dressed in another century, bright blue and white. The husband was carrying their baby. With all the machismo of Turkish men, I saw fathers carrying their children, over and over.

He asked if I would take their picture at the tomb of the Mevlana, but I explained that it wasn't one of those cameras where the picture came out at once. He pulled his wife back and posed. She explained again to him that it wasn't the right kind of camera. She was obviously a little more sophisticated than he was, but he insisted. After all, he was the man, the *erkek adam.* So they posed, and then he held out his hand for the picture. Finally she made him see that I could not give it to him.

He started to laugh at us. He had made his gesture as a joke. She and I had been trying to explain for several minutes, and I saw that in our feminine foolishness he had just let us run on. He had simply wanted a record, no matter who had it, that he had brought his child to be blessed by the Mevlana. He thanked me, and he took his wife by the arm and they walked away to stand in the line that was already forming in front of the ticket office, made out of one of the dervish cells.

By nine o'clock there was already a long line. When we went in I found out why. Atatürk may have made it into a museum, but to the Turkish country people the Mevlana's tomb is one of the most sacred places in Turkey.

Like the Hellenist fragments, the imperial Roman columns, the ancient tribal habits, designs, and way of life; like the artisans of Armenia, who were there long before the Romans; and the early Turks who mingled their Asian blood with the Gauls, the Phrygians, and the other indigenous people they found in Anatolia, nothing is ever really lost there. It is only planted and saved to come again. Religion there has waited, too. Perhaps its influence is more dangerous for Turkey since it has suffered so much derision. The man with his wife and baby and daughter had had taken away from them a setting for their connection with their past. They had simply waited. They have waited in Anatolia before.

When Aladdin became sultan after the death of his gentle poet brother in 1219, one of the first things that he did was to invite to Konya, the capital, a host of poets, religious men, architects, sculptors. It became, as the years went on, the most widely known welcoming and safe place to work in the whole of the Middle East. The Mongols had already started their inexorable movement toward the west, and they drove before them all those who make a civilization civilized. They had gathered in Konya from all over the mid-eastern world for safety and to be a part of what was the center of the great renaissance of peace and prosperity, the first they had known after two hundred years of raids and warfare.

The Mevlana's father was a famous religious teacher. He had brought his family from Afghanistan, via the inevitable pilgrimage to Mecca, the *hadj* that Mohammed demanded of good Muslims. Aladdin invited the family to Konya and asked them to stay at the palace. But the Mevlana's father answered that as a holy man he belonged in a *tekke,* and so, on the ground where many of the royal family of the Seljuks had been buried, Aladdin gave them a place to build. It is where the Mevlana's tomb stands now.

Here, organized by the Mevlana's son, the mystic order of the

Whirling Dervishes grew and was given rules and a structure in a way that the practical, down-to-earth wanderer and dreamer, the Mevlana Celâleddin Rumi, would not have recognized. He preferred the streets, the sound of the hammer in the goldsmith's shop, the clop of the horse's hoofs, the music from the *hamam* and the wandering musician. Nobody has given a more detailed picture of what daily street life in Konya in the thirteenth century was like than he did in his vast output of poetry. Alas, most of what has been translated makes the airy-fairy mistake so often made about mystics. The translations are made when God and love are mentioned and leave the homely metaphors to less enlightened souls. So the Mevlana's love of day and people and earth and the objects and pleasures of life is hard to find, and yet, it is there, still there.

The entrance to his tomb is through what was once a gilded door. Now the silver plate underneath shows through, set in carved walnut. The entry is called "the Entrance of the Lovers." The first thing I saw was a quatrain of the Mevlana's.

> Come, come again, whoever,
> whatever you may be, come;
> heathen, fire worshiper,
> sinful of idolatry come.
> Come, even if you have broken
> your penitence a hundred times,
> Ours is not the portal of despair
> and misery, come.

All the way up to the Ottoman dome, with its delicate reds and whites in tile, the walls are covered with large cobalt blue plaques with Sufic calligraphy, in gold, of the Koran, of the Mevlana's poems, or of the Mevlana's warnings that are not warnings. "Either you seem as you are, or become as you seem," was one that had been translated. I translated it again for myself, "If you don't stop you'll stick that way." The sayings reminded me of the warnings of my grandmother.

The whole place was domestic, down-to-earth, and sacred. From the Seljuk sultans to almost the last of the Ottomans, all are represented there in the rich coverings for the catafalques, the green and red silk embroidered with gold, the gold on the walls—a residue of rich sultanates—carpets from centuries ago around the tombs, and, over it all, nineteenth-century European crystal chandeliers.

The tombs are set along high platforms on either side of the room, under high vaulted ceilings of three domes. The central dome, over the Mevlana's tomb, is Seljuk. The room holds many of the tombs of the dervish masters and the family of the Mevlana. The Mevlana's tomb is magnificent and glows with its own atmosphere of holiness. The large turban at the head of it rises high above the rest of the room, so that he seems to be standing behind all of the riches and color, that simple man who liked to drink wine and dance in the street.

Long lines of people from all over Turkey had come there on pilgrimage. They knelt and kissed all the way along the silver railing of the catafalque. There was a murmur of the welcome that they give to the dead, as if they were alive, *"Selamünaleyküm";* and of the *tabrih,* from the first *sura,* or chapter, of the Koran; and high above, very softly, the sound of the *ney* floated down, the flute music the Mevlana said was the sound of the reed that longed for its home, a lost, lonely sweet sound. In one of his poems, he says of the music, "Day and night, music, a quiet, bright reed song. If it fades, we fade." There was no other sound in a room that was solid with people.

Then the tourists came, with one noisy guide pushing the way for his Germans, another with his English, through the quiet people saying their prayers, giving their lectures in loud voices, competing with each other, drowning out prayer and quietness and the sound of the *ney.* It is this split, this noisy contempt for the simple people who had come so far that I saw as the danger of a reactive anger in Turkey, where tribal and conservative religious people have been so patient and grown so bitter.

At the other end of the street, the life of Aladdin spread over the hill, the fragment of wall of the royal kiosk, the Aladdin Mosque where he and many of the other Seljuk sultans are buried, the *medreses* that have been made into museums.

Ibn Bibi Duda, the thirteenth-century historian, is the only chronicler contemporary with Aladdin's time. From his pages, suddenly, there is Aladdin, a young man, riding out "on his steed, with the emirs of the court and his army captains, in the fields and gardens outside of Konya. He looked toward the city, ornamented with people and riches a day's journey in length." Konya then was a city of a hundred thousand people.

"People from all the lands had gathered there," wrote Ibn Bibi Duda, and "created for themselves a fatherland in that city of happiness." Aladdin saw that, "like unto the blade with both edges exposed from the sheath it lacked a city wall, a city like a graceful bride" was unprotected.

He ordered, according to Ibn Bibi, "a city wall around this city and around Sivas that the ominous hoe of deceitful time cannot plow down." And he said that every man who worked on the wall should sign his name on one of the stones in gold. Alas, deceitful time, and war, and neglect did plow it down. The wall is long gone from Konya, and only a few stones, signed by the men who built it, and two angels, guarding nothing, are left.

The İnci Medresesi, finished 1265, has been made into a sculpture museum. Its door is decorated with a great plait that looks like woven stone. Its truncated minaret was partly destroyed by an earthquake, but it still has green tile facings wound among its brick designs. The two angels from Aladdin's wall run in bas-relief across a field of stone. With their wings, their crowns, their long braids of hair, and brandishing swords, they look the way the angel should have looked at the gate of the Garden of Eden.

The Karatay Medresesi, built in 1251, farther along the street that circles around the Phrygian burial mound, is the most beautiful building that survives from the Seljuk period. It also adds another clue to the search for this astonishing and forgotten thirteenth-century renaissance sultan.

The Greek slave Ibn al din Karatay started as a page in the palace. He was freed by Aladdin and made tutor to his sons. He rose to be a minister of state, and an ascetic follower of the Mevlana. For years he kept the Mongols from sacking the city by a mixture of diplomacy, bribery, war, and guile. It was his *han* that we had found in the little village, beyond Elbaşı.

The gate of the Karatay Medresesi is interlaced with white and sky-blue marble facing. Columns stand on either side of the door. Its Sufic calligraphy is a swirl of carved marble. Inside the main room, which has replaced the open courtyard of more traditional *medreses,* the domed ceiling seems to shed its own light. It is a field of blue-and-white starlike, flowerlike tangles and circles of tile on a deep purple background. The calligraphy all around the walls and the *iwan* is a tiled purple so deep it is nearly black, and like other Seljuk calligraphy it seems to grow and twine like living plants. The triumph that defines all this is the quartet of squinches, or *muqarnas,* the "Turkish triangles," that are like half-opened fans of tile on the four corners, as if the ceiling itself grew out of them. The watercourse to a small pool in the center of the floor is shaped like a stone snake, and designed to burble with water so that the students studying in the room could be calmed by its sound.

In a hall built from students' cells in the 1950s, when the building was restored and made into the tile museum of Konya, are the tiles from Aladdin's last palace. According to Ibn Bibi, the sultan drew the plans "to his determined command." A palace was built that was "more glorious than the souls of the chaste, and roomier than the plain of modesty . . . their vaulted domes competed with the *muqarnas* of the highest heaven, . . . because of its turquoise and azure decorations."

There is nothing left of that last palace but a few ruins and these tiles, and there they are, in all their color: the dancing animals, surprised dragons, here a hare caught in mid-leap, there a comic donkey being lifted by a girth around its middle and looking deeply offended. Two birds face each other in branches of vine; a panther is as playful as a pup. A woman's face on a bird's body smiles like a sly sphinx, horses rear, all are fragmented reflections in the eye of Aladdin, his choices and a record of his wit and pleasure.

When other Eastern medieval men are mentioned, there is a picture in the mind—of Saladin, the Kurd who had been a vassal of the Seljuks; of Genghis Khan; and later of Tamerlane, Timur the Lame; but of this man, who was known in his time as the greatest of Seljuk sultans, there are only the ruined *hans,* the lost palaces, the broken walls, the stone angels, the beautiful tiles, and the words of Ibn Bibi, translated from medieval Persian that few people can read any longer into turn-of-the-century German.

Aladdin's "hoe of deceitful time" has covered over the memory of the man who opened the center and the east of Anatolia to commerce and safer living. Christians were not persecuted under his reign. Artists and artisans found work in Sivas, in Kayseri, in Tokat, in Amasya, and then in Konya, the cultural center of the kingdom of Rum, whether they were Armenian or Persian or trans-Caucasian or Turkic or Afghan. With the taste and choices of the Seljuk sultans who welcomed them, they produced, out of all their techniques, a new, composite architecture.

There is a final glimpse of Aladdin in Konya before he is blotted out by time, tourism, and concrete. He is a young man, who pauses, according to Ibn Bibi's history, "between bottle and cup," in the midst of banqueting with his friends and listening to minstrels who sing "unceasingly to him." Like Prince Hal, he remembers that he is a king, and announces preparations for war.

The order goes out to the army that "every ant will become a dragon and every sparrow an eagle" to lay siege to the mountain fortress that towers today over miles of white buildings of the Turkish resort that Alanya has become. He commands that the army be divided in three parts, that one section should "dash like a panther to the cliffs and the rock and storm them. One section should creep as a crocodile from the seaside to the battle and one division should roll to the fortress in ships as a mighty wave."

Less poetic and more practically, he wanted to open the port, then called Kalonoros, so that his trade route, already beginning to be dotted with the safe houses, the *hans,* across Anatolia from the Mediterranean to the Black Sea, would have a port built to his own plans.

Antalya, on the Mediterranean, was already in the hands of the Seljuks, but farther along the coast, a Christian king, Kurt Vart, held "a merciless mountain before which heaven is like a flat plain, a fortress having the sea as moat and marble cliffs as fortress walls."

It was this fortress Aladdin decided to besiege so that "the ocean pearls of this territory will be added to the strand of pearls" he already had.

"The scribes of the court sprayed musk-colored black ink on the camphor-white of the paper and ornamented the whole face with lines that were like the locks of moon beauties and the ringlets of Jupiter-like heart-breakers. They made their firmans in majestic copy and dispatched them by relay messengers. In less than ten days an army came which caused by the hooves of their wind-swift steeds such clouds of dust to be stirred up that the face of the sun and of the moon were veiled in dust.

"The sultan commanded that the mountain be stormed. They climbed at once like a flying eagle and a speeding panther up that marble cliff and the army positioned itself on that mountain for battle, that mountain to which not even thoughts had been able to penetrate before. They posted a hundred mighty catapults around the fortress in a circle."

For two months the battle went on. There is a legend that Aladdin tied candles to the horns of a flock of goats at night, lit them, and set the goats loose on the mountainside so that Kurt Vart would think his army was two or three times the size it was. The ruse is supposed to have worked better than the catapults. Kurt Vart surrendered.

That is where Aladdin won his Christian wife, the daughter of Kurt Vart. In the center of the fort he captured, a small Byzantine church was left intact in the middle of the new palace and fortifications he built. He changed the name of the port to Alanya, and it is still called that, after Aladdin.

Alanya is the southern end of Aladdin's crescent. Down from the Taurus Mountains, past the lakes, the villages, the change is so abrupt that it could be, and has often been, another country.

I was alone there in tourist land. I hadn't been handed, for once, from *arkadaş* to *arkadaş*. I felt, for the first time, that I was watching Turkey instead of being in it. The mountain that Aladdin captured rises up over Alanya on the coast, a steep sugarloaf with his fortress walls laced around it, reaching, it seems, almost to heaven, but it overlooks, not the dust of battle, not the banners, not a thousand tents, but a coast that, between the beautiful mountains and the sea, has been ruined. It reminds me of that green algae that warns divers that they have dived too near a built-up coast, a mixture of sludge and life, even the color disgusting.

One white concrete hotel after another stretches along the coast, and if anyone looks toward the mountain, they must do it only as a duty, to remember that they are not on a cheap package tour to Spain or Florida, or any other resort coast where the modern crop of holiday-makers turn their faces to the sun like the moon flowers of the high fields of Anatolia.

As Gertrude Stein said about Oakland, "There is no there there" in a place where at least five kingdoms have flourished and been blotted out. The remains of the fortress and the extended walls designed and ordered by Aladdin still spread across the skyscape of the sharp mountain that thrusts into the sea, but few go to see them. The small Byzantine church, left within the fort that became his summer palace, is only a roofless skeleton that seems to be made of stone lace. On the top of the mountain where I walked to see the place, stood the only camel I saw in Turkey, its owner waiting for tourists to have their pictures taken on it. It looked profoundly bored, but, then, camels do.

There are two other places that still reflect what the place might have been like in Aladdin's time. The massive red tower that looms over the pleasure boats and the seaside promenade is now a museum. When it was built, it was a pivot for the fortifications. The hidden docking for his navy, arched over the water, graceful and harsh, is still in use. For centuries, whatever emir or pirate ruled Alanya sent narrow black ships from Aladdin's secret docks out to attack shipping in the waters of the eastern Mediterranean.

There is only one more glimpse of Aladdin on the coast that was the southern end of his crescent kingdom. I turned off the road from Alanya to Antalya. There, thrusting up, more sharply than the mountain at Alanya, is another mountain that was once a religious retreat, so high, so steep, that "the sentries' backs were curved because they were so near the heavenly dome." It is the fortress of Alara. The brother of Kurt Vart, a Christian contemplative, starved himself to death rather than give up the fortress to Aladdin. It is so out-of-the-way of the traffic on the so-crowded coastal resorts, that it seems strange that it was once on the main road to Konya, a *han* on Aladdin's new safe trade route.

There is a little village, a small hut, a few tables shaded with a roof of summer vines, a hospitable local *bakkal* and cafekeeper, a few workmen digging out Aladdin's *han,* forgotten for so long. In the distance, boys played in the lovely river that was once said to be as wide as the Nile, but is now a gentle, deep blue vein through the summer fields.

CHAPTER
TEN

DEATH
IN THE LAND OF
THE TROGLODYTES

FOUND MUCH OF Aladdin's life in Konya, but in Kayseri I found his death. Yusuf and I drove into the city after a day of *hans* and spaces, and there it was, the place where it had happened. The castle, the *kale*, rose high on the left of the round town center, called the Centrum, as if the Romans still controlled Kayseri. The castle had been built by the Romans and enlarged by the Seljuks and the Ottomans, so that the close-fitted, huge lower stones of the walls and the smaller upper stones, in layers of age, could be read like a geological calendar of stone.

A wedding party roared past us as we came into the town, the wedding car wrapped with tricolored streamers, all the horns honking. Everyone got out of the way. They move fast, and Turkey does not have the strict Muslim taboo against drinking, and never has, so weddings, except for the very strict ones like the one we went to in Erzurum, are usually massively, joyously drunk and unabashed. Right there, and at once, was the difference between that conservative and this exuberant city.

Kayseri has survived by being in the right place and always at the right time, as now, when there is boom there, industry of the past and the present, and the Mercedes has replaced the horse-drawn heavy carved cart with its silk curtains of the Seljuk ladies, for a little while. One of those "nows" no more permanent than "then" through which Kayseri has survived all this time.

There is no past in Kayseri, only—so strong that I became part of it, the pace, the stroll, the bargaining, the industry—a perpetual present. Its citizens have the reputation of being the most industrious in Turkey. Many of the ancient walls and the buildings are intact because they have been in use, with only a few lapses for invasions, tribal quarrels, decimations, sieges, since they were built. If one wall has been torn down in an ecstasy of war, another layer of wall or castle has been put in its place, time after time.

The past and the present intertwine in Kayseri as closely as those marble interlacings over the doors of the Seljuk arches. There is no self-consciousness. The walls are there, the castle—more fortress than castle—the mosques, and the *medreses,* an essential part of the busy, commercial, pragmatic, lively city—a city of much the same size it must have been when it was Caesarea Mazaca to the Romans and to Saint Paul, and then when it was the Danishmend capital, then when the father of Aladdin made it the second city of the Seljuk empire.

In my search for Aladdin, I was getting nearer the illusion, for it could only be that, which might contain more truth about him than the meager facts. But like the search for God in the poem of Celâleddin Rumi, where he uses the metaphor of the wind, which you cannot see but see only the dust rising from the road or the grass swaying, the search for Aladdin was still part legend, part rumor, part stone, or roads, or customs. Then, in Konya and in Kayseri, I began to find a man, ruler.

The *kale* was, to me, more than a castle. It was the place where, after several days of games, jousting, fights, the revels of men, Aladdin appears and disappears, now praying in his royal tent, now playing at fighting one of his emirs with spear against mace, all this in 1236 on the playing fields outside the city.

After the games in honor of the heir he had chosen for his throne, Ibn Bibi wrote, with more baroque truth than mundane fact, Aladdin commanded that "every Ambassador and emir present in Kayseri should come to a royal feast. The feast was prepared, the voices of the musicians were heard singing beautiful melodies. Cupbearers with gold belts and silver thighs encircled the revelers like moving cypresses. The enchanting flute played and the song was sung, *Take your share of wellbeing and pleasure, for everything, even though the goal be far away, shall end."*

But, Ibn Bibi said, "The cawing wailing bird of bad luck finished the song with a terrible voice. How many have our eyes seen, who mixed wine with their clear water, and after this were confused in the morning? So it is that fate changes from one state to another. And as they drenched themselves with wine from the goblets, the chief servant brought in a roasted bird garnished with lentils and carved it for the Sultan. He took several bites and then, a terrible change showed on his highness's face. The guests ran away in horror. The sultan was driven to the *Kale Kakubadiyye,* his pavilion outside the city, and had to vomit many times on the way.

"On the 31 May, 1236, he journeyed forth from the *Kale Kakubadiyye* to the eternal peace of paradise. . . . The well-kept order of the Sultanate broke like a strand of pearls."

There is the story, in the buildings around the wide space of the Centrum and the statue of Atatürk, where the traffic moves fast in modern Kayseri. Across from the *kale* is the Honat Hatun, with the mosque and tomb of the Christian wife he called Mahperi, Moon Fairy. Her tomb and *medrese* were built the year after his death. Inside she lies, placed there by her son, in a marble tomb that you reach from one of the *medrese* rooms up a flight of stone stairs. You are asked to remove your shoes. Muslim tombs are considered holy ground.

One of the daughters of Aladdin is buried in the Döner Gümbet in the center of a fine open park, between the lanes of the highway that goes to Erciyas Dağı, the mountain that looms over Kayseri. It is a twelve-sided building with a conical roof, like a monumental tent. The sides have carved shallow niches with the animals and birds of Aladdin: the double-headed eagle in the tree of life, the Seljuk lion, twin birds on branches.

Isolated from the others, what is called the Çifte (twin) Gümbet, even though one of them has disappeared, is the tomb of the second wife of Aladdin, the mother of his chosen heir. She and her two sons were murdered by Kaykushrau II who had planned his father's assassination.

So there, in Kayseri, I met Aladdin's death at the hand of his sixteen-year-old son by the wife he called Moon Fairy, the Christian daughter he had won in the treaty with her father after his defeat at Alanya.

Kayseri is crowded, but as a walking city is crowded: the wide streets, the sidewalks, and the lanes and passages. I thought then that the center of the city must always have been much the same way, the smell, the racket—not noise, for noise can be undirectional. This is the racket of celebration and of business. It is the sale of yogurt and cheese and milk from the large wooden vats under umbrellas in the little bazaar at the foot of the citadel wall. Who cares if it was built by Justinian or Aladdin or anybody else? It provides shade for the yogurt and the perfectly picked vegetables that might wilt in the morning sun.

This was a Hittite city three thousand years before the Seljuks, so for a minute, in the evening, the Seljuk buildings seemed new. There are fragments of all this past in the two museums there. The Turkish government has divided, in almost every city, the archaeological museum, which contains the Hittite, Roman, Phrygian, and all the other ancient relics, from the ethnographical museum, which has the remnants of Turkish culture from the Seljuks on through the Ottoman centuries.

The archaeological museum at Kayseri is one of the best in Turkey. It too, like the city, seems to offer itself as a record of lives and a vitality that has not been lost. Two Hittite lions stand side by side at the door, guarding nothing. Inside, in a modern building where skylights catch and throw the sunlight so that the objects seem to bask in it, there is the skull of a lost king, his hollow eyes sealed with gold, his mouth covered with a gold gag, and a gold diadem on his crown of bone. There is a sphinx, a line of coffins like *dolmas,* of baked clay, a huge Roman eagle—gross compared to the delicacy of the twin-headed eagle of Aladdin. The headless torso of a Roman citizen, a little larger than life, stands on the porch. All of it echoes who the people were and, in the streets of this old-new city, what they remain.

To walk into the ethnographical museum, which is made from the *medrese* that contains the tomb of Moon Fairy, is to walk into a curious, comfortable intimacy, containing death but full of easy life. Someone had planted flowers in the courtyard, where a snake rose in the center of a low fountain. Twin carved dragons from one of the Seljuk palaces, twin fighting cocks, were on the walls, and in one corner of the *medrese* there was a complete Türkmen tent, unlike the wide-flung black wings of the nomad tents we had passed in the fields.

This tent was more permanent, constructed the same way such tents have been constructed for century after century: the rounded roof, the staved sides, the stones—sometimes carved, sometimes plain—that hung down like pendants to keep the animal-skin roof on during the heavy storms of winter.

This was the shape of death for the Seljuks: round or hexagonal buildings to entomb them, with the same rounded roof, and the added protection of a pointed, conical overroof from the snow and wind and space. It was sometimes plain, sometimes hexagonal, angled to a high point to let the snow slide off. We had seen them when we went across the lonely plains, where death had struck so far from home. I wonder, remembering the death-tent imitations, if the basic poem of the wanderer is not that of Celâleddin Rumi, who said, "The reed fife moans for the marsh it has left, the bird wails for home. . . ." But what home could these nomadic people remember but birth, who had wandered for so many centuries?

People strolled along through the old bazaars with arches much the same height and the same shape as the arches in the Sultan Han. I could no more have not joined them than I could have ignored the bustle of the present and tried to weed out only the dead past.

Yusuf and I wandered through the bazaar, where the finest rugs and wool in Turkey are said to be sold. Arch after arch, cobbled streets, a huddle of ancient men sitting in the last of the evening sun outside the Ulu Camii, survivors of the soldiers of Atatürk. A boy brought them tea on a tray that hung from chains, and bowed, not because they might have been the *ghazis* that he was brought up on but because they were old.

We walked past building after building, courtyard after courtyard— a maze of walking spaces, some fine shops, elegant as Turkey can be, some old shops that sold only copper pans that caught the last sun, too. Once in a while a small van was urgent about getting through the crowd, but people paid little attention. Feet were made before cars. The driver nudged his way carefully past them. Nobody minded. He took his turn.

We turned into the courtyard of a *han*. There was a strong smell of sheepskins, of blood, of food, of silk. High piles of wool waited to be carded, raw against the old dark stone walls of what had been, at some time past, an *iwan*. We climbed the stairs to the second floor.

Boys of what were obviously well-known local teams were playing volleyball in the courtyard below. All the way around the balcony in front of the shops and tiny workshops that were inside the cavelike rooms men stood cheering for their chosen team. They called to each other, or down to the boys in the midst of it all playing volleyball in the courtyard of a *han* that from the arches must have been seventeenth-century Ottoman. There was no sign. Nobody cared.

Work had stopped for a little while, and after the game was over men drifted back into their workshops or stood beside their wares, rugs thrown over the balcony railing, carpet shoulder bags with leather facings hung on hooks against the walls. The hand-and-foot-driven sewing machines revved up again. Below us, men began to card the wool, to move the piles of sheepskins, of sheared wool, and someone used the hose that ran from the stone *çeşme,* the water fountain, to clean a corner of the courtyard where a sheep had been killed. The blood and water ran slowly down to a drain that had been there several hundred years.

Yusuf had told me that if I liked anything I saw, not to show it. He sounded like a professional poker player instructing an amateur. So when I found a shoulder bag, made from a small piece of the carpet that is so famous from Kayseri, I said nothing until we had gone past. It became a game. I told him which one it was, and then walked on, slowly, elaborately casual, around the balcony.

By the time I had got back, a price had been arranged between them. They waited. The bag lay between us. By that time I had entered completely into the game that was expected and was being enjoyed by several men who stood around watching. Silence. More silence. I finally said I didn't like the shoulder strap, which was made of wool rope. I said it looked tattered. Consternation—as the word would be written in the stage directions in a play. One of the men stepped forward. He told us that he had made the black leather seaming on the bag and that he would make, then and there, a strap that I would like. I agreed, still elaborately casual, and swanned into his little workshop in my best bored *hanım efendi* (ladylike) manner. It seemed only polite for me to play my part as they played theirs. Everybody was having a little moment of pleasure in it on a summer evening.

We sat in his workshop. He was a maker of hats—all kinds of hats: camouflage material, leather, wool, shepherd's caps that must have been brought to him from the country villages for lining, a little cave of caps of all colors and designs, caps with bills that Atatürk wanted men to wear.

Kaskets, şapkas, hats, for centuries they were, in Turkey, the mark of the *gavur.* No self-respecting Muslim would wear one. They wore either fezzes, or the turbans and *kalpaks,* the military's high fur shakos that showed their rank and often their beliefs. In 1925, Atatürk outlawed the fez, which had been the symbolic head covering for the Ottoman Turks, and commanded that the Turks should wear the *kasket,* the peaked cap, so that they could not bow their heads to the ground when they prayed. He considered it demeaning. It seems such a minor thing to do, to order a change of fashion, but it was more than that and blood was spilled. A man who wrote an attack on hats on a wall in a village near Sivas was hanged. Near Trabzon, two devout Muslims were hanged, and several others were sentenced to imprisonment and hard labor, for refusing to give up their fezzes. So there we sat, nearly sixty-five years later— less than a lifetime—surrounded by hats, and a memory of blood, and not a fez in sight.

The hatmaker worked, silently and slowly, at his old black leather-sewing machine and punch. It took an hour of careful, concentrated good work. Finally there was a wide black leather strap exactly like the binding. He handed it to me with some pride and said that the work and the strap would be (the equivalent of) three dollars. I had had enough by then. "It will not," I said. "It will be five dollars." The whole bag had cost ten dollars.

All the way around the balcony there were men at work. I had wondered innocently how so many children could afford American blue jeans, and I found out. In a corner of the balcony a quiet man sat making them at a treadle sewing machine, all sizes of pants and jackets, with all of the labels of French, American, British jeans. He was using the labels, not in any dishonest way, but as the names of things, so that they would be true copies. They hung overhead, moving a little in the evening breeze that had, at last, found the *han,* and was cooling it.

There were no doors to the shops, only the arched entries to the old inn rooms. Maybe at some time there had been wooden walls there, with their own doors. But now they were open, and obviously, as at Sivas in the *medrese,* they stayed that way, with their wares and their machines left through the night.

An old man sat at the most ancient leather-sewing machine that I saw there. He got up when he saw me come by for the second time. I had had no idea he even noticed me on my first stroll around. He pointed to the leather belt bag I was wearing, and asked Yusuf, not me, if he could inspect it. I gave it to him, and again the men gathered. He and the other leather workers around him, all old men, turned it, measured it, looked at the seaming, the way the belt was attached to the pocket, and approved. He gave it back with a bow, and we went away, but I knew that in a few days a woman walking past would see leather-belt bags exactly like mine hanging on the wall outside his shop.

He would tell them, in the *miş* tense, that they might have come, or were rumored to have come, or could have come from California, or

Florida, or whatever state he thought of at the time, or even knew. Nobody would believe this, or would be meant to, or care. It was simply part of life, of the legends men work by, of time and places, and that form of politeness known as the *miş* tense, the rumor, the white lie.

Yusuf never stopped. He went, and stayed all the time I was with him, beyond the call of duty. He had sought out the oldest mosque in Kayseri while I took a much needed nap after lunch. In the late afternoon he took me with some pride to the mosque, in the middle of a Kayseri slum. The *imam* was drinking tea with some friends in the local *kahve* in the shade, but when we asked him, he got into the car and came with us to open it.

My constant shift of reaction to the religious people that I met was extreme here. I had decided so easily that the new mosques in villages and towns all through the east of Anatolia, and the little boys intoning an Arabic they could not understand, were a mixture of right-wing manipulation of naive people, of innocence, and of the danger of hired death-squads.

Then I met the *imam* in Kayseri. He was a young man, well-educated, polite of course; at any other time of meeting him I would have taken him for one of the *müdürs,* the government-appointed mayors who are in the small towns and who come from Ankara or İstanbul and long for home. I realized that, just as you would find them in the West, there are educated, dedicated holy men among the Muslims, who go where they are needed.

This was a slum, very poor, and the mosque so old—pre-Seljuk— that it was sunk several feet below the modern ground level. A chicken and a child played on the hard dirt in front of the mosque door. Although it was early twelfth century, it had been reconstructed, perhaps after an earthquake, in the early thirteenth century. The high squared tiled surface around the *mihrab,* the niche that shows the direction south to the Turkish Muslims so that they can face Mecca, their holiest city, when they pray, was the color that the Seljuks used, cobalt blue and eggplant purple and turquoise, the tiles delicate.

The *imam* uncovered for us an old well under the floor where the ablutions had once been done. Through a grill the *medrese,* which had been connected to the mosque, was shut away, dangerous, waiting for revival in a place where the local people needed their roofs fixed. We walked through the detritus of the slum that surrounded it, and took him back to his friends and his tea.

He would never have mentioned a contribution to the poor he served, but I noticed that Yusuf, who tended to be cynical about what he thought was religious reaction like most of the educated young, kissed his hand in thanks, and when we settled our accounts in the evening, he had given him alms for the poor. Even with very modern Turks, tradition runs as deep as the blood, and without needing to, they fight it consciously all the time, instead of accepting its riches.

Looming over Kayseri, protecting it, and always there to destroy it, is the main reason for its choice as a capital city, not only of the Seljuks but of the Hittites, the Romans, the Phrygians, the Byzantines. Erciyas Dağı is one of the highest mountains in Turkey, an extinct volcano where in late August we could see snow on its peak. Its fantastic explosion millenia ago formed the strange landscape of Cappadocia.

There are none of the famous carved pinnacles in the city, but there is, underground, said to be another city of rooms and tunnels, hollowed out of the soft volcanic rock, where the people hid until whatever swirl of trouble, natural or man-made destruction, was over and they could come up again.

Erciyas Dağı and its sister mountain, Melendiz Dağı, dominate the flat land west of Kayseri. Eons ago, they spewed out the new world of tufa and granite rocks for hundreds of miles around them. Gradually, through time, the slow sculptor, water, carved out river valleys, hills, caves in the soft rock. Much of Cappadocia looks like a desert tossed by the wind. It is some of the richest agricultural land in the country.

The mountain seemed to follow us as we drove for miles west from Kayseri along the central plain. After a while it was as if the car weren't moving, a sensation like being on a ship at sea, motionless, going nowhere. The land moved past around us. The plains were flat to the horizon, so far away we seemed to see the earth's curve, blanketed in August with huge fields of sunflowers all turning toward the east. In Turkey they are called moon flowers; like the moon dependent on the sun's reflection for their color and light.

From time to time we saw cars and the ever-present tractors with carts behind them parked beside the road by green fields. We stopped, too. People from the villages were bent over the low vines, picking grapes. Yusuf went into the field and brought back large bunches of fat white grapes, but he would not let me eat them until they had been washed. He said they had medicine on them.

Beyond the fields, stone sheepcotes were scattered over the low hills that were the first glimpse of a changing land. They looked so like ancient houses that the locals say that once people did live in them. They were built on solid stone plateaus with such thin topsoil that the stone showed through, and runnels that might have been old drainage ditches or ditches made by snow melt. The protective cotes foretold winters of deep snow when the sheep, part of the lifeblood of the central plains, have to be sheltered from the winds that blow all the way from Asia, and from the deep snow that in the spring melts and pours down into the hidden valleys and makes the land so lush.

Cappadocia was once the name for a great plate dominated by the two mountains, where, during the second millenium B.C., the Hittite Empire covered a huge area of central Turkey from Ankara southeast to Malatya, and from the Black Sea in the north to the Taurus Mountains in the south. Now Cappadocia is the unofficial name for a much smaller area, pitted with deep valleys, roughly between Niğde in the west and Kayseri in the east.

Ahead of us, a high hill was pierced with caves as small as windows in the honey-colored rock. We dipped, down below the plain, on a steep Ottoman road finely paved with square black stones so that I had a sense of hands, thousands of hands, carefully placing them there. The road curved around the first of the tufa hills, and there they were, the buildings of the troglodytes, carved into the rock, the first sight of the villages, the churches, the dovecotes where, for centuries before what we think of as historic time (which seems to be pushed back every year as we find out and learn to read the signs), people have lived, protected themselves, and carved perfect retreats for religious anchorites.

Think of a huge cave without a top, where the stalagmites, some of them as high as ten-story buildings, are exposed to the sun and the deep blue sky. Think of them as blush pink. It is as if suddenly the moon landscape which we are now familiar with in its desolate beautiful skeletal forms, were to become a Garden of Eden, for they are surrounded and permeated with vineyards, with fields of bright vegetables and fruit, with lush river valleys and lines of formal cypress trees growing along their banks, green below the brown and fawn level of the high plains of central Anatolia.

Xenophon and his hoplites got drunk in one of Cappadocia's underground cities. Early Christian saints carved monasteries in its hills. There are Byzantine cave churches. More than a hundred underground cities, like the one rumored to be under Kayseri, have been found there, and more are being discovered all the time.

Once it was thought that djinns carved the cities. Medieval travelers said that the strangely shaped cones were huge religious statues. To Muslims, the cave churches were haunted by figures with the "evil eye" that they found in frescoes painted on the walls, so that the eyes of many of the figures have been carefully scratched out. But the natural carving of the soft rock is more fantastic than fantasy, more eerie than ghost stories.

Cappadocia was lost to the Western world for centuries until the early twentieth century, when Père Guillaume de Jerphanion, a French Jesuit priest, riding on horseback through central Anatolia, happened on "valleys in the searingly brilliant light, running through the most fantastic of all landscapes."

We drove down from Avanos into the steep gully that hid the monasteries of Göreme from an alien world for so long. Göreme, now deserted of people, has been made into the most famous of the outdoor museums of Cappadocia. Even filled, as it was the day we saw it, with tourists from all over the world, there is still the strange atmosphere of secrecy that it depended on when it was a Christian monastic retreat. Most of the churches are hidden behind the camouflage of small windows that make them look from outside as if they were houses or storerooms. They hide, like a vast beehive, up ladders, in caves, through labyrinthine entrances, around the steep walks of Göreme—here a church with tenth-century frescoes, there an earlier one, probably second century. But once within, their wall paintings are vivid. Some of them have columns like theatrical sets, since they are formed within the soft rock and need no such supports.

Some are primitive, some like more sophisticated Byzantine churches. The earlier ones are decorated with the red ochre that has been used in sacred places since prehistory, with drawings of animals and saints, hieroglyphic signs, secret symbols.

I followed Yusuf up rickety ladders, through tunnels, around the steep sand-colored paths. In one, we stepped over shallow, empty graves carved into rock, some small enough for children. In another we found life-size frescoes of the fourth-century Emperor Constantine and his mother, Saint Helena, holding between them the True Cross, which she is said to have discovered on a pilgrimage to Jerusalem.

A fresco of a strange hermaphroditic figure with a woman's body and a man's face is life-size too, an image once sacred to the Mother Goddess, the most powerful deity in Asia Minor long before the foundation of the coastal Greek cities. She was served by priests who were castrati, and one of her incarnations was as a bearded figure dressed as a woman. Here, the figure has been turned by legend into a Christian saint. She was a beautiful woman, they say, so pursued by men that she prayed for protection for her chastity, and her prayer was answered with some extremity. She was given the face of a bearded old man.

The most elaborate church at Göreme is called the Church of the Buckle, after a carving in the inner dome. Inside, it is a pure Byzantine church—the carved columns, the story of the Virgin Mary around the walls, the intimate side chapels. Sunlight streams in from the barrel entry, and turns the underground vault into gold. Beyond it, deeper within the small, elaborate main body of the church, concealed lights re-create the illusion of candlelight. The place commanded such quiet that I forgot that I was under a high hill, surrounded by tourists. The whole place is a carved and painted version of a prehistoric sacred cave.

It would take weeks to see all of the churches of Cappadocia. It is estimated that there are more than four hundred of them in the area, and there are more to be discovered.

For centuries, Göreme was a training ground for priests; tradition has it that it was visited by Saint Paul, who saw it as a perfect place for teaching missionaries to go into a still-shamanistic country.

The colors in all of them are rich. Why they have not long since faded is a mystery. But at first an even greater mystery is why these rock formations have provided homes and hiding places since pre-Hittite times. Coming from the east, the pathway of Hittite, Persian, Greek, imperial Roman, Byzantine Roman, Turkish marauders for so many centuries, you can sense why.

In a wonderfully fertile land, these were sanctuaries for people, their animals, and their goods, out of sight of the great sweeps of armies and of nomads that passed by on the high steppes of central Anatolia, above their hidden valleys.

Many of them have been occupied ever since. Up until about thirty years ago, the village of Zelve was a fully populated, working town. It is carved into the rocks around a natural amphitheater, with two deep ravines opening into it. There is still the rock-carved mosque at the entrance to the Muslim ravine, and churches, hard to reach, in the Christian ravine.

I climbed up into the Christian ravine, and there was a mill with the mill wheel still on its cave floor, and a church with stalagmite columns. There were storerooms, houses, some of them out-of-bounds because they were dangerous.

Christians and Muslims seem to have lived amicably side by side for centuries. With the fine farming around them, the cave mills, the hidden stores, they were self-sufficient people.

But after all the years, the village reached its capacity. The walls between the cave rooms were too thin. There were rock falls. The rooms were becoming overcrowded and dangerous. So the people have been moved to the new village, Yenizelve (New Zelve). We passed them, the women still veiled, riding donkeys to their fields. Now Zelve is deserted, except for the thousands of tourists who come to see a ghostly and silent village of stone.

But for centuries, people lived there and carved homes out of the tufa hills and the volcanic pinnacles. They were so easy to carve that a family simply whittled out another room for each child born. The rock is so soft that it cuts like soap, but it hardens as soon as it is exposed to the air. After centuries of exposure to air and wind and water, the curved surfaces seem to have gone back to being organic shapes.

Nowhere is this more true, and eerier, than in the underground "cities," carved deeper and deeper into the earth, which shows the depth of the volcanic tufa. The largest known one—only rediscovered in 1965—is at Derinkuyu. Eight levels have been opened to visitors. Stone tools and graffiti have been found that prove that it has been in use since pre-Hittite times, at least five thousand years ago and probably more.

The carving of the low corridors is like a living intestinal organism. I became a troglodyte, head down, following the single file of tourists deeper and deeper into the labyrinthine rooms, past the mills, the churches, the baptisteries, the empty graves. There were round sculpted stones that were used as doors to close off whole sections in case of discovery or attack.

It was cool. The temperature never changes and the air, all the way down the eight levels that have been opened to visitors, is as fresh as the surface. I looked down a deep air well. It seemed bottomless—there are at least twenty more stories, not yet fully explored, below.

When I went, there must have been hundreds of people moving slowly along the dimly lit corridors, following the arrows that pointed the way. Otherwise, it is easy to get lost in a wrong turning, deep underground. What had been protection for the people who made these places through the centuries is a modern nightmare. Sound is muffled. The cavelike "city" demands silence, the silence of wonder and not a little controlled fear.

About three stories down, there was a large central room with five or six exits. We found a French girl, crying. She had lapsed into blind claustrophobic panic, and she was frozen against the wall, afraid to move. Yusuf offered to take her back to the surface, after making me promise, which he didn't need to do, that I would not move until he came back. In one of those lacunae of emptiness that can happen, even when there are so many people, I found myself completely alone there. I could feel the panic rise like a temperature, but curiosity outweighed fear, and when he came back I went on with him, down to the pit bottom, where the corridors were little more than waist-high and the rooms dead.

To go from life underground to the town of Ürgüp, as old and as new as all the rest, is to witness the birth of cities, from cave to mansion, still going on today. When I walked along a street of Ürgüp, I could hear truck engines revving in a garage inside the mountain. When I went to one of the small hotels, the rooms at the back were carved out of the high hill behind it. The exterior stone trim on the doors, the balconies, the dentils of houses in Ürgüp reflect a history of kingdoms. There are beautiful Seljuk-Turkish facades, Greek columns, a half-fallen Roman temple facade to a tomb, an Ottoman-Turkish gateway, all sculpted of honey-colored stone that gleams in the sun.

Ürgüp is a green city, a city of flowers. I sat in the section of the park reserved for women and families and had tea, surrounded by a garden and huge funeral urns, like the urns Ali Baba hid in, that had been found underground. I could glimpse, as I passed, the flower-decked columned courtyard of a restaurant that was once a *medrese,* or perhaps a palace, for this has been a kingdom, lost for centuries to the outside world.

But the people who have lived there since their ancestors, and in some cases their own parents, came out of the caves, go on, unaware of being lost and found and lost again, from the time of the Hittites or Xenophon or the Byzantines or the Turkish tribes. They have made the best wine in Turkey in the mineral-laden volcanic soil, raised fruits and vegetables, and hidden their beasts and their food and their families down below the ground when they had to.

There is level after level, ancient and modern, of Cappadocia, from the underground cities to the latest tourist hotel perched above a honeycombed hill, to the fortress of Uçhisar. The fortress is one of the highest points in Cappadocia. It is carved out of a great pinnacle of tufa, corridor after corridor, room above room. We climbed outside steps in the wind, going up and up until we came to shallow graves at the pinnacle, hollowed out of the rock like the graves at Göreme.

It is a natural skyscraper above the surrounding country. We looked, as Hittite, Greek, Roman, Seljuk, Ottoman soldiers on watch had done, over the tangled, deceptively desolate valleys, their towers and castles and statues and chimneys formed not by men but by time and water. We could see all the way to the horizon of tableland above them, and to the mountain, Erciyas Dağı, that began it all with its ancient eruption, said to be one of the greatest ever on earth.

It was my last day with Yusuf—lank, handsome, graceful young man, Laz and Turk—and when he said *Allahaısmarladık,* I am putting myself in the hands of God, he brought me a present, a tape of sad, lost songs about loss in a minor key, and in the marble lobby of the Ankara Hilton we kissed each other on both cheeks, as we should.

CHAPTER ELEVEN

A HAUNTING
OF CHILDREN
AND MONUMENTS

ATÜRK WAS RIGHT to choose Ankara as the old, new capital of an old, new country. From the great Iron-Age Hittite symbolic sculpture that stands in the middle of Ankara as its symbol, to the silk evening scarf of that modern *ghazi* and dandy, it is the essence of Turkey. Its whole history is there: the Hittites, the Augustan Romans, the Byzantines, the Seljuks, the Ottomans, the modern parliament.

It was a part of the Phrygian kingdom, which occupied central Anatolia for several centuries, until it was finally incorporated into the Roman Empire in 85 B.C. In 264 B.C. the king of Phrygia imported wild Gauls as mercenaries to guard his frontier, but they proved to be so troublesome that he exiled them to the land around Ankara and the ancient city of Gordium, to settle their families. For centuries this part of Anatolia was known as Galatia, the land of the Gauls, those wild tribes who had overrun France and eastern Europe, redheaded, red-bearded, blue-eyed barbarians.

They invaded not only the blood of the indigenous people, who had lived there since the Hittites, but the language as well. When I had come back once from Turkey when I lived there, I talked to a friend who was Gaelic-speaking from the outer islands off Scotland, and there were Turkish words he understood. Saint Paul wrote to them, warning of false prophets. "Oh foolish Galatians," he wrote, "who hath bewitched you, that ye should not obey the truth?"

Ankara is gathered around the mountain-high citadel, which is the center, the ancient nest of the city, and then it stretches across the hills and valleys of the modern capital: the finest museum in Turkey, the temple of Augustus and the great mosque of a dervish saint, the wide modern streets and the parks, the modern "Hittite" hill tomb of Atatürk with the revered relics, the silk scarf, the evening cape, the swords, the uniforms.

I went on Sunday morning to see the first-century Roman temple, but the greater present trapped me behind an iron fence, for the temple has a common wall with the fifteenth-century mosque of the saintly dervish Hacibayram. Coffins had been lined up on trestles in the courtyard, looking small under the great trees, for the funerals of those who wanted to be buried near the saint, and the whole front of the fence on the street was covered with huge floral funeral wreaths. The mourners mingled with the little boys who were being circumcised that day, and who were brought there by their families for the saint's blessing.

The temple once was the temple to Cybele, one of the names for the Mother Goddess, then was rebuilt as the temple to Augustus Caesar when imperial Rome ruled all of Anatolia. On the common wall Augustus had carved, as earlier kings had done, the history of his exploits so that they form a huge Latin and Greek plaque, temple high, the best record in existence of the Augustan age.

Sometimes I wandered through the old citadel city of Ankara with Ihsan's American wife, Toni Cross, who loves Ankara and knows it well. She writes, every week, for lucky members of the American Embassy in Ankara, a guide to where to go, what to see, where to eat, where to shop, how to pet an Ankara cat, in the embassy paper. She shared with me the things she had found in the ancient city over the years. I caught familiarity from her as we walked along.

The huge walls of the old fortified town loom up, a mountain above the fine modern city. It was quiet there away from the traffic and the transistors playing Michael Jackson in the shops, the bright young Turks in their Western clothes. We were walking to another city, another time.

The citadel walls are Byzantine and then Seljuk and then Ottoman and above them, using them as foundations and sometimes courtyards as high as penthouses, watchful over the tops of the massive walls, are the old wooden houses, still lived in, with their flowers and their branch-covered courtyards and their laundry in the wind that once flung Roman banners. The walls can be read like a geologist reads the cuts in rock seen from an American highway for the eons of stone, shale, coal. Fragments of an old water system have been used to repair and rebuild. The system was built to draw water up to the heights when this was the fortress for a Roman provincial city of probably two hundred thousand people.

We wandered up the long steps and through the labyrinthine gate, designed to keep battering rams from being wheeled inside the fortress, and there, on the left, is a fine Ottoman house, with a stray cat in possession on its porch of traditional carved wood.

Across from it, on the inner side of the great wall, there is a long line of Roman satyrs, lying end to end, all of their penises smashed, built into the wall by the Christian Byzantines.

There the welcoming children found us and began their chant, *"Alman?"*—German. My answer was the fine and final *no* of the Turks— *"Yok."* They followed us and called out, *"Fransiz?"*—French?

I said, *"Dün akşam, aydan geldim"*—Last night I came from the moon. Instead of it stopping them they were delighted, and when a new little girl ran up to see what the laughter was, I heard her friend say to her, *"Aydan gelmiş,"* which, translated, with all the spirit of Byzantine intrigue, means "She *says* she comes from the moon, she thinks she comes from the moon, or maybe she does come from the moon."

They followed us along the narrow street, with the wooden Ottoman balconies making shade for us, children and cats who seem to know something when Toni is around. The cats wound around her legs and purred.

We went to a Seljuk mosque that contained, that morning, the whole past in its simple forest room of wooden columns, which for the Seljuks was a late introduction after the earlier ones of stone. At their tops, below the carved ceiling, were the capitals from the classic city, Corinthian and Doric. Around the *mihrab* was some of the finest Seljuk tile I had seen.

We covered our heads with scarves and crept up into the women's section, the balcony, where the old rugs were thick lying over each other, and we were face to face with the capitals, and a slow murmur came from down below by the window between the *mihrab* and the *mimbar,* a wooden Seljuk carving, dark and so old it seemed to have turned to stone.

Against the light of the window a *hoca,* a teacher, was surrounded by little boys sitting cross-legged on the rugs of the floor. He was teaching the Koran, and from time to time a long, skinny finger would wave at the boys. His profile against the window, with his pointed beard, his admonishing voice, the waving finger, could have been as old as the mosque itself. The beard wagged, once in a while a boy giggled, all in the silence of the high room with its dark ceiling.

We walked on through the village of Ankara, the new city below forgotten in a trick of pace and time. The sounds around us were village sounds. Women in *şalvar* stood in the doorways watching the narrow streets, saying *"Günaydin,"* good day, to us; people lazed through the old bazaar of shops, the copper pots caught the sun, so did the tall hookahs: The iron dog collars with their spikes reminded me that we were still, and always in Turkey, near the country. We walked as slowly as the others, by the radio shops, all the *bakkals,* and the people sitting in the shade.

We stopped to look at restorations of Ottoman houses within the citadel. It is beginning to be fashionable to live there again, as in the old times, above the turmoil of the city. But as we walked toward the south gate to the outdoor vegetable market a small rock hit me, and when I turned there was a little girl, about four years old, grinning, reminding me of where we were. She had the bright red hair, the pale skin, the blue eyes, of a little Galatian imp.

The Ankara museum nestles below the great walls of the citadel in a reconstructed sixteenth-century covered bazaar and the *han* that was beside it. The *han* was built by the Grand Vizier to Mehmet the Conqueror in the late fifteenth century. Inside, the museum seems thoroughly modern, and that is no surprise. Except in the decadent later years, Ottoman architecture had a grand simplicity about it, the spaces, the round domes, the interlaced marble door lintels.

There are the sculptures and the friezes from the nine-thousand-year-old neolithic settlement of Çatal Höyük, its bull heads, its kissing leopards, and its flying vultures. There is its Mother Goddess too, a small statue. She is giving birth, with two lions as her midwives. She is the earliest Mother Goddess that has been found, sedate and hugely fat, this tiny figure, who will be worshiped in so many forms and in so many ways, and with so many visual changes and legends and truths, and hopes: *mater matria,* all the way from this nine-thousand-year-old woman in the Ankara museum to the mountain above Ephesus where they say the

Virgin Mary, Mother of Christ, spent her last years and died, finally evolved from this chthonic figure to the reality of a quiet woman you would pass in the street, not knowing or noticing her.

There in the open display rooms, which were shops for the horse traders and the silk merchants, the Mother Goddess grows thinner and more mysterious as you pass a thousand years from case to case. The wonderful Hittite stags and the Urartian animals seem to move as you move around them. There are mirrors and gold diadems, comic ewers with duck heads, here a long unsolved hieroglyphic puzzle on a fragment of stone wall, there the head of an emperor.

The lions and the bulls in the center of the museum, in what was once the covered courtyard, are formal and silent. I began to realize that there is a timeless aesthetic, and you can see it. One leaping Hittite stag is beautiful; another, its contemporary, is awkward. One artist was better than another, in whatever century the work was done, in Ankara or Çatal Höyük, in Perge or Ephesus or Divriği.

It was the privilege of Victorian writers to lapse into essays, sermons, and opinions from time to time in the middle of novels, travel books, and even phrase books. (*The coachman is drunk, the front right horse looks ill-fed,* etc.) I want to claim that privilege now to talk about art, ruins, and museums—the museums and ruins of Turkey, which, with all the riches gathered there, are some of the finest in the world. From the most beautiful museum that I saw—Ankara—to the simplest—Van—there are treasures in all of them, not to be missed.

One of the most fortunate things about the late discovery of the most ancient kingdoms of central Anatolia is that they were found and excavated after the Turkish people realized that they were treasures, and after the Ottoman pashas had sold so much of the Anatolian past and let it be carted away by the British and the Germans, who for so long thought they owned Turkey, especially the Greco-Roman coast. That is why you must go to Berlin to see much of Perge and to the British Museum to see most of what was built into the Crusaders' Castle in Bodrum of the Mausoleum of Halicarnassus.

But the second millenium B.C. empire of the Hittites, the cities and sculptures of the kingdom of Urartu, which existed around Lake Van from the ninth to the seventh centuries B.C., the wealth of new discoveries of the Roman provincial cities are in Turkey, and they will stay there.

Most of the finds are housed in the nearest local museum instead of being carted to Ankara or İstanbul. So the local people have a part in the digs, and they are very proud of it. Turkey is so rich in its taken-for-granted past that every town could have such a museum, and most of them do.

No place is the timeless aesthetic of beautiful art better realized than in the museum in Antalya. There, among the usual display of Roman senators, emperors who look like Rotary Club members, and their dumpy wives that I had grown to expect along this provincial coast, was some of the most beautiful Roman sculpture I have ever seen—slim, flying, graceful figures, made by a long lost, unnamed sculptor in the ruined city of Perge. An elegant Nemesis stares over your head, ignoring everything but fate. A dancer carved from black-and-white marble has been caught in midwhirl for two thousand years, as if she danced and paused yesterday, and froze there. She is what originality is, made by hands that released her into that frozen life, by an eye that caught movement and distilled it. It may have been based on a Greek original, but that is all. The eye, the vision is individual and always new.

Perge was the home of a school for sculptors, and the quality from there is well beyond anything else, except for a figure of Hercules and of the three Fates in the Roman bath that has been made into the museum at Side, which look like they may have been made by the same artist, or are of the same school.

Perge, Side, all of the gaunt ruins of the Greco-Roman cities along the coasts of the Aegean and the Mediterranean bring me to a prejudice masked as opinion.

People tend to make statements about ruins, roses, murder, love, conjure whole memories from a stubbed toe on a shard of marble. So I will talk about ruins, the ruins of Turkey. I don't like the way they are seen. I remember joining the crowds one day in Ephesus, the greatest of all the Greco-Roman cities in Asia Minor. We shuffled by the hundreds past the magnificent tombs of marble buildings. There were few Turkish people there. I trudged the marble streets lost in an international crowd as polyglot as it must have been when Ephesus was the leading port of the Aegean. I swore then—and that was seventeen years ago—that one day I would go back, and find a way to be there alone, not shoved, not pushed, not herded.

The ruins of all the kingdoms are popular with tourists and rightly so. But all too often the archaeologists and the tourists treat the modern

Turks as if they were some kind of algae that has grown on their surfaces. There is a belief in Turkey that foreign tourists only care about what is left of the Greco-Roman kingdoms. This is understandable when they see foreign money spent on digs that concentrate only on the classic and preclassic past, and when the tour buses vomit out people who treat the Turks as if they were in the way of the ruins and the rocks. I remembered an archaeologist who looked at the sacred mound in the center of Konya, layer upon layer—pre-Hittite, Bronze Age, Phrygian, Seljuk—and grumbled, "Look at all that stuff. Why don't they get rid of it and dig here?"

What she wanted "them" to get rid of was the mosque where most of the Seljuk sultans, including the great Aladdin, unknown to her, are buried, and where, if you read it, you will find Iconium and the Phrygians, and the marks of Crusaders in its walls and its columns, and the builders of a great and short-lived empire.

Her remark reminded me of the complaints of lovers of the dead past that the great new dam in the south near Diyarbakır, which will bring water to the poorest and most arid part of Turkey, is in the way of the ruins.

There are legendary places that don't disappoint when you first see them. Venice is one of them, and, for me, Diyarbakır, on the banks of the Tigris, which the Turks call the Dicle Nehri, with its black granite Roman walls, is another. It is magnificent and you can see it in full glory from the banks of the river.

It looms in air, high above the river valley, tower on tower, huge walls, which in other places are only foundations now. Slim, handsome, arrogant Kurds in their elegant traditional dress walk in the streets of Diyarbakır, two by two. The older women are veiled. It is conservative and nearly Arab in feeling.

The city is packed with refugees. Without much fanfare by the Turkish government, hundreds of Kurds were allowed across the Iraqi border when Saddam Hussein of Iraq used poison gas on the Iraqi Kurdish villagers. Nobody else helped them. It was considered injudicious by the Western countries, including the United States, to offend Saddam Hussein, because of his popular war with Iran. Only the Turks acted, and for their pains they were asked by the International Red Cross to submit to a refugee inspection before any aid was sent.

Since 3500 B.C. Diyarbakir has been conquered, owned, laid waste, rebuilt, over and over. It has belonged to more than thirty kingdoms in its time. The walls stand where borders need to be watched, and even these days, an unacknowledged civil war by bands of Turkish Kurds whispers around them.

The land between Diyarbakir and Malatya is like a Valley of Desolation. The fields are covered with large black granite rocks coughed up from long-dead volcanoes. The gorges are deep, and the road in places seems only a ledge halfway up a cliff. I could not imagine how people could survive there. Its dry gorges, its great boulders, are the landscape of one of Eliot's more despairing poems, without water and without hope.

There must have been forests there, once. Now there is country poverty, the worst I saw in Turkey. It is caused not by the inefficiency of the present but by the profligacy of the deep past when the trees were cut, and by the heavy hand of earth heave and the lack of water.

It is in this arid land that the greatest dam ever planned by the Turkish government is nearly finished and ready to flood and irrigate fields, make electric power, do all those things that man-made solutions do for a parched and poverty-stricken land. Part of it will be flooded over by great reservoirs. Archaeologists have been given some time—they complain that it is not enough—to retrieve what they can from a place where nobody has lifted a finger to help hungry people until the planning of the new water system.

But the sources of the Tigris and the Euphrates will be affected, and will, once again, revive a Middle Eastern trouble spot as old as the murderous and thieving invasions of Sargon II, the eighth-century "King of the Universe" from the Assyrian Empire in the land that is now Iraq. The dam will control much of the water that flows into Iraq and Syria, and their supply can be shut off at any time.

CHAPTER
TWELVE

MIDAS
AND SAKARYA

AM NOT A vicarious watcher, like Yeats's "world besotted traveler." Even though it may be a romantic illusion, I want to live where I am. So for weeks in Turkey I had been walking, driving, floating, dawdling, talking on the easy street of being part of the places I went to, the way of living by the day, however short the time. But because there seemed no other way to see it, I joined a tour to go to see the Gordium of King Midas.

Once I went by hydrofoil up New York City's East River. It was supposed to be a dramatic sensation of speed and waves without any danger from either. I felt like I was jailed in a pill. It was the same in the high, arrogant, air-conditioned Mercedes tour bus. I was seeing Turkey under glass—literally, the glass of the bus window. I had the sense that we were pushing the present out of the way as if it were underbrush. The dead were our prey—the ever-living, fascinating, usually tidy, very ancient dead.

We floated like skaters across the great plain west of Ankara, and people on the bus bet who would see a camel first in a land that has in the last twenty years been converted to the tractor.

The road we took had been the Silk Road, the great trade route, the road of Alexander, the Crusaders, the Seljuks, the Ottoman and the Türkmen, the Phrygians, Tamerlane, Genghis Khan. It is the artery of Turkish history from east to west and, for the Eurocentric historian, from

165

west to east, across Anatolia. It should clang with the shields of the hoplites. Armor should shine in the sun.

Instead, today, the road is wide, the trucks, huge and powerful and showing it at every blind hill, every turn, cruise along it, owning it. Modern conquerors from the Mercedes factory snort and whinny like the warhorses, except when some local farmer and his family, going at five miles an hour in a cart pulled by the family tractor, which has replaced the camel, simply refuses to get out of the way, or even to look behind him as he goes slowly, slowly across Anatolia as he always has, ready to be killed but not to be bullied, changed, speeded up, or suppressed. He is the maddening, surviving strength of Anatolia, and he always has been, with Alexander fuming behind him, Tamerlane cursing, Genghis Khan sighing.

Then we came to that huge desert the color of fawns, with thin lines of black cypresses drawn in the distance across it, dotted with natural and man-made hills. Under the man-made tumuli of Gordium there are tombs, and they are so like the natural hills that they made those of us who were amateurs at archaeology wonder which were tumuli. Lulled by the bus, we could dream of treasure, still unfound, in lost tombs.

After an hour or so, we turned off the main road and began to roll across the flat land toward a river, the ancient Sangarius where the reeds of the river whispered in the wind, "King Midas has ass's ears. King Midas has ass's ears."

I have a horror of battlefields, being endowed, or cursed, with a little of the second sight, and I need to be warned that I am getting near one. The chills of recognition began with me as we began to cross the desert, and at first I thought that I was ill. Then I realized where I was— Sangarius, Sakarya.

We were crossing the site of one of the longest, bloodiest battles of the twentieth century, where, in 1921, Mustafa Kemal Atatürk finally turned back the Greek army.

Across this huge desertlike expanse, they fought what Atatürk called the longest pitched battle in history, twenty-one days.

Churchill described how the wives and the daughters of the soldiers did the work of the camels and oxen that they lacked. They came from Erzurum, from Sivas, from Trabzon and Kayseri. Atatürk had gathered their strength from all over the east, where I had come from, and I could see them still, like the women in his statue in the center of Amasya, women in their *şalvar* with their head scarves, their feet bound in rags, pulling, coaxing the ox carts, the farm wagons, whatever they could find and use to move supplies and ammunition. They dug them out of the mud. They trundled them across the great mountains, the steep valleys that I had seen, slowly, slowly, with that terrible surviving patience that had always come from the east.

It was in August, the same month when we drove across their battlefield protected by the air conditioning of the bus, that under that heavy indifferent sun there was the groan of heavy carts. There were the silent women, trudging like Mother Courage along the dirt roads under artillery fire; the thousands of men in rags, some of them with uniforms made of cut-up carpets, fighting the modern battle for Anatolia, the last, so far, over this ground that has been coveted and fought over for eons.

The Greeks were better equipped, but they were too far from home. They had been force-marched under the orders of a commander so insane that he thought his legs were made of glass and might break, so he had to be carried. They had scorched the earth and they were hungry, and the August sun was their enemy. When Greeks were captured the first thing they asked for was water.

The two armies met in a final battle along the Sakarya River, where we were on the sunny morning in the modern silence where exhausted land has been left to the tourists, the archaeologists, and the geese in the small muddy ponds.

On a hill, like the tumulus where Midas or not-Midas was buried, Atatürk, who had fallen from a horse some days before and broken a rib, sat in a mud hut on a seat from an abandoned railroad car and directed the battle. It was long. It was savage. He had driven the British and the Australians from Gallipoli; he had drawn the Turks together out of the shards of war; he had, like the *ghazis* before him no matter how modern he considered himself, come from the east, as conquerors always had.

In two years only, from 1919 to that August in 1921, from the time when he had been exiled from İstanbul as a troublemaker on the advice of the occupying English and he and his friends had made plans for a revived Turkey over a table in Amasya, he had pulled together an army from a population in the east that had been laid low by circumstance and war. Several million people had been lost there, not only to the Russians on the

Eastern Front but to the Armenian revolt. From 1915 on, Armenians and Turks, Muslims and Christians, had slaughtered, starved each other out, lost homes, in one of the most vicious civil wars of modern times.

In every town in the east there is a statue or a bust of Atatürk, the father of modern Turkey, and if there was a place where the nation was born, with the attendant blood and pain, it was not in speeches and meetings and decisions but in this harsh desert, nearly in the center of Turkey, threatening Ankara, at the Battle of the Sakarya.

We finally arrived at Gordium, where the brash, young, barbarian king Alexander took his sword and slashed the Gordian knot. It was so quiet there. Hot and quiet. Across the sand, we trudged to see the Bronze Age, then Phrygian ruins of Gordium. Great walls were sunk by age and sand drift below the level of the decimated land. At one time there had been the massive gate of Gordium, but that morning it looked unassuming in the heat, dwarfed by the space around it. Somehow, as do so many digs, it looked too neat for what it was, where men had died and crowds had gathered and invasions had happened. There it was gone back to earth, a graveyard of empires in the sun.

We went inside the highest tumulus, called the tomb of Midas. The huge petrified logs of the burial room are the clue to what this land must have looked like covered with virgin forest, before more and more people and animals ate and built and wasted through the centuries and made a desert. In the little local museum there are fragments and a portrait statue from the tomb. Maybe it is King Midas himself and maybe it isn't. At any rate he looks like a grumpy little man with a pug nose, self-comforting and fat, so maybe he did have ass's ears. It is easy to believe.

There too, under an awning, are fragments of what archaeologists say is the earliest mosaic pavement ever found, but they have not been to villages on the coast where, with the same kind of black and white river pebbles, they still make the same simple mosaic floors today.

We were playing games with the deep past in a place permeated with a more immediate violence. There were only a flock of geese, a single donkey, a man in a cart in all that wide space, to interfere. The wild Galatians are gone, as are the Persians, the Phrygians, the mounted Scythians whose grandmothers were Amazons. We ourselves were a clue to the Scythians. We all were wearing comfortable trousers, probably the most important inheritance from them. The fields are full of shards of the

Phrygian kingdom still, and there are signs of the old road built by Darius, and gun emplacements from 1921.

One of the people on the bus, who knew more about modern Turkey than the others, insisted that we stop in the town of Polatlı, between Ankara and Gordium, on the way back to Ankara. There, on top of the highest hill, is the war memorial that marks the point that the Greeks reached in the War of Independence. The monument rises in a series of snagged concrete points, higher and higher, until it covers the crest of the hill, as if the soldiers of Jason had gone back to being dragon's teeth. Yet this place is not mentioned in guidebooks that direct tourists to the legends and the more ancient dead.

When an artist showed Atatürk a "heroic" painting of the Battle of the Sakarya, he said, "That picture should never be exhibited. All those who took part in the battle know very well that our horses were skin and bone, and we were hardly any better ourselves. Skeletons all of us. In painting those fine warriors and sleek horses, you dishonor Sakarya, my friend."

Later, I drove again with my friends, Martie and Paul Henze, along the main road through the vast battlefield of Sakarya. They had been in the American Embassy in Ankara, but through the years they and their six children had covered almost the whole of Turkey. They spoke Turkish, and had camped, delved, inspected, and cared about almost every place that I had seen in the east, and many that I never would.

We drove the back roads through the country of battles and volcanoes. When we passed the black spears of basalt, as high as small mountains, some with their crests showing ruins of castle fortresses in places where the builders must have flown there, I remembered Ibn Bibi's description of the fortress at Alara where the sentries' backs were bent because they were so near the circle of the sky.

Beside the turn in the road that we took to go to Sivrihisar, there was a fat and pleasant statue of Nazrettin Hoca astride his donkey, a modern statue to lay claim to his birthplace in Sivrihisar, although he is claimed by several cities.

Nazrettin Hoca is Turkey's comic wise man. All that is known is that he was born somewhere in the same district as Aesop, the slave. They are alike, except for one great difference. The morals of Nazrettin's tales have a reverse wisdom that shows, as well as Aesop's, a way to live. They simply use the ridiculous to make their point, instead of the solemnity of a parable or a moral.

His tomb is the prime example. Maybe it's his tomb and maybe it isn't, as the Turks begin fairy tales: *Bir var miş bir yok miş,* maybe it happened, maybe it didn't. The tomb is only a facade with a large lock, but the back is open, the last joke of the Hoca, and the lake he poured the yogurt in did not turn into a lake of yogurt, but it could have, so why not try?

We were stopping in Sivrihisar to see one of the last of the pure Seljuk mosques still in use, and, as usual, we ran into modern Turkey because the mosque was closed until time for prayers and nobody could find the key.

He was eight years old, a little Turkish boy in Sivrihisar. He came up to us, surrounded by a gang of interested boys. I suspect that he entertained them this way when there were strangers. He spoke with a strong Australian accent. Every year, he told us, he and his mother came back to see his grandfather who was one hundred years old and a *ghazi.*

He took us up the hill where Sivrihisar—spear city—had been built so long ago under the shadow of crags that looked themselves like spears, where we could see what could have been remnants of a Byzantine citadel, but which had grown so back into the rock skyscape it could have been a natural strange shape against the sky in this place of weather-carved lances.

He was very formal. He took his guiding seriously, as a Turk. No matter how long he had lived in Australia, Sivrihisar was his family home, he told us, and it would be until his grandfather died, which would not be long. That was the way it was.

He walked up the old streets past some of the most beautiful Ottoman-style houses that I saw in Turkey. They could have been built a hundred years ago, or fifty, or yesterday. Their style could have been Phrygian or earlier, as some of the archaeologists say now. They are so traditionally constructed and carved and decorated that once the wood weathers it is all the same there—the dark carving, the upper stories that look like Tudor houses with their crossed lathing and the fill of rubble and plaster. This is earthquake building in earthquake country, the cross beams strengthening the walls, then the rubble, which can fall and be replaced without the loss of the basic shape.

They looked so much like early Tudor houses that I wondered if the early Crusaders saw houses like this, part of so much that they saw on their first forays into Anatolia, and took the way of building back with them. There is some evidence, if only in function. The upper stories are built out over the street, for protection from rain, to catch the breeze in summer, and to provide communal shade when the sun is a killer in August. We took photographs and looked at the ancient walls around the gardens, and wandered, and then we realized that our small, self-appointed guide was telling us a story, in the same voice he would have used to tell us the dates of the houses, or who lived there.

"My grandfather tells me these stories every year and I write them down in a notebook so that I will always remember them after he dies, which will be soon. Here," he pointed to the snagged hills beyond the town, "the Greeks came over the rocks, and we were thrown back."

He was not telling us about the classic wars, but about part of the Battle of the Sakarya that happened in Sivrihisar. It was the same language. "They came here," the little boy pointed toward the sharp cliffs, "and we were ready for them. We put pointed sticks, I think they would be called staves, don't you?

"My grandfather said we put them there in rows below the mountain, and the Greeks fell on them and then they could be shot." He had wandered out of the clutch of beautiful houses and was leading us into wasteland.

"Here," he said, "was the Greek part of the town. Everything is gone but the church and the baths, which I will show you. My grandfather said that they had all lived together as friends for so many years that he and his friends could not understand why the Greek people of the town suddenly turned against them like that. When the Greek army came they joined it, and they made the Turkish men they caught be baptized in their church, and I have seen the place. They called it a baptistery and you walk into it on the floor, like a pool. But they put boiling water into it and it burned them all over and many of them died.

"The church is here but nobody uses it. You see, my grandfather says they thought the Greeks who were their neighbors were their friends, their *arkadaş* we call it here. When they turned on them like that, many were killed on both sides."

We had come to the nineteenth-century church, left as it was in 1922 when the Greeks left in the exchange of populations after the Treaty of Versailles, not the one that ended the First World War, but a second one that, after Atatürk's victory, secured the borders of modern Turkey.

It was a tomb. Too many had died there and it was haunted, he told us. He thought there was machinery inside it, and maybe it was haunted and maybe it wasn't, because in Australia things were not haunted and so he didn't believe it. But it was, he said, a tomb anyway.

He pointed at the wall. "It was right there, in that spot—my grandfather showed it to me many times when he could still go for walks—that he was wounded, not with a bullet but with a knife, and he has showed me the scar many times right across his belly. But his friends dragged him away before the Greeks could take him and baptize him.

"Now come and you must see the baths. Maybe they are Roman. I don't know. We don't use them. They are a ruin and people from America and Australia like ruins, because they don't have any of their own. I know that. I show many people the town when I am here because I speak perfect English."

We climbed up the bare hill, past foundations, half-covered, past large stone and brick basements that now were caves in the hillside. Obviously, it had been a rich Greek suburb. Before war rolled over them, the houses had looked out over the great valley that we had come along from Ankara, the valley of the Sakarya.

Not a house, not a wall was left. In many places in Turkey the local people moved into the houses left by the Greeks when they were exchanged, but not in Sivrihisar. The memories were too painful for that. They were simply gone, and the hillside was as bare and full of clues as if it had truly been an ancient Greek city, instead of a suburb destroyed in 1921 or 1922.

When we walked along the narrow lovely streets with their flowers wherever they could be planted, and the designs painted on the white plaster walls of their houses, and the grills of lathing set geometrically to hold the walls, we walked again through civil war, for the war in Sivrihisar was smaller and more intense than the great Battle of the Sakarya that was raging around them. It had been a war of neighbor against neighbor, back to the weapons used since prehistoric times, the long knives, the wooden staves, and the boiling water that could kill as well as modern bullets. War as it had always been, man to man, what is called, without imagination in the military annals, close combat.

We waited outside the mosque on a sunny wall, after several little boys had gone to the *imam* and the *hoca* and the *müdür* to find out who would have a key. They kept coming back and reporting politely that if we waited just a little longer someone would be there.

As a matter of fact they were having their lunch and it was Friday and nobody was going to move until the time for prayers. So we wandered a little more, this time alone. We had lost our friend from Australia. He was being very active in trying to find the key, in a panicked surge of pride.

We bought white cheese and good Turkish bread and a bottle of wine to take for a picnic, and we had coffee in the bakery with its few tables, and we waited in the sun where the town was gone quite still at dinner time, and I'm sure nobody thought much anymore about the battle that had been fought through every street only a life span ago, except a little boy and his grandfather.

CHAPTER
THIRTEEN

AN INCIDENT
OF TIME

NOW, HAVING SAID all this about archaeology in Turkey, I must eat some of the words. One of the most fascinating experiences I had when I returned there was among the dead and those who find more life there than in the present. Hattushash, the Bogazköy of modern Turkey, was the capital of the once-powerful Hittite Empire of the second millenium B.C., unknown, except for a brief mention in the Old Testament, until the twentieth century.

It stretches over isolated hills, abandoned in the sun at the head of a valley. On a day in late August, when the other ruins of Turkey would have been full of tourists, I went to that vast, empty place with a group led by Dr. Emily Vermeule of Harvard. Without her knowledge and her graceful introduction to the place, it would have meant nothing to me— only a huge checkerboard of piled stones and massive walls as mysterious as they were for centuries to the people of Anatolia, who called them "Cyclopean" after the giant Cyclops, because they thought they were built by the "giants in the earth in those days," of the Old Testament. Well-cut blocks of limestone that look like great pillows are piled there. The local people still think they were put there by djinns. The only Turkish people at Hattushash that day were those at the gate who seemed to be guards, and a few small-boy descendants of the great Hittites, selling their own hand-carved versions of tiny Hittite lions.

We went first up the stark hills to natural corridors of rock that from a distance hide what is there, and make you think there may be more and more like this wherever there are upthrusts on the mountains, places to hide, to instill awe, gnostic places.

Yazılıkaya, the most sacred spot of the Hittite Empire, is nearly a mile away from all the rest of Hattushash, haunting in its nature and its place. There was no need to carve a labyrinth; water had cut one deep into the cliff rocks, making the cliffs into high walls that dwarfed us and our cameras and our serious learning and our wash-and-wear traveling clothes. We seemed to disappear into a natural maw of the hill among the rocks of the sanctuary, where there has been ritual and murder.

A god carved into the cliff protects a small carved king of Hattushash. A goddess stands on a lion. The most familiar from the pictures, smaller than I expected, is a two-foot-high column of soldier-gods in lockstep, brutal and alive. They march in place and have for so many centuries, long hidden there.

All that is left of the huge temple complex of Yazılıkaya are these natural rock chambers that were the *sanctum sanctorum,* the most secret places of the religious cult of the Hittite kings. Neat lines of white stones are spread out toward the valley below, looking like some vast children's game of hopscotch, to show the area of the once great temple.

All over the hills and into the valley below, the building sites are marked with these too-neat white stones, the inevitable tidiness of archaeological digs. At Hattushash, that capital of an empire that ate its neighbors and brutalized central Anatolia for centuries in the second millenium B.C., this dead tidiness is as out of place as genteel Colonial Williamsburg with no drunks and no slave market.

Yazılıkaya and Hattushash are the most carefully organized and kept digs in all of Anatolia. They have been, for more than forty years, the main archaeological site of the German Oriental Society. The dig and the discoveries are not yet finished, as we found out the day we were there. I had the sense that the search would never be finished, for here was a long-lived culture and a huge, hidden city.

We climbed the steps of the citadel and walked through a strange triangular tunnel, until we stood where Hattushash spread out before us down the hill and almost into the valley below. We posed for each other in front of the gates where the lions are carved. Cameras clicked. Small boys sold Hittite lions they had carved.

The heavy, chthonic sphinxes at the Sphinx Gate are reproductions.

One original is in Berlin, one in İstanbul. Beyond the gate, the replica of the storm god, which is in the museum in Ankara, is almost sleek-looking, and, of course, a soldier.

The palace was just below the man-made heights where back and forth for centuries the soldiers marched and watched over the valley. From there the Hittite rulers controlled the world that they knew and they did it for an obvious reason. No matter how brave, how fertile, how civilized the smaller kingdoms that they swallowed, the Hittites were soldier-merchants and it was a lethal combination, as we still know from the industrial-and-military complex that Eisenhower warned against.

They welcomed trade, and kept records as carefully and neatly in clay tablets as the German archaeologists who have, through the years of digging there, piled and spaced and measured the rocks that form, like stone diagrams, the shapes of their houses, their storerooms, their palaces.

Suddenly it was all new, all alive, and we were a part, by an accident of time, of one vicarious burst of elation at what it would be like to discover the past and see it give up answers. We were taken by Dr. Vermeule to meet the head of archaeology at Hattushash, Peter Neve, who for more than forty years has dug there. He is a sun-dried sixty-year-old as weathered as the stones he plays with, and who moves over the rocks and hills, so familiar to him, as lithely as a young man.

He took Dr. Vermeule to see the newest dig, and we tagged along, quiet, ignorant, and curious, in a schoolchildren's line behind them, picking up crumbs of information in a nearly secret language as he told her about the newest find. It was a tomb just under the citadel.

There, in a crude retaining wall that nobody paid attention to, set sideways like the satyrs in the Byzantine wall at Ankara, were several fallen soldiers of the Hittites. Maybe the wall was Galatian—the Galatians lived here as well.

But neither of the archaeologists paid any attention to it. He had just discovered a large keystone at the door of the early Hittite tomb, a cave back into the hill under the citadel. It was about three feet long, carved in an arch. They stood together, marveling at it, elated at the fact that the discovery had put the invention of the keystone arch back more than a thousand years. They were both in their sixties, and had both worked as archaeologists for years, but for that minute they skipped like lambs as they clambered over the huge stones. The sun shone on them and work was never finished for them. There was always another place, another discovery, and I envied the timelessness of their work.

We went on to the smaller city of Alacahöyük, older than Hattushash, and less neatly dead. The city itself is small, and the original head-high sphinxes at its gates smiled on the evening, colored almost pink by the late sun. They were beautiful, like much of Hittite art when it is not being aggressively massive—the comic wide-eyed animals, the stags, the lions, the long-bodied horses, which have their own angular magnificence.

The day had drawn toward evening. In the little square of the town a girl drove geese to drink at the town fountain with its mix of Hittite, Hellenistic, and Ottoman stone, whatever had been there to make a bowl to catch the water for the town *çeşme.*

I watched them take turns, quietly. The geese drank, then the cattle came, and the whole village slowly gathered, ignoring as best they could the large bus sitting in the midst of their evening. Three men came staggering along, blind drunk. It was the ritual of the second day of a village wedding, the masculine mourning for the abdication of the groom's kingship, for there is a Turkish saying that a man is a king until he marries. The groom was between them, hanging onto the shoulders of his friends like a drunk in the comics. The geese, the cattle, the people, the tourists, all quiet toward evening, paid them no mind.

I wandered away there, to what someone said had been the old museum and was now a half-abandoned building where the gate sagged on its hinges. It screeched when I forced it open. In the courtyard, as I had hoped, were Hittite lions and a horse, too large to move to the newer and finer museum near the ruins. Heavy brute survivors, there was something monstrous about them. Most of the lions I had seen in Anatolia are connected in style, a species, a pride. I had found them from the east to the west, the favorite symbol of kingship for all the centuries, all the way to the avenue that leads to Atatürk's tomb. But these Hittite lions had no descendants. I could see why that powerful empire had been so lost for so long. Maybe to the always-returning indigenous people, they were a bad memory, an evil eye. Abandonments reflect this all over the world. The sense that a place is haunted, the evil eye, is older in the human mind than the name of any god.

CHAPTER
FOURTEEN

THE ARK OF VAN

WITH SOME NATIONAL self-consciousness in modern Turkey, Hittite art has been revived. You find it in the iron sculpture that is the symbol of Ankara, a circle with an antlered stag, and on the cloth that is hand-blocked with the same symbol. But survival is a different thing. Hittite art has been lost and found again, unlike much of the other ancient kingdoms that have survived without any lacunae of time in the habits and eyes of the people of Anatolia. All through this account there have been these traces, found in a gesture, a manner, a legend, an old saw, a way of shipbuilding, a superstition.

On my living-room floor in Virginia there are *kilims,* those indigenous Turkish woven flat rugs, unlike the more familiar thick carpets of the Middle East. They are peasant rugs. They are covered with comic animals, chickens, dogs, here a camel, there a red-and-yellow tiger—an animal that has not been seen in eastern Turkey for some centuries— peacocks, imaginary beasts, eagles, goats. They are Hakkarı rugs that are only made in the district of Van and farther east into Russia, in what was once the kingdom of Urartu. On one of the rugs, a mounted warrior on a striped horse lifts his arm in greeting or threat, a twin of a warrior on an Urartian stone box from the eighth century B.C. In the mountain villages, the Kurds still weave animals and birds and fantastic beasts and these warriors into their rugs, unlike the strict geometry of the Islamic *kilims.*

The Seljuks, who passed this way, were strongly affected by Urartian methods of building and seeing, centuries after they had been forgotten as a kingdom.

The Urartu were a confederation of indigenous tribes of the area that covers much the same terrain as the later kingdom of Armenia in eastern Turkey near Lake Van. The word *Ararat* comes from them. The Armenians claim descent from them. So do the Turks. It is thought now that the people who became the present-day Armenians came down from the Balkans, and the people of the region that became, for a little while, Urartu, had been there for centuries when the Asiatic Turks poured across into Anatolia.

Sometimes we tend to think of the change to new kingdoms as a wiping clean, a *tabula rasa,* and then the resettlement of the land in a new way, but it is not so simple. People and their ways of being tend to be left over to haunt the tidy-minded scholar. Whatever the mixture was, and whatever the settlement and resettlement of these valleys between the high mountains in the east, of which Ararat is one, Urartu was a wild kingdom, made safe by its own terrain.

It was short-lived, like the later kingdom of the Seljuks. It lasted only from the ninth to the seventh centuries B.C., but it left as evidence, like the Seljuks, an oasis of superb art, of a way of seeing, of wit and charm and fine building, between the more powerful, harsh kingdoms of the Hittites and the Assyrians.

I wanted to see what was left of this kingdom, another of those that has only been noticed again in the twentieth century. I flew to Van, called Tushpa by the Urartians, which was the ancient capital of the kingdom. The plane flew over the bare, sharp mountains, and there it was, an inland sea, Lake Van, once called the Sea of Nairne, turquoise blue below. The mountains were honey-colored and they carried black sharp escarpments like spears.

An old Turkish man had been helped by his younger wife onto the plane at Ankara, obviously very ill, but he sat there, straight and dignified, being taken home to die. But he died in the air over the mountains, a little too early to set foot on his land. It was so quiet, so calm, this death. His body sat there, still dignified in death as we got off the plane and the medical team got on. A woman doctor who was a passenger had leaned over him, but it was hardly noticed by anyone else. Dying is private, even on airplanes over the Caucasus Mountains; there was not a voice raised, not a quicker footstep.

Van is one of the oldest towns in Turkey. I was struck at once by how new it seemed. There was something not yet ominous, like hidden evil, but honestly harsh and violent about the place, a dusty frontier with the bare mountains looming over it. It is strangely sophisticated at the same time and I wondered about that.

The atmosphere of Van is volatile; there are too many troops. It is a military post not only for the Russian border but for the Kurdish guerrillas who are ever present in this part of the world.

It seemed like an American frontier town, with rug salesmen meeting the buses instead of bully boys from the saloon. Three-quarters of the population is Kurdish, and they come from far more colorful villages than the people in the rest of Turkey, which has been all too blanketed with dress reform. A man walked across the street followed by his two pretty young wives. They held hands, the two women, obviously happy friends, dressed in bright printed *şalvar,* their waists encased in metal belts that would have fetched a fortune in İstanbul, their shirts studded with metal spangles, and their veils of almost transparent cloth, seductive in the slight wind and falling away quite prettily around their young faces.

To show how old the culture here is, and how little changed, the first clue to the art of the Urartians is found in prehistoric cave paintings in the mountains around Van. They were painted there as early as 15,000 B.C., but the animals and the humans are drawn with the anatomical care and visual wit that has always been the mark of indigenous artists in this part of Anatolia.

There are more clues to the Urartians in the small local museum at Van: the bronze belts, the gold, the libation vessels. But instead of the stolid trudge of the Hittite soldiers and gods, or the stability of the Hittite domestic animals, there is grace and fluid movement. The Urartu horses prance and toss their heads, the cattle even flick their tails. I thought of the graceful, haunting, dying lioness in the Assyrian Lion Hunt bas-reliefs at the British Museum. They are so much more beautiful than most Assyrian sculpture that I wondered if perhaps a captured Urartian artist had carved that wall.

The horsemen of the Urartu turn and face you, like the horsemen on my *kilims,* unlike the marching men and the animals of the Assyrians and the Hittites. The Urartians seem to have enjoyed themselves, too. Two terra-cotta boots have been found, flared at the top like Cavalier boots, only they are wine cups, an early notion of drinking champagne from a slipper. Even their fragmented storm god, standing outside the museum atop his bull in the conventional stance of the gods, has grace. Their lions have the delineated formal sinews of strength, and their goats gambol, and their bulls kneel on their forelegs like the kneeling animals in Renaissance paintings of the Nativity. But the most beautiful, and the most telling single object that I saw, was a wall in the newly exposed royal city at Çavuştepe—a simple wall of what looked like black basalt. The large stones were so perfectly fitted that for nearly three thousand years before it was dug up, even covered over with the detritus of time, not one bit of earth had crept into the interstices.

Çavuştepe was carved out of bedrock on a hill above the plains. It was looted and burned by the Assyrians. I thought of the people there, dressed in the fine belts and the gold ornaments I had seen in the museum; sophisticated people decimated by the power-driven, heavy-faced Assyrian marauders, whose lists of loot are almost the only evidence we have now of Urartian civilization, except for a few artifacts. The Assyrian raiders made their careful lists of gold and silver and animals carved and covered with bronze, wall paintings, fine clothes, and mountain courage. The stones of this city still show marks of the Assyrian assault and the burning of it that they recorded.

The Assyrians, who were trading partners of the Hittites and who for centuries invaded the east of Anatolia, are more familiar because of their translated writing and because of our own Bible. They called themselves no less than the Kings of the Universe. Sargon II, Sennacherib, all their words on walls, on clay, are so graphic that you can hear the creak of their chariots and see the heads they boasted of, piled in pyramids in front of defeated cities destroyed with fire, their smoke covering "the face of heaven like a cyclone."

There, on the high hill, we could look across the bottom land, still watered by canals the Urartians dug there, and the village near the foot of the hill is built on Urartian foundations. Now the fields are rich with ages of topsoil from the now bare, denuded mountains, long since washed down to make the dark lush fields you see. The place that Sargon II saw when he invaded it has to be imagined. Once these fields and mountains were covered with forest so thick that when Sargon had the exploits carved in stone, he became a young prince, a warrior far from home for a little while, among the lists of his booty.

He told of "... high mountains covered with all kinds of trees, whose surface was a jungle, whose passes were frightful, over whose areas shadows stretch as in a cedar forest, the traveler of whose paths never sees the light of the sun." In his own history of his exploits he keeps coming back to this, to forests that were "as dense as a reed marsh," to darkness and flowing wild rivers, and places where his chariot had to be taken up with ropes, and his soldiers and their mounts narrowed down to a single file, trudging through the thick forest.

Then, suddenly, there is, in the Assyrian chronicles, another human voice, another tired young prince, Sennacherib, a younger and more human "king of the universe." "I, like a strong wild ox led the way. Gullies, mountain torrents and waterfalls, dangerous cliffs, I surmounted in my sedan chair. When it was too steep for my chair, I advanced on foot. Like a young gazelle I mounted the highest peaks.... Whenever my knees gave out, I sat down on a mountain boulder and drank the cold water from a water-skin to quench my thirst."

It is obvious that the people of Çavuştepe had too much, and they aroused the envy and the cupidity of those stronger and more brutal than themselves. Sargon's lists of loot from here and Tushpa and other Urartian strongholds are long and rich, and he mentions, which is odd, the perfection of works of art. When I read of the cars, stolen from the Kuwaiti showrooms and streets, going back to Iraq piled high with loot from Kuwait, the gold, the computers, the televisions, the medical instruments, I thought of the lists of Sargon, who came from the same land as the present-day Iraq, and how little had changed.

It is obvious that as long ago as the Urartu, the bad drove out the good. But maybe not. The eye, the genius survived. The Armenian stone masons had learned, centuries ago, from the indigenous people, and up until the late nineteenth century were the best in Turkey.

The Seljuks had the sense to use Armenian craftsmen. At the tenth-century Armenian Church of the Holy Cross, on an island in Lake Van, there is a carved riot of animals and Bible stories around the outer walls. It reminded me of the wonderful excess of the mosque door at Divriği.

On the way to the island, I found the most beautiful tomb I have ever seen in all my search for the Seljuks. It was built of a stone that seemed to blush in the sun. The carving was incredibly delicate, a perfect transition between the Seljuk pointed arches and the flatter carving of the early Ottomans.

There it was, six thousand feet up among the ungovernable and independent mountaineers who still make what they want as they always have. A sign said it was built by the Lord of Van and Hakkarı for his daughter in 1335—a long-lost ruler, a long-lost princess—in the traditional shape of the *yurt,* the Central Asian tent of the nomads, surrounded by Muslim graves. Children had made the cemetery a playground and I was, as always, an entertainment and a moment of quick ephemeral friendship. They said, in their soft voices, "Hello, hello," and one little girl took my hand and said, *"İyi arkadaşım,"* my good friend.

Lake Van is the blue of the Turks, a pure turquoise. The island of the Akdamar Kilisesi, the Armenian Church, is a favorite place for the local Turkish people to go for picnics on Sundays. The little boat for the half-hour journey from the mainland was packed beyond the gunwales, for the local boatmen know that Sunday is the day they can make enough money to last them for the week.

Both on the boats and in the rug shops there seems to be a desperate fear that no more buses will come, no more planes, no more cars, and that they will sink back into neglect if they don't trade now, here, and at once. It is a game beyond a game, and when they wave you good-bye with those nice, sad Turkish and Kurdish faces, as if you were their last friend leaving, it is a form of politeness before they meet, as in the Old West, the next stagecoach, bringing gold and news.

It was an idyllic day to wander in the island breeze, cool under the sparse trees, and look at the lavish wild carvings of the church. It had been built when the land of Armenia was ruled by the Abbasids, the rulers of Persia before the Seljuks. They had obeyed the Koran to the letter and let "the people of the Book"—the Christians and the Jews— follow their religion and their building without interference.

But unconscious dilution from the early Türkmen can be seen in the Mongolian eyes, and a seated figure sits in the Asian manner that two hundred years later can be seen in the cross-legged figures on the tiles at the Karatay Museum in Konya. David and Goliath stand half facing each other, exactly as two Seljuk warriors face each other two centuries later on a piece of carved wood at the Museum of Turkish Art in İstanbul. The animals, boats, saints, vines, on the outside walls of the church read as a history not only of the Bible but of a way of life in the tenth century at Lake

Van, two hundred years before the Seljuks won at Manzikert, and Alp Arslan, the brave lion, opened the way for the main body of Türkmen tribes to come over into the highlands and finally all the way to the Aegean.

When it was time for the little overloaded boat to start back to the mainland, a wind came up and nudged it onto a large rock that was just below the surface of the water. We began, quite gently, to sink. The Turkish boatman, who seemed brokenhearted at the damage to his hull, stripped, forgetting or ignoring his passengers, and dived over the side to inspect his livelihood. He came up dripping with water and maybe tears; I couldn't tell.

The stolid patient Turks sat through yet another near disaster without moving. Nobody panicked. Nobody vomited. Nobody jumped overboard. All together we went slowly deeper into the water. The boatman managed to put us ashore on a huge pile of rocks. We clambered across them and back to the little pier to try again, in another overloaded boat. The next day when I passed the island on the bus to Diyarbakır there, tied to the rock as we had left it, was a very small, very waterlogged toy boat in the distance, all alone.

All too often, in this part of Turkey, as it did at Sakarya River, the present bursts upon the past with such silent violence that the safety of age is ripped apart.

On Sunday evening toward sundown I did what all tourists do at that time of day in Van. There is a huge, long, natural citadel of rock, now isolated in mid-plain, but once on the shore of Lake Van. It is shaped like a ship that has been left high and dry on a shoreline that has receded through the centuries.

But the huge cut stones below it were once piers. It was the citadel and capital of the Urartu kingdom, and I wondered when I saw it if that isolated rock was the beginning of the legend, the human historic memory of a flood there, on the inland sea, and, surrounded by the waters of the flood, a shiplike rock where people survived. There had been people there living on the rock for millenia, surrounded by a bulwark of mountains since the Rock of Van was, or might have been, the Ark of Noah.

There are as many levels of legend about the Rock of Van as there are levels of building, but the basic surviving building is Urartu, put there when it was Tushpa. It is the tourist sight of Van, and day after day, to see the sunset, people climb its steep, once impregnable sides and bask in the past there.

I wandered where Sargon II piled the heads of the vanquished in front of the gates in the valley below. Then I climbed like all the rest of the tourists, in sensible shoes, up and up the steep path, over stones and slides. There, cut into an unseemly rock face, approached in fear and trembling, at least by me, down rock steps, with sheer cliff for several hundred feet below and with a sort of guardrail that was, as I thought then, as frail as silk, was the same billboard brag that you find from the Assyrians all the way to Augustus at Ankara. It was the brag of a long-forgotten Urartu king.

There, behind the stone billboard, is the tomb of the Urartu kings, empty long since. There too are the beautiful fitted rocks, as at Çavuş-tepe, but they are hidden by the Phrygians, the Assyrians, the Byzantines, the Seljuks, the Ottomans, all the people who used the rock as a fortress after the Urartu.

Over and over the place has been put to fire and sword and now it is a pleasant climb in the evening, a nice time to look out over Lake Van from so high up, and sit along the stone benches that are old or new or ancient, and you can rest from history and events. It is a lulling place.

Then I looked down into the valley on the south side of the great rock. It was a graveyard the size of a town, all that is left of the Turkish section of ancient Van after the revolt when the Armenian guerrillas raised the standard of the Republic of Armenia in the city of Van in April of 1915.

For years the imperial Russian government had backed Armenian nationalism in the area in the hope of having an indigenous population to come over to them when they succeeded, after so long, in taking the Dardanelles. It was to be the last in a series of wars the czarist government fought, including the Crimean War, to gain access to the Mediterranean.

When the Russian army retreated hordes of Armenians went with them. The whole of the Eastern Front had become a place of disease, starvation, a no-man's-land. When the Armenians left Van, they fired the Turkish section and, in a few days, killed thirty thousand Muslims, including Armenians who had become Muslims, but mostly Turks.

It was during this revolt that the order went out to clear the Armenian population from the war zone, with its tragic, unforgivable results. They were forced out of the grave they had made of Van and from all the country around, those who had not followed the Russians. The awful march to the coast began of neglect, starvation, and tragic cruelty. Sometimes I think that march has gone on ever since in both the minds of the Armenians and the Turks, never to end, never to be forgotten by either of them. It is old, fetid, solidified hatred, hard to clean away on either side.

Now grass grows over the foundations, a few shapes of mosques stand out from the grave mounds of houses and shops and people. Where so much else was burned by the late August sun to fawn color, the dead city had stayed green, fed by its springs and its dead.

It is one of the most tragic civil wars on record, a half-forgotten and mistold story of a people with ancient hatreds between them who had lived in some kind of amity for centuries, and who were roused on both sides, partly by the Russians and partly by the fears of the dying Ottoman Empire. The bloodbath that resulted killed nearly a million Armenians and more than two million Turks with the same inhuman weapons of massacre, neglect, and starvation.

I wanted to run from it, but the cliffs were too steep, the paths too precarious for that. So it took an hour of stumbling into deserted Byzantine basilicas, into broken Ottoman barracks, into the whole stone labyrinth of the place to get down off the ark of a mountain that once must have seemed so safe.

CHAPTER FIFTEEN

THE ROAD BACK

HE CIRCLE OF time and space and kingdoms was almost complete for me. I had traveled from İstanbul along the Black Sea, to the towers of Trabzon, down along the route of Xenophon, through the lands of the Urartu, along the great crescent of the Seljuk kingdom. I had seen the now-dead power center of the Hittites, the Pontic kings, the battles and the paths and the War of Independence, and the new capital of Atatürk that was so old.

I flew west again to Ankara and joined Paul and Martie Henze to drive back to İstanbul where I had started the search. We followed the slow, worn paths of the most contemporary and best known to the modern world of all the kingdoms of Anatolia—the Ottoman Empire.

The tribe of the Osmanlı rode out of tribal legend into history and legitimacy in the thirteenth century, during the Seljuk reign of the great Aladdin.

Bir var miş, bir yok miş, as the fairy tales begin. Maybe it happened, maybe it didn't. Four hundred horsemen under the command of their tribal leader, Ertoğrul, had fled before the Mongols, looking for new lands for their flocks and their families. They came upon a battle between two groups of soldiers, both unknown to Ertoğrul. He chose the losing side as a gesture of chivalry. It was the army of Aladdin. The choice turned the tide of the battle, and Aladdin rewarded Ertoğrul with the lands around the city of the present-day Eskişehir.

Aladdin bestowed on Ertoğrul a banner and a drum, the signs of sovereignty over the land he had given them. The first settlement was Söğüt, near Eskişehir. It was a policy to put the more warlike *ghazis* on the borders as buffer tribes, and Söğüt was near the border between Aladdin's kingdom and the fragmented Byzantine Empire.

The Osmanlıs had been pagan animists, like most of the tribes of the thirteenth century that were driven west before the Mongols. But there is an Islamic legend of their conversion too, the story of a man, a stranger who was given shelter in the house of a pious Muslim, as hospitality demanded. The stranger had stood all night one night and read a book that his host had given him. It was Osman, the son of Ertoğrul. The book, of course, was the Koran. Osman dreamed when he finally slept that a great tree grew from his loins. It was the classic prophetic dream of empire.

Osman grew in strength and captured the city of Bursa in 1326, after a seige of seven years. He died there soon after he conquered it; the Osmanlıs, which is what they called themselves, the children of Osman, stayed there for two hundred years. It was the first capital of what was to become the Ottoman Empire, an empire that lasted under the Osmanlıs until Atatürk exiled the last pathetic remnant of the great Osmanlıs— Mehmet VI—and proclaimed the Turkish Republic on 29 October 1923. The Ottoman Empire had lasted for six hundred years, twice as long as the British Empire.

On the way to İstanbul, we drove into Söğüt, where it had begun. There were soldiers in the streets, conscripts far from home, walking in the afternoon, slowly.

There, as a sacred center of modern Turkey, is the simple tomb of Ertoğrul. The Islamic and the Turkish flag had been placed at the head of his catafalque. Two young men stood with their hands held up in the Islamic attitude of prayer. This is the font of the Ottoman Empire; it was from this small center that Osman began to take the exhausted and neglected lands nearer and nearer Constantinople, as Alp Arslan had taken the eastern lands in his time.

The Osmanlı had been only one, and a minor one, of the many tribes into which Anatolia disintegrated with the fall of the Seljuks and then the Mongols. But they had something the others lacked. They had a new religion from which they drew their zeal. They had a sense of organization. And they were not too stubborn to learn from the mistakes of their predecessors. Sometimes the lessons were brutal.

Beyond Ertoğrul's tomb, in a large semicircle, is a modern open pantheon of the founders of all of the successive kingdoms of the Turkish tribes that ruled Anatolia. Bronze busts of Alp Arslan, Attila, Genghis, Timur the Lame, Osman—seventeen of them altogether—stand in niches. They look like brothers. Only their beards and their helmets are different. In the center is a bust of Atatürk, the founder of the most recent of the Turkish states.

It is the place where Turkish officers take their oath of allegiance in the army. Beside it is a small museum with a Turkic tent in the center, the kind of tent that the Osmanlı came in at first, and from which they began the raids that would turn, in time, into empire.

Genghis Khan, Attila the Hun, Timur the Lame, Mustafa Kemal Atatürk are still the heroes of the Turkish people. I was once giving tea to a friend in Bodrum whose last name was Genghis, a name his father had picked when Atatürk sent out the order in 1934 that everyone in Turkey should have a surname, which they had never had before. My young friend, Attila, was fixing the fence.

I said, "Where in God's name am I? Genghis is in the living room and Attila is fixing the fence."

My friend, slightly offended, said, "One nation's heroes are another nation's villains."

Boys in Turkey are called Attila and Genghis, and Timur after Timur the Lame, and Osman and Orhan, Mustafa and Kemal, although only Atatürk can have the name of Atatürk—"the father of Turkey." Some are called Emre, for they care for their poets, too.

Söğüt is an attempt to create a modern "sacred" place. Seyitgazi, near Eskişehir, has been a holy place since before the Greeks, and it has, on its hill, every evidence of century after century of sacred change. Its caves were sacred in 35,000 B.C., as caves and mountains have always been since the Mother Goddess came out of a mountain cave. Gods and saints and legendary lovers have slept in them since Endymion and the Seven Sleepers of Ephesus. It has a temple facade of the Phrygians, which still has the carvings of its sacred lions. Animals, caves, mountains—in all the sacred places that people have made into centers of prayer and sacrifice, neither names nor time matter. Now the place is called Seyitgazi after Seyit Battal Gazi, the Arabic hero of an eighth-century battle against the Byzantines.

Its skyline is the dome of a Byzantine basilica, an Ottoman tomb, a pre-Ottoman mosque. A marble-paved Roman road leads into it, its walls are Byzantine and Ottoman, and part of its *tekke,* its monastery, was built in the time of the Seljuks, to house the Bektaşi dervishes.

Nothing has been lost at Seyitgazi. The kitchens where the sacrificed lambs were cooked are still in use, after the long time when war rolled over Seyitgazi in the twentieth century and the place was deserted. When I went there with Paul and Martie Henze, who had been there often before, it was full of Turkish people who had brought their lambs and their food to the kitchens to be sacrificed and cooked, and there was blood on the stones. We were the only Westerners, and probably the only ones who recognized that a baptistery from the Byzantine church had been built into the corner of the courtyard, and that the columns were Roman.

At the tomb of Seyit Battal Gazi women in their *şalvar* and their head scarves moved slowly around the twenty-foot-long catafalque and kissed along its sides. Then they kissed along the small tomb beside it where a Christian princess is buried. It is said that she fell in love with Seyit Gazi, and when she tried to warn him of danger, she drew attention to him and he was killed. In grief she killed herself and she, or someone, lies there in her little tomb. I remembered the saint at Tokat, the same story, and the story in *Dede Korkut.*

Unlike so many other shrines in Turkey this one was full of women cooking, praying, and, when they saw us, smiling and wanting to have their pictures taken with the *gavurs.*

It was there, below the altar in the apse of the Byzantine-Christian basilica that had been turned long ago into the mosque of the *tekke* of the Bektaşi, that I found the last clue to Aladdin. There is argument over whether his mother was Christian or not, and there is the inevitable legend that she was a Muslim convert and that she asked to be buried at the Bektaşi *tekke,* but there is mystery there. She is buried beneath the altar, and that is where, since Christian churches were built, Christian saints and rulers were interred.

Seyitgazi is a mystery, and a continuity, and a link that holds the past in a still center of the present. But the past is everywhere, knitted into daily life. I think of the goat I once saw being sacrificed and the handprint the captain made with its blood on the prow of the boat that was launched at Bodrum, and the red ribbon tied to the goat's horn as the red string was tied to the toe of Esau to show that he was the firstborn, and I think of the basil plants they take aboard the boats when nobody remembers that basil is sacred to the Mother Goddess.

I remember that every year on a certain day people swim at Trabzon, not knowing or caring why they do it, and the baptistery at Sümela, where they toil three thousand feet up that perpendicular mountain bringing their children to be blessed where there was a sacred cave and then a church built in it and a monastery that lasted for more than fifteen hundred years. Turkey is new as a nation, and it is as old, literally, as the hills that are still sacred, stripped and bare and lion-colored.

I think of Bursa, the first Ottoman capital near the Sea of Marmara, as the most eastern city in the west of Turkey. It has not lost, at least a part of it has not, that atmosphere of quiet dignity that is in every place in Turkey beyond Ankara. But Bursa is three cities. One is a frantic, busy modern place of factories in the valley that is the center of the growing Turkish automobile industry. Hidden behind it, as if all that noise and speed were a moat to protect it, is the old city, green and quiet. It was the most Western place where I did not hear Michael Jackson on loudspeakers.

The third Bursa is its prison, where Nazım Hikmet, Turkey's finest modern poet, was imprisoned for his poetry. There have only been ten years, the years after the revolution of 1960, when the Turkish people have been able to read and to publish what they wanted to. Censorship is a part of a way of life there that has never been reformed, and it is an irony that most of the liberals who have tried to reform the government, which still today leans so heavily on the mind, were educated at what was, until recently, the Presbyterian Robert College in İstanbul, where, because it was an American college, censorship did not exist.

Nazım Hikmet was jailed because young army officers had been caught reading his poetry. He stayed in prison for twelve years, and his greatest work, which is, to me, no less than a history of modern Turkey in human images never to be forgotten, is the epic *Human Landscapes,* which he began in Bursa prison in 1941. He was released in a general amnesty in 1950 and driven into permanent exile.

The history of political imprisonment is a tangled one though. Yilmaz Guney, Turkey's most famous actor, was imprisoned as a communist, released, and then killed a man when he was drunk and was imprisoned again. He escaped to Europe, where he completed the film *Yol,* which has become an underground classic there. There is only one thing wrong. He is presented in the beginning as a political prisoner— there is no mention of the fact that he was imprisoned for the second time on a charge of murder. There is much of the *miş* tense in the political propaganda of both the left and the right there.

Old Bursa, where the famous spas are, lies along the foothills of one of the tallest mountains in Turkey. The mountain, Uludağ, now a ski resort in the winter, was once called Mount Olympus. It rises at the western beginning of the great high plains of Anatolia.

To find it, we drove through maniacal traffic, horns honking, past concrete, glass, and steel buildings, then had to slow to the pace of a mass of people wandering through the busy *pazar,* up toward the mountain. It was Saturday evening and darkness was falling. We reached the old city. The factories were behind us. We began to hear, instead, the play of water.

Evliya Celebi, the seventeenth-century Turkish traveler, called Bursa "a mine of living water." It flows with fountains and streams and waterfalls and hot mineral pools. Cypress trees stand as straight and tall as the minarets of the old mosques. There are ancient plane trees that were there in the fifteenth century. The city has grown from the austere piety of nomads new to cities to the opulence of the later culture.

It has never forgotten that it was a capital, a sacred city, and the leading spa of Asia Minor from the time of the Roman Caesars through the nineteenth century, when pashas came with their wives and stayed at huge baroque hotels taking the waters. Now the hotels are new and modern, and the hot water still flows from the mountain.

Its physical beauty, its small houses of pink and blue and yellow, its splashes of green trees and shrubs and flowers and water, its ruins, its great monuments, and its luxurious hotels, reflect its past and its own sense of pride and being, like a family that has been a long time in the same place and held the same land.

The great mountain feeds it. The streams rush down deep ravines where there are still narrow walking bridges on their graceful Ottoman arches. As in most of Turkey, marble hints of the Roman Empire are used in the ancient citadel whose fragments still partly enclose the oldest part of the city. There are hints of Rome in the walls of the old houses. Time is an element of architecture in Bursa. It seems to be enshrined in stone.

Bursa is also the most luxurious city in Turkey. The twentieth-century hotels that have grown up around the hot mineral springs have their own pools. I lay in the marble pool at the Çelik Palas, with its high dome pierced with tiny openings, and watched the sunlight come in like stars through the mist made by the steam. The water was hot, and the mineral had stained the dome walls so that it was streaked with Turkish blue and green as if it had been painted by Monet.

There are hot mineral baths all along the foothills, in the hotels, in medieval buildings. Eski Kaplıca (the old bath) was established by Justinian in the sixth century. The present building was built in 1511. The new Kervansaray Hotel has been built on the steep slope of the hill below it, using the old domed bath as its focal point. It is one of the most beautiful examples in Turkey of the integration of a modern building into the cityscape, and into the past.

At the center of old Bursa around the Great Mosque and the smaller Orhaniye Mosque, both built in the fourteenth century, a traditional complex was built at the same time: soup kitchens, a hospital, a *medrese,* and a paved square with fountains that tossed high plumes of water into the air and the wind, for to the Muslims public water fountains are considered a charity by a religion born in a parched land.

This is one of the pious gifts to the public that for centuries have been built all over Turkey. Turkey runs with water. Even along the large highways you will see trucks stopped, people talking together as they drink the water given by some vizier, *ağa,* pious villager, long ago. The Turks are descended from nomads for whom water was scarce, so I was never in a place where I was far from fresh, sweet water for long. There is a *çeşme* on corner after corner, wall after wall in the cities, against public buildings, and always in front of the mosques where they are put for ablutions for worshipers. The Koran orders that feet, hands, and, in the early days, genitals, be washed before prayer.

It was also a tradition to build *pazars* whose rent paid for these acts of piety. So spread below the Bursa complex toward the valley there is still street after street of the old *pazars,* some covered, some open, where you can buy anything from food to books to gold (in the covered section), to those satin and fur uniforms with bright red or blue capes, and gold-painted crowns that the boys wear when they are circumcised. They look like Principal Boys in English pantomimes.

The paved square and the fountains are still there, a good place to sit, as people always have, drinking tea and watching the crowds. Behind the fountains, in the Koza Han—the word *koza* means silk cocoon—is a fifteenth-century building that looks unassuming from the square.

When we went in we saw that it was an ancient inn, built and integrated into the hillside so that we were standing on the balcony of the second story. It is the silk center of Turkey. There are bolts of cloth, scarves, ties, whatever can be made of silk, and some of the finest leather in the country. The shops go all the way around the second-floor balcony. In the center of the courtyard below is a small, very elegant mosque in the Seljuk style. When Bursa was the capital and the caravans were in, the courtyard was full of honking, spitting camels, those imperious animals with their *havuts* filled with goods for Sultans and their courts—ivory and sables and fine china from the East.

Now, if you go there in July, the courtyard will be full again, this time of the villagers who are bringing their silk cocoons to be auctioned in the open market. The growing of the silkworms and their feeding on mulberry leaves is a cottage industry around Bursa, and in almost every window of the shops around the upper court, you will see the small white bundles that are the source of silk thread, as if the merchants are reminding themselves—and you—where all the opulence came from.

The Great Mosque, to the left of the square, is, to me, the finest building in the city, even though the Yeşil Cami, the Green Mosque, is the most famous. It is the largest mosque in Turkey, a transition building between the old Seljuk style, with its stalagmite shaped pointed doorways, and the grand space of the first simple Ottoman interiors. Here the transition is evident, and it is beautiful. There is—because it is Bursa?—a large fountain in the center so that the ablutions of the worshipers can be done inside the building.

The fountain is directly under an opening in the roof so that the sun streams down to weave the plume of water in the center with sparks of light. Shoes are neatly placed around it by the worshipers.

It is said that the fountain was built within the walls because when the Sultan Beyazit wanted to place the mosque there, one woman held out and refused to sell him her house. When she was forced to move, the fountain was placed where her house had been, since men could not pray in a place that was taken without the owner's consent. So it stands, her legend and her monument, in the center of the vast building, where the calligraphy is some of the finest in Turkey. There are huge murals of graceful black Sufic scrolls on white backgrounds; *trompe l'oeil* around the doors, over the windows and the arches; calligraphic designs of the names of Allah, the sultans, and the prophets.

Karagöz and Hacivat were born here too. Karagöz was a hunchback who was working on the mosque when it was built. He was caught making fun of the Sultan by using his hands to cast shadow figures on the wall. In a fury, the sultan had him executed. It was out of Karagöz's joking that the Turkish shadow puppets were born. The shadow puppets are still everywhere, as familiar as Punch and Judy.

There are mosques and tombs—*türbes*—of Ottoman sultans the length and breadth of Bursa, from all the periods of Ottoman rule. The Green Mosque has a balcony for the Sultan and his family that is the gold-splashed gaudy that would become a mark of Ottoman taste and replace the austerity of the Seljuks. To the right of the *mihrab* is one of the most beautiful of the tiled and carved rooms in that baroque, rich architectural style.

Bursa had a devastating earthquake in the mid-nineteenth century and much of it had to be rebuilt, but Islam is conservative and traditional. It was put back exactly as it had been. It is a place whose riches come from a mountain that can destroy it. Like Karagöz's shadow play in the Great Mosque, there is a sense of amusement, and beauty, and vastness and danger.

But when I lay in the hot thermal bath at the Çelek Palas and looked up at the beautiful dome, I was Roman and Ottoman and a part of the mountain, for this luxury comes from the same source as the earthquakes, deep in the earth. The same water feeds silkworm and sultan, devastation, luxury, prison, and the mulberry trees.

When we drove into Beyazit, into the roil and crowds of İstanbul, and I finally had made full circle around Turkey, this time I came from the east, the path, the *yol* of the Seljuks and then the Ottomans.

İstanbul did seem like the center of a world, now Ottoman and modern European in feeling, instead of the Byzantine city I had come to nine weeks before. I had traveled through empires, and wastes, and deserts and mountains, coasts and cities. The best part of it was that I had been, mostly, with Turkish people, and all of them were a part of their land, whether they were professors from Ankara, or Laz from the Black Sea, or little boys from Australia. That is what is wonderful about Nazım Hikmet's poetry. The place he called "a precious silk carpet" is, as he said it was, theirs.

CHAPTER
SIXTEEN

THE MIME

I T WAS TIME TO close the smaller, personal circle of my wanderings, to go back to Bodrum. I had delayed it all through the journey; I had heard that Bodrum had turned into the Portofino of the Aegean, and I was afraid of disappointment at what I saw as destruction of a small, dear place. So instead, I lingered on the road south from İzmir, keeping the promise to myself that I had made so long before, that I would go to Ephesus, and stay, and wander.

Near the coast of the Aegean, about an hour by car south of İzmir, three mountains form a triangle above the valley of the River Cayster. On the first, the foothill nearest the main road, is the modern town of Seljuk. It is also the oldest settlement. Tradition says that it was begun by the Amazons, and there, in a marshy grove, they sacrificed to the chthonic Asian Mother Goddess the testicles of their enemies, chanted, clashed their shields, and sang the song that centuries later the Bacchantes sang.

Probably by the tenth century B.C. the settlement had already moved to the place between the other two of the three mountains where the Greek city of Ephesus was to grow, about a mile from the ancient shrine. It became, through time, one of the largest and most important commercial and religious centers in Asia Minor. By Roman times it had become so large a city that nearly 130 years after it was rediscovered it is still being excavated.

Through the later centuries the city shrank and the Byzantine walls grew higher, built of fear and stone, as if the future the people could already read could be kept out. It was destroyed slowly, by silt, politics, religion, raids, earthquake, and malaria. Finally the old port, clogged by earthquake debris and the new river delta, was completely abandoned.

By the fifteenth century A.D. Ephesus was only a village. Its people had always rebuilt some kind of shelter after disaster, but the last time there was no more building. Three earthquakes had decimated it. After the third there were too few people left to build.

It was then that the last of the Ephesians moved back to the hill settlement that was the first in the valley and where it has, for one of those short presents which on the Aegean coast can change and rechange, ended for the time being as the Byzantine, then Seljuk, then Ottoman, now modern town of Seljuk.

The modern town surrounds the holy hill that was a place of Christian pilgrimage, where the ruins of a Byzantine church built over the grave of Saint John lie behind an ominous gate made of Roman fragments, called the Gate of the Pursued.

A citadel crowns the hill at Seljuk, with walls that were built by the Byzantines and rebuilt by the Seljuks. In the middle of it, with a view of miles of the fertile valley and the mountains of the ancient city, there is a small Byzantine church, centuries ago turned into a mosque. When I went up to the top of the hill, through the remains of the great labyrinthine fortress gates, Turkish boys were flirting with tourist girls and daring them to climb the broken minaret.

The abandoned port city of Ephesus was lost for nearly five hundred years. There were only upthrusts of stone, often of marble, fragments plowed up by the farmers who tilled the fields over it, to tell where it had been. It lay under five to ten meters of silt from the Cayster and the Maeander rivers.

It was rediscovered by a man with the lovely name of John Turtle Wood, an English engineer who was building a railroad down the coast in the 1850s and 1860s. He was an amateur archaeologist, who wanted to find the temple of Diana of the Ephesians, mentioned in the Bible.

Wood worked for some years and found much of Ephesus: the streets, the port, the huge theater where Saint Paul had preached against the goddess. There the silversmiths—who made their fortunes by selling silver votive statues to pilgrims—had started a riot. The populace, led by one Demetrius, shouted, "Great is Diana of the Ephesians." Saint Paul barely escaped with his life.

Wood had begun to uncover the most complete Roman ruins that exist, but he could not find what he wanted most, the temple to Diana that had been one of the ancient Seven Wonders of the World. Finally, he found a description on a stela, a monument stone, of a ceremony and procession that started at the temple, went to the theater through one of the main gates of the city, the Corresian Gate, which he had not found, and then went from the theater up the Sacred Way and through the Magnesian Gate on the other side of the mountain back to the temple.

He realized, as an engineer, that it should lie at the apex of the two sacred roads that had been described, and he thought, or hoped, that it would be somewhere near the then tiny village of Seljuk. On New Year's Day 1870, he found the first clue to his treasure, a few exposed fragments that stuck up above the surface of a swamp. He drained as much of the water as he could, and began to dig there.

He had found the place where the grove of the Amazons had grown through centuries into a religious center as large and as important in its time as the Vatican is today, the center of worship of the Great Mother, Ma, Cybele, Aphrodite, Artemis, Diana of the Ephesians—called by the Greeks the Artemision—the place where Xenophon sent money to thank the goddess for the rescue of his soldiers. It had been stripped, fallen in earthquakes, raided, looted, the marble destroyed by centuries of burning in the lime kilns he found around the site. The Byzantines, the Seljuks, the Ottomans, had denuded it to build baths and walls and churches, first in classic Ephesus, and then in Byzantine and medieval Seljuk.

The Mother Goddess had been a warrior, an eater of men, a sacred whore, a virgin huntress, a moon goddess, a witch. Her temple is still there in the drained swamp, and in the walls, the pavings, the columns strewn across the valley, hidden in the newer ruins of Ephesus and Seljuk, that place of worship called the most important in all of Asia Minor, and then, by the Christians and the Muslims, a cave of evil spirits.

The church that replaced it was the first ever dedicated to the Virgin Mary, who, according to legend and Christian tradition, was brought to Ephesus to live in her later years by Saint John.

It was built more than a mile away from the Artemision, lost already by the third century, down by the docks in the classic city, in the place where in pagan times the sailors could find their temple to Aphrodite. The building that became the church had been a large market, with the little house that the Virgin had lived in beside it. The apse is said to have been built over her house, for now the Mother Goddess did not come to the valley of Ephesus in thunder, or as hermaphrodite, or as a warrior of the Amazons, or as a whore or huntress, but as the aging Virgin Mother of Christ.

It was in this church that three hundred bishops of both the eastern part of the Christian church, whose center was the then Roman capital at Constantinople, and the western part, from the Vatican in Rome, met in solemn session in A.D. 431 to argue whether the Virgin Mary was the Mother of God or, as Bishop Nestorius of Constantinople preached, only the mother of the man Jesus. So, while Bishop Nestorius had to be protected by soldiers from the religious riots that raged in the streets, the bishops sat for several months, making one of the holiest metaphors ever conceived by the religious and poetic mind into the dogma that she was the Mother of God.

That church, too, is a ruin. There is a path across waste ground from the church to the bazaar at the commercial entrance to the fenced-in ruins of Ephesus, a bazaar that sells everything from clothes to copies of the ancient images of Artemis with the bull's testicles, which replaced the human castrated offerings, hung in several rows over her bosom. The little statues are not gold or silver anymore, but clay.

Beside the path, unnoticed, is a line of beehives, set there by someone who probably never knew that the bee was sacred to Artemis, that her priests were called Essenes or beekeepers, and that she, as sacred queen bee, was on the ancient coins of the city.

I thought that, instead of going by the main road, I would try to find and follow the path that Wood had discovered from the Artemision to the theater, if any trace of the sacred road still existed. I decided to search for it and, if I could find a trace, follow it around the mountain to the place where archaeologists think the Corresian Gate entered the city walls, although the gate itself has never been found.

So I, a foreign lady dressed in a large sun hat and sensible Reeboks, started one morning in the early sun, at the single standing column that is all that is left above ground of the hundreds of columns that were once the great temple. I set out on the main road until I saw that there was a dirt road, more direct, that ran at an angle through farm fields and up the mountainside.

I dodged invaders in tour buses and private cars on their busy ways, and in a few minutes I had found a path through country silence, headed toward the mountain that is on the north side of the ruins.

I walked past orchards and farmhouses. The little path grew faint beyond the last farmhouse. I began to climb the hill, watching the shadow of my hat on the ground. Nobody had climbed there for so long that weeds had grown high in the middle of it, but it was still marked if only by the slight dip in the otherwise weedy cover and tangled vines. I began to thrust my way through them.

In the middle of what had become a ghost path, I saw the bones and a little of the torn pelt of a large animal—a cow, a deer—eaten there by wild things, and I knew that I had found something of what that world was like when there was no civilized modern overlay. I told myself that whatever beast it was, wolf or wild dog, it was asleep. At least I hoped it was well-fed and asleep.

I went on climbing in the sun that was getting heavier, searching the ground and the undergrowth. At the crest of one of the lower foothills, I looked, and looked again, afraid of being fooled. There it was, a fragment of marble that had been exposed by years of weather, and beyond it, a long straight edge of white marble that glistened in the light.

I had played at being Wood and I had found it, the sacred road. I went all blithe and brave in the morning, a nice lady in a big hat. I parted weeds, and struggled through vines, and when I parted two small saplings I found that I had walked to what I first thought was a cliff. It was not.

Down below me, still far away from the ruins of the ancient city within its fence and with its guides and crowds, was the small marble atrium of a lost suburban house. Weeds grew in an empty shallow pool. On either side of marble steps, there were still two dolphins that had once been fountains that poured water from their mouths into the pool. I slid down the hill to the level of the floor, and I walked a short path of marble to its door, where the two truncated columns on either side still showed the grooves where, at night, they would have closed the house to marauders.

But one night the marauders had come to this house, and it had been so long abandoned that nothing of any world was left there but a Roman atrium, a little pool, two dolphins, a threshold, and silence in the sun.

I went on past it, up along the crest of the hill again. I slipped and slid and felt a fool, and at one point thought, if I break an ankle or my leg on this hill, I won't be found until I am a lady skeleton in a big hat, picked clean. I parted the underbrush and looked down upon another atrium, this one large and complete, with a fountain base in the center, and roofless rooms beyond it. The wall looked about ten feet high, and I skirted the top of it, holding onto small trees for balance, to look for a way down.

I hadn't heard anything move, yet he stood there in front of me, smiling, quite silent, a large strong Turkish man, holding in his hand a small bunch of sweet wild thyme. He held it toward me, saying nothing, still smiling. There was something so gentle about him that I could not be afraid. I took the wild thyme, and I thanked him, in Turkish. He smiled again and touched his mouth and his ear. He was deaf and dumb. I still have the wild thyme, pressed and dried, kept like a Victorian lady's souvenir of the Holy Land.

Dumb was the wrong word for him. There was no need for speech. He was an actor, an eloquent mime. I pointed to the atrium below and held my hands apart to show I didn't know how to get down into it. He took my arm, and carefully, slowly, led me down a steep pile of rubble.

He mimed the opening of a nonexistent door and ushered me through it. He showed me roofless room after roofless room as if he had discovered them. He dug and threw imaginary earth over his shoulder to show that it had been dug up.

I think that he had scared people before, and he was happy that there was someone who would let him show his house, for it was his house. Maybe he did sleep there. I don't know. I only know that he treated me as a guest in a ruin ten feet below the level of the ground, and that he took me from room to room where once there had been marble walls and now there was only stone, where he was host and owner for a little while.

He showed me a small pool, held out his hand the height of a small child, and then swam across the air. All the time he smiled. He took me to a larger pool and swam again. Then he grabbed my arm and led me through a dark corridor toward what I thought at first was a cave. It was not. He sat down in a niche in the corridor, and strained until his face was pink, to show me it was the toilet. Then he took me into the kitchen where there were two ovens. They were almost complete, except that the iron doors were gone. The arches of narrow Byzantine bricks were graceful over them, and the ovens were large as if there had been a large family there.

For the first one he rolled dough for bread, kneaded it in air, slapped it, and put it in the oven. Then he took it out, broke it, and shared it with me. I ate the air with him. The other was the main oven, and he picked vegetables from the floor of the cave kitchen, hit air to kill an animal, made a stew, and placed it in the stone and brick niche. We ate it and then we walked out into the sun of the larger atrium. Behind it, in the hill, he gestured that it had not yet been dug up, and then he pointed to a marble votive herma, whose head was missing, and knelt behind it, grinning, and set his own head there, to show me what it was. The grin was ancient, a satyr's grin.

We stood beyond his house on the edge of the hill, looking down on the buses and the crowd in the distance. Across and behind the noise and crowds, in a field, looking abandoned too, was the church of the Virgin Mary. The house where we stood had looked out over that and the harbor, and although it has not been found, I knew that it was near where the Corresian Gate had been.

When I gave my friend, my *arkadaş,* some money, he kissed my hand and held it to his forehead, and then, pleased with the sun and me, and the fact that someone had not run away from him who lived like Caliban in a ruin, he put his arms around me and kissed me on both cheeks. Then I went down the hill to Ephesus. When I looked back to wave he had disappeared.

What was the place? I've tried to find it in the books that tell what digging has been done at Ephesus, but this was outside the walls and not important enough to document, except for one obscure mention, that someone had dug there in 1926 and that there had been suburban mansions on the mountainside, and I already knew that. It exists across the tradition of a road, near a lost gate, near the stadium where Porphyrios the Mime was martyred as a Christian. Or maybe it was another Porphyrios; it was so long ago and there were so many martyrs.

CHAPTER
SEVENTEEN

CIRCLES OF SPACE
AND TIME

COULDN'T AVOID going to Bodrum any longer. So after sixteen years of nostalgia and memory, it was time, if it would ever be. I went with one of my dearest American friends. I thought of him as imported friendship in case all my old friends were gone, or changed, or rich, or had forgotten me.

As we got nearer Bodrum, my worst fears were beginning to be realized. There was a constant traffic jam along the wide new paved road that ignored the ancient monuments so that vacation vans and cars and buses could speed into the town.

I recognized nothing as we drove in, not one landmark of the place I had known for three years. We turned into the main street along the Turkish harbor, and at last I saw something I knew—the little mosque beside the sea, with its slender minaret insignificant against the masts of foreign yachts.

Where there had been local *bakkals,* small groceries, and food stores that stayed open half the night on hot nights in the old days when nobody could sleep, hotels and rich villas gleaming with new white paint and concrete stretched along the quays. There were offices for Avis, American Express, and Benetton; a private yacht club; a limo service; rug after rug after rug shop.

When we walked out along the wide elegant new quay, built over a shore where I used to watch the tide go in and out, I counted a hundred yachts from all over the world, nestled beside each other in the *liman* where once in high summer there might have been ten. There were no fishing boats, no sponge-diving boats among them.

All the way up to the walls of Halicarnassus, the empty hillside meadows were covered with holiday houses, all alike, that looked from a distance like white skulls. When I went to look for the ancient theater I found it, after a hard climb, beyond the new noisy highway, full of traffic, dangerous to cross.

It was Friday, but the *pazar* had moved away from the main square. That had been made into an informal parking space for taxis, parked nose to nose. They roared and sped and honked day and night up and down the narrow streets. I saw not one *dolmuş;* any self-respecting camel would have scorned the place. There were no donkeys, no carts from the country. Bodrum had been completely mechanized.

There were no country people at the *pazar.* The beautiful vegetable market was organized and permanent, stretched under awnings along the main road into Bodrum. The display was as colorful as it had always been. But the booths in the clothing and hardware *pazar* were full of shoddy imitations of Western clothes and souvenirs for tourists.

It was no longer my sweet, kind, quiet town. It was, to me, a place that had been changed by invasion, as the cities I had seen in Anatolia had been changed and overlaid centuries ago. But this was twentieth-century invasion, Yenibodrum, New Bodrum. It is busy and shining and very, very rich, white as bone, too elegant for the country people I had known to live there any more.

They are all gone: the carpenter, the fishermen, the sponge divers, the *dolmuşes* stuffed with country people. When I looked for the place where I had lived, I couldn't even recognize the street.

All the way along the Greek side of the town there were bars and hotels where there had been *bakkals,* fairly primitive *lokantas,* and small houses. Large charter boats clung together out at the end of a pier, some advertising belly dancers. The old Halikarnas Hotel on a point at the end of the bay had become a chic and noisy motel-cum-disco that I was told pulsed through the night. In front of it, new Greek temple columns thrust up against the sky—a folly of "ancient" ruins.

At our secret beach east of the town, where I had gone with my friends and lain on the beach and thought of Vietnam and seventeenth-century England, a grand complex called TMT Motel has been built, with gardens, a swimming pool, and tennis courts. I could have been in Florida.

There are retreats though. At the Mavi Ev, one of the new small bars and hotels, we sat in the evening in a charming, quiet, wood-paneled room. It was already October and there was a fire in the fireplace, and, modern or not, it was as welcoming as a private house. Artemis Pansiyon, the old family-run hotel at the Greek end where scuba divers have always stayed, had changed least, even in clientele. So there are places to escape noise and planned confusion.

The museum is now organized and safe and full of treasures, but the sense of discovery is gone, and at night young Turkish men dress up like Crusaders under the new floodlights. It is far too regimented to allow anyone to risk life and limb climbing to the top of a broken tower to see the harbor. The ancient harbor is no longer visible under the water, anyway. It is completely covered with yachts.

The two little streets to the modern harbor, where Ahmet had his shop and where I used to buy Turkish shirts, where there was a tiny bar to meet friends on quiet evenings, had been changed into a *pazar* that has the reputation of being "the best boutique in the Med," with all the jet-set customers that the language implies. Well-dressed visitors from the yachts strolled there, buying in the early evening, to the sound of Western music from the shops, and then crowded the expensive restaurants. In a country whose cuisine is superb, it is indicative of what has happened to Bodrum that the most expensive and highly recommended restaurant is Italian, a charming place called Langolo Italiano, hidden up a side street, far from the music and the noise.

The new shops are wonderful, all the color and smell of gold and silk and leather and fine rugs, a scent of luxury that must have been in the bazaar in Bursa in early Ottoman times. And they are fun. At Dirava Pazar you can have your portrait made of Turkish carpet from a passport photograph. The whole outdoor boutique has the color and shape and gleam and texture of riches, but there are fine bargains, too. A narrow street is overhung with inexpensive comfortable *şalvar*. At the end of it a tailor, Yilmaz, made attractive Turkish jackets of quilted cotton to wear with jeans or jewelry, and made them in a day.

It seemed churlish to mourn. I stopped searching for what was gone and began to enjoy what was there—a new Bodrum, shining white in the sun. I stayed this time in the house of Ahmet Ertegün. My room was the size that my house and my courtyard had been, and there was a bathroom at either end of it, this time all the way indoors.

The house is the most beautiful restoration in Bodrum, rebuilt from the ruins of four Ottoman houses surrounding an overgrown garden, where once, when it was still a ruin, I used to go for picnics among the old neglected fruit trees, the wild flowers, and the fragments of fluted columns from the ancient city of Halicarnassus. The reconstruction reflects traditional Bodrum: old wooden harem screens, traditional white walls against fine carpets, local crochetwork used perfectly, lush shrubs, well-cared-for trees. This is, in essence, the change in Bodrum at its best.

Then I got off the chic front streets of shops and sought out, with little hope of finding him, Ali Güven, who used to make the best sandals I have ever worn. I found him. When I walked in after sixteen years, he looked up, and looked again, and shouted out, "Marileeyim," My Mary Lee! We hugged each other for pure joy.

The sandals are more than ten times the price they were; Ali Güven is now known as the best sandalmaker in the Aegean. But his shop is exactly the same: the same smell of leather, the same piles of useful junk, the same smile, the same hugs, the same cups of tea, the same superb sandals—but a clientele of famous names.

I used to buy jewelry from eastern Turkey that my dear friends, Lale and Haluk, brought back from their winter travels. Now they have become internationally known jewelry designers, and their tiny shop at the corner of the quay serves a steady stream of chic European customers. They also make fine replicas of museum jewelry and coins for the Turkish government.

Lale and I went to lunch at Gümüşlük, the ancient town of Mindos, on the other side of Bodrum peninsula. It has been protected against the newness and, in a lot of places, the exploitation of Bodrum by being declared an historic zone. There we sat at a table on the quay outside a restaurant that we had gone to all that time ago. It was exactly the same. We ate *barbunya,* the red mullet that is the best fish in the Aegean. Time stopped for me. I sat at a table I had known and looked at the calm sea. There was even the same fragment of a Greek column, used as a doorsill.

İsmet, my other best friend, who taught me to scuba dive so long ago, is still the same kind and thoughtful seagoing man. He runs his own fine charter boat along what is now called in the brochures the Turquoise Coast, and to Gökova Bay, where we used to anchor in nearly empty coves for the night. Now the coves of Gökova Bay are crowded with boats.

His is the family that still runs Artemis Pansiyon. He is captain of the same boat that I saw launched more than sixteen years ago, and it is a photograph of the bloody handprint that Ismet put on the side of the boat in the traditional way after the goat was sacrificed that is on the cover of my novel about Turkey, *Blood Tie*.

Sandalmaker, jewelry designer, sea captain—they all greeted me as if we had seen each other the day before instead of fifteen years ago. I was at home again, in that place where the word *friend* carries the weight and warmth of centuries. Bodrum became the place I had known and remembered as if I had dreamed a new city. Streets fell into place, familiar again, with all the affection, the kindness that had made Bodrum one of the happiest places I had ever lived.

It was still there, as it had been for three thousand years, I am sure. Cities don't change in spirit. Bodrum is still Bodrum because it has never lost what made it unique—a capacity for easygoing, insouciant friendship.

It was only on the surface that the new Bodrum had overlain my memory, as Bodrum had overlain Halicarnassus so long ago. When I had to leave, and it was as hard as it had been sixteen years before, I climbed up beyond the new houses to see if the city wall was still there. I had been afraid it was gone because I had not been able to find the floor of the temple, which had been on top of the ancient acropolis, and the deep well behind it with the snakes was long gone, filled in. Where the snakes had gone I hesitated to think.

There was the wall, forgotten on the mountain, the titanic stones, the Mindos Gate. I looked from there down at Bodrum, in its cup of a valley below the mountains, for the last time. What had shrunk to a small village for a thousand of those years had grown again to the size of Halicarnassus when it was one of the leading ports of the civilized world.

There was one more place to stop before I went back to İzmir, to İstanbul, to New York. One day in the spring of 1974 Lale and I decided that we would go and see the ancient city of Heraclia-under-Latmos on Lake Bafa, tucked into a gorge of the mountain where Endymion is supposed to sleep, visited at night by his lover, Selene, the moon goddess.

It had been a seaport and a sacred place on an inlet of the Aegean during the time of the Carians for a thousand years before the invasion of

Alexander. Slow silting up of the Maeander had cut it off from the sea, so long ago that the water in Lake Bafa, the lake it made, is clear, pure, sweet water. The port is long gone and the shore has changed so that some of the graves cut into rock are beneath the water, and at night the empty graves are underwater shadows glimpsed by the moon they once worshiped.

Time, and the slow fall of buildings no longer needed, the invasions of wild herdsmen, and the loss of its people have turned Heraclia, which means holy city, into a ghost place. We thought that anyway, going there.

We left at 5:30 in the morning on the bus from Bodrum, two hours away, while it was still dark. There had been a lot of teasing about our going, for the town and the mountain are owned, or were then, by one of the more powerful *ağas,* who was said to keep a private army and to shelter bandits, but this was late in the twentieth century and armed bandits belonged in movies and, after all, we were to go only a few miles off the main road to İzmir, one of Turkey's most civilized cities. So amid taunts from our friends that we would be kidnapped, raped, kept prisoner, shot, we set out in the early morning on the bus with passengers going to Muğla, the provincial capital. All of these jokes were called out in the predawn as the bus left Bodrum. The Turks will make a celebration of getting on the bus, and their jokes tend to be violent.

We watched the dawn come up from the sea in the distance. At Muğla workmen got on, and the bus smelled of men and sleep. A boy with a tray held by a chain sold *ayran,* the drink made from yogurt and water, in the little marketplace.

We had no idea how we would get to Heraclia when the bus let us off under a tree beside the road in the clean, empty morning. It was an adventure. They are easy to have, a few steps away always in Turkey. There was the ever-present Turkish taxi, its driver waiting, half-asleep in the shade, in case someone got off the bus. He seemed ready to stay there, lodged at the side of the road, for however many days it took for a passenger to turn up.

This was not the tourist season; it was early spring, the best time to travel in Turkey, that and the fall, when the air is crisp, the roads emptier, and the days cool.

When we got into the taxi, the Turkish between Lale and the taxi driver already far too complicated for me to follow, an old man, who had been sitting on a rock under the tree, came over and simply got into the front seat.

Lale explained that he had been waiting for someone to take the taxi so that he could ride up to his village, which was four miles around the mountain from Heraclia. He, too, had been prepared to wait all day for the next bus or the next or the next. The pace of Turkey was catching. We set off slowly up the rutted road.

Mount Latmos loomed, cragged and fearsome, over the whole end of the lake. The local people call it Beşparmak, five fingers, for the dagged shape of its heights. It seems too diminutive a name for such a huge, lowering mountain that has contained so much legend and still contained, in its crags and in its heights, hidden terror, although that morning we didn't know it. But perhaps the new name wasn't so much lack of imagination as that quality that makes us turn the old and formidable gods into fairies, so that we can bear their presence without fear.

All the way around the end of the lake, the old man asked questions. I could only catch a few words. He asked Lale where we came from, how many children we each had, where our husbands were, why they allowed us to come to Kapikiri, which is the modern Turkish name for the little village that perches on the ruins of Heraclia.

Lale told me later how she had answered the questions. She made me into a widow, because she said he wouldn't understand anything as farfetched as a woman who traveled alone, much less one who was a writer. I had only caught one word, *melek,* which means angel.

We let the old man out at the road to his village; he would walk another four miles around the base of the mountain to get there. Melek, Lale told me, was his cousin. She said he had told us to say that we were his friends, an open sesame in Turkey, and that he had sent us to her. He said that we would find Melek in the village and she would welcome us. We drove into the tiny town square, where there was a central well with an ancient carving, nearly obscured by weather and time, and there she was, the head of her family, dressed in *şalvar,* with the familiar bright striped shawl over her head that has replaced the *yaşmak.*

She was a small rosy woman, with a face of such satisfaction with life and such kindness that she made me feel bedraggled. When Lale asked her if there were a place to stay, she said, of course, that we would stay the night at her own house. She explained that there was no place else, and that she could not accept any pay or, she said she would, Lale told me, be shamed forever before God.

The present-day village of Kapıkırı was built on a white table rock. Melek took us up the hill along a steep, rocky path. What age the houses were I couldn't say. But they had been there for so long they seemed to grow out of the rock surface of the small plateau between the mountain and the great ancient wall of Heraclia that we could see up to our left.

Melek's house was behind a pure white wall with a small wooden door painted bright blue that I had to bend down to go in. Inside the courtyard, on the right, there were stalls for a goat and two sheep, so that the immaculate courtyard smelled of animals and spicy geraniums in olive-oil cans. We left our shoes at the door, and walked into a minimal whiteness that would have warmed the heart of the most modern aesthete.

The only color came from the bright *kilims* on the whitened stone floor, Melek's clothes, and a few copper pots. There were two other rooms that seemed at first not to have individual functions. Melek made a tiny fire with a few sticks in the fireplace of the first of them. She must have whitened the fireplace with lime every morning for, with the hundreds of years that it had probably been used, there was little sign of fire stain.

At whatever age they are, Turkish women in the villages can sink to the floor like ballet dancers. Lale and I followed Melek down, our more civilized muscles groaning. Melek rolled out dough for *börek* on a small round wooden table about eight inches from the floor, and baked it in an iron dish directly over the embers of the fire. It was superb. The little table, which looked like it had been made in the village, was the only piece of furniture I saw in Melek's house.

This is the way she made the flat bread that would be *börek,* a meat or vegetable pie, for our supper. "This is their manner of making them; they have a small round table, very smooth, on which they throw some flour, and mix it with water into a paste, softer than that for bread. This paste they divide into round pieces, which they flatten as much as possible, with a wooden roller of a smaller diameter than an egg, until they make them as thin as I have mentioned. During this operation they have a convex plate of iron placed on a tripod, and heated by a gentle fire underneath, on which they spread the cake and instantly turn it, so that they make two of their cakes sooner than a waferman can make one wafer."

That is not my description but that of a sixteenth-century traveler, Brocquière, but Melek did exactly the same thing. I recognized the *börek* table. I had had the carpenter make me one to use in my own small house in Bodrum.

Melek's house and her courtyard could have been the house of a family three thousand years ago when this had been a holy city. The walls were thick to keep the heat and the cool inside, like Saracen houses around the Mediterranean. There was a fireplace in each room and a pile of pillows in the corner of the larger room, where we went to have our tea. A raised platform stretched along one wall.

By the time we were sitting there having tea, the women had begun, silently, to filter into the room and sit around the walls, while Melek took Lale through the same series of questions that her cousin had in the taxi. Lale went on with her Byzantine story of my life for them. When I asked her why she had made it up, she simply said that she had told them what they were familiar with, as if she were speaking their language. It seemed somehow to be rude there to be so direct as to tell the bald and brazen truth instead of a story, the best use of Byzantine circumlocution that I had heard in Turkey.

Outside the glassless window of Melek's larger room the mountain loomed. She saw me watching it and she told Lale to tell me that they went there to gather wood, but that they never went alone, that there were dangerous *periler* there. *Peri* is the Turkish word for fairy.

I knew then that I was going to climb the mountain. On the way to a narrow gorge that looked easy to climb, I crossed the small fields where the low rock walls defined pasture for the goats and sheep. I realized that these were not farm walls, but the ruins of houses, an *agora,* and beyond the rock-fenced fields a long wall that had been colonnaded once.

Beyond me, nearer to the mountain, in one of the last of the house ruins, I saw a man standing under a tree, looking at me with that sad watchfulness of Turkish police everywhere. He was not doing anything; he was simply watching. I had a feeling that he wished I had not come so he could go back and sit in the rustic *kahve* we had passed near the town well. I recognized him, too, by the neat boots, the air of being well dressed but poor, unlike the village men that we had passed on the way to Melek's who wore the male version of the *şalvar* with ragged Western jackets. He did nothing, only watched sadly, until I had started to climb the side of the gorge, up the mountain that rose above my head for five thousand feet of geologically new raw crags, for this is earthquake country and the mountains are young and very much alive.

I climbed what I thought at first was natural rock, then I saw that I was following ancient steps all the way up the cleft in the mountain, and at the top of the gorge, way above me, was a titanic wall of huge square stones. It seemed to have no use. It was not for protection. It was too obscured for that by the higher cliffs behind it. I wondered if the wall was, quite practically, to catch water in the winter. Melek had told us that the village was deserted in summer, partly because the whole village moved to camp near down in the valley of the Maeander, where they earned a living picking cotton. She had added that they would have had to leave anyway since the rock base became too hot to live on, and there was no water in summer.

Somewhere higher up the mountain, long since lost in this gorge or another one, lay the cave of Endymion, whose name means "he who finds himself within." He is within Latmos forever and within the tender caul of the love of Selene, the moon. He lives still as psychic truth, deeply resonant and acceptable, a form for something known and loved and hated and feared: the deep unfathomable love of son for mother, once worshiped as lovers, then tabooed as incestuous, then honored in reality, unless the mother appears as the destructive goddess.

As Selene she rose above Mount Latmos at night, horned by the new moon—huge, chthonic, protective and terrible in might—and sought out the beautiful, dying or sleeping lover-son, the sacrifice. This time, unlike the dead Adonis, Endymion was not killed but condemned to its substitute for human sacrifice, to sleep forever, containing in his legend, beyond new taboos, new beliefs, a black stone of basic primal truth.

Somewhere on the mountain, where I leaned against the rock wall to keep from falling, the unknown cave still protected his legend—the hidden, deceptively safe young man. When the Roman Empire became Christian, monasteries were built on the mountain and on islands in the lake, and Heraclia became a bishopric. The monks turned Endymion into a Christian saint who went to the mountain to sleep and dream the secret name of God. When he died they made his tomb in a rock wall like the one I leaned against, and when they opened it once a year at his festival, they could hear him humming, trying to tell them the name.

Far away below me, down the slope of the village, I could see the rock tombs of the monks shadowed under the water of the lake.

There was, I tried not to admit it, something, not sinister, but beyond understanding about the mountain as I climbed higher, and the wind found me and pushed me to the mother rock, and I could feel my hackles rise. I tried not to let it bother me. Maybe I thought that I might find my own Endymion's cave or, like the monks in the sixth century, hear the whispered name of God.

I had got to the path directly below the wall at the head of the gorge. It rose above me, a useless giant monument of dark brute rocks, a man-made cliff. Then I heard something that did raise my hackles, so alone there, so far from anything, with no human in sight.

But there was one, a small boy who had followed me up the mountain. I stood still. When he caught up with me he said, or I thought he said, "Your friend is crying." When I seemed not to understand enough, he did wipe his eyes and point down to the roof of Melek's house. Slowly, again, he said, "Your friend cries for you. Come. *Gel*," he said. "She is *tasali*," and to show her worry, he wrinkled up his forehead like an old man and wiped his eyes again.

I began to follow him down the mountain, with a strong sense that there was something behind me I hadn't quite found there. When he saw that I was on my way, he bounded ahead. Whether he was running to get off the mountain or was just released from his duty, I never knew.

I remembered that Melek told about gathering wood, so I picked up as many sticks as I could find to take back. This seemed to be received as almost an imperial act of politeness, as if they were surprised that foreign widows would know to gather wood. I asked Lale to tell them that I, too, was from the mountains.

Lale was surprised to see me back. When I said that I understood that she was worried about my climbing the mountain, she laughed.

"No," she told me, "Melek wanted you to come back, so she told the boy to tell you that." Even on a small walk up a mountain, everybody, including Lale, seemed involved in a legend more acceptable than truth.

At six o'clock we sat around the small *börek* table on the floor and Melek spread a cloth that covered the table and our legs. We ate *börek* again, with glasses of *ayran,* and thick dark hunks of the good bread that Melek had baked in the village oven, and a salad gathered from the fields among the ruins.

There were five of us—Lale and me, Melek, her daughter-in-law, and her granddaughter, who had the Greek name of Zefir, a lovely child of fourteen. Where the men were or if there were men in that house I didn't know yet. I had seen none except the men at the *kahve,* the small boy, and the plainclothes policeman.

But in the early evening, while it was still light, the whole village, men and women, began to file into Melek's room as if they knew exactly when Zefir would take the remains of our dinner and the table away again. Dignified and tattered, they came, one by one, and sat on the floor around the walls. When an old man walked into the room, the younger men got to their feet and one, who, Lale whispered, was his son, came up to him, bowed his head, took his father's hand, kissed the back of it, and touched his own forehead with it. The manners of the Ottoman Empire had fetched up there in an obscure village. From the time the old man came in his son, who must have been about thirty, never sat down in his presence, but leaned against the white entry to the room, where I could see that the walls were more than a foot thick.

I watched the mountain glow in the sunset and then darken as the night came on and there was only the light from the fire on their faces, and the bright end of the old man's cigarette. None of the younger men smoked in front of him. The mountain had disappeared into blackness. The villagers, too, seemed to go into the night slowly, as the mountain itself did, not expecting any more than the lowering of day, the fire, the voices.

The silence got heavier, punctuated only by short questions to Lale from the old man who sat imperiously smoking a cigarette. Then he began to speak, as if he were telling a story, and everybody listened and nobody interrupted.

Later, whispering in Melek's storeroom, we lay in the pitch dark on straw pallets on the floor with *kilims* over us, still in our clothes, for it was cold below the mountain, while small creatures scuttled among the sacks of feed. Lale told me that Melek was a widow and the old man was the head of the family, Melek's brother. The story he had told was that he had been once to Bodrum where he saw naked women, and women with hair on their arms, and women who went into the bars—a terrible place. He intended to go back sometime, but none of the rest were to go there; it was too sinful a place for them.

"You don't know the trouble you have gotten me into," Lale said before she went to sleep. "These are Shiites, you can tell by the manners. You may find them romantic, but I am a Turk and I have accepted their hospitality and if I don't give it back the same way, it would cause a blood feud.''

The next morning at dawn, when the place was cool and washed clean by the night, Melek gave us breakfast the same way, sitting around the eight-inch-high wooden *börek* board. She told us that Zefir would show us where all the ruins were.

I could read Melek's house in a new, or old, way in the new light. It had no age; it had simply risen there around a courtyard—the size of the rooms, the thick walls, the way people there had always lived. It could have been a thousand years old, shored up each year—all the houses I saw were cared for in this way, whitewashed, so neatly patched that I had to look carefully at the courtyard wall to see where human or animal had driven into it and left a scar. When? It had ceased to matter to me as it had long ago ceased to them. The world was alive around them, whether it had happened yesterday or another day or another century.

Zefir moved ahead of us, lithe as her ancient namesake, the west wind, through the small central square where the baker was already shoveling bread into his open brick oven with a long pole, flattened at the end, and the men who had sat around the room the night before had already gathered at the *kahve,* looking as if they had come straight back there after they left Melek's house, to wait for the morning.

We climbed to the temple floor on the left foothill that made a natural platform above the fountain. From there, where the marble floor and the walls were still intact, we had an Artemis-view of what had once been the harbor and now had only a few fishing boats pulled up on the shore. A tiny Byzantine monastery had been on the little island in the old harbor, and now it lay in ruins, reflected in the morning calm of the water. Beyond the dry ditch that had been the Marsyas River, the sun already drenched the mountaintop.

It was getting hot on the marble platform, where the statue of Artemis must have looked through the open front of the temple down on the port activity on such a morning, in the days when this was a busy seaport, before the Maeander closed the end of the inlet and made it into the lake we were watching.

We climbed slowly up the footholds carved in the left side of the huge wall that surrounded Heraclia, higher and higher up the main gorge of the village. The stones were even larger than I had thought, and, while ghosts of the small men with their armor shining no longer climbed there for me, not on a sun-splashed morning anyway, the sheer size of the high walls told of the constant, taken-for-granted danger that would make a ruler build such a massive shield—against what?

Sometimes the answer was as simple as the nearest towns, for Kapikiri is not the only modern village to hide within itself a city of the past. There were, clutched around the foothills of Latmos, several towns that had been on the borders of the Carian kingdom when Mausolus ruled. They had, even then, a history of raids on each other. Was it for trade, for religion, for the always longed-for, obsessive pleasure of power? They seem to have had constant wars in this part of the world tucked under the mountains, and only what for them would have been short periods of peace, sometimes five hundred years, sometimes a thousand. Those numbers are small in a land as old as this.

Across the little hollow made by the river we saw the shrine to Endymion. Zefir led us down to it and we sat under the one small tree that grew between the ruined floor stones and the great pile of murex shells that lay so deep on the open floor of the shrine that they had become, long since, a part of the ground itself.

These are the seashells, sacred to the Mother Goddess as Aphrodite, from which Tyrian purple dye was made, the color of royalty. There has been no saltwater here for nearly two thousand years. The shells have simply been left where they were dropped after whatever feasts or sacrifices took place there.

The shrine is small, and its shell-shaped opening looks up toward the high platform of Athena or Aphrodite or Artemis. Whatever the Mother Goddess and her lover-son were called they were metaphors for the same beliefs, the holy family without father, or later with the recognition of a father in the demiurge, and the mother, enclosing "the one who finds himself within" her again, as cave, mountain, and temple.

Zefir stood in front of us, like a good storyteller, while we all ate the bread and cheese that Melek had given us. She pointed to the mountain. Lale told me that she said that an anarchist had been caught there by the gendarmes and that her village had helped them. It had been, she said, very exciting.

Lale and I both remembered that there had been an item in the paper about an anarchist student leader from, I think, İstanbul, who had been hiding in the mountains and had been caught. Zefir said that her own village had helped the gendarmes because they had found out that people in their enemy village, a few miles away, were hiding him. Lale asked her what had happened.

"They found him on the mountain and they brought him down into our village and they beat him and beat him to death," Lale translated what Zefir said while she waited, smiling in the sun, "and then the gendarmes congratulated us for helping and we had a great feast."

"Ask her," I said, "what an anarchist is."

"Oh," she answered, "they are human like you and me, but they have long beards."

We found out later that the young man had not been killed, but had been beaten and then jailed. I asked Lale when I saw her again after so long, if she had heard of the man again. She laughed and said, "He is editing a weekly paper in İstanbul."

Zefir's story was more dramatic, more ancient. This country has been raided and laid waste, and memories of drama are old, and how was a young student from İstanbul to know he had fallen into an ancient village feud? Maybe the story of Endymion had as real a beginning: the young shepherd found and beaten and beaten and left to die, turned in memory to sleep, protected by the Mother Goddess—a story to cover a sacrifice.

When there is so little thought of time, only of winter when they live on the ruins in their already ancient houses; summer when they go down to the Maeander River where there is work in the cotton fields and there is water; the time the young man was found on the mountain; the time the walls were patrolled by Carians, then Romans, then Seljuks, then Turkish soldiers; or when the Mongol herdsmen came, more and more of them, more inexorable than savage, to the small gorge below Mount Latmos; it all flows together, seasonal, timeless, the way things are, and nothing is forgotten.

So I asked my taxi driver to turn off the main road to İzmir, this time fifteen years later. We drove around the end of Lake Bafa, toward the mountain. We passed farms. I had forgotten that there were farms below the mountain, wherever anything could be grown. Then there were open fields, and then the hollows where house-size rocks had been thrown down by the mountain as if sometime it had been besieged.

It was the same, but I didn't know it. I had been there once, for so short a time. I walked up what I thought was the right path, looking for a blue door with little hope of finding it. The village was on a steeper slope than I had remembered, and it threw my direction off. Then I saw it, a little house with a blue door and a courtyard, below the level of the road.

There was nobody there. The place was silent. I turned to go back down the hill. A woman was coming up the hill, a village woman with a rosy face. I said, in my slow and labored Turkish, *"Melek nerede?"* Where is Melek? I was afraid to hear the answer.

"I am Melek," she said, and then I recognized her. I said, "Fifteen years ago my friend Lale and I came from Bodrum . . ."

I got no farther. She hugged me and kissed me on both cheeks, *"Hoşgeldin, canim,"* she was so excited that she called out to her neighbors. *"Iyi arkadaşım! Iyi arkadaşım! Gel! Gel!"* My good friend! Come! Come! She brought wood down from the mountain for me!" She had remembered me through that small incident. I couldn't stay, so I promised that I would come back and stay with her again, and neither of us believed it but it was part of the affection, the politeness. In the road I looked back and she was still standing there, smiling and waving. I called out the Turkish good-bye, *"Allahaısmarladık,"* I am putting myself into the hands of God. She answered, *"Güle, güle"* Go happily. Then I went on to İzmir, and İstanbul, and home.

I have a friend in Virginia who, nearly forty years ago, was in a prison camp in Korea. His life was saved by a Turk. He told me that hundreds of GIs died there. "We didn't know how to look after ourselves, and the Turks took pity on us. They thought we were babes in the woods. My friend was Hakim. When I was sick he brought me food, and he looked after me as he would have another Turkish person. They knew how to survive." He was silent for a long time, back there, and I was not a part of that.

Finally he said, "I won't tell you the bad part. I will tell you the good part. When we were caught, most of us had American GI scrip in our pockets. It became the rate of exchange in the camp and, in a year, the Turks had all the scrip. When our sweaters and socks wore out, they picked the wool apart and reknitted it. Hakim made me a pair of socks.

"Every day they knelt and prayed to the southwest where Mecca was, and when the Chinese soldiers hit them in the butt with bayonets to make them get up, they stood and said, 'Kill me. I will go straight to Heaven.' Then they turned their backs on the soldiers and knelt to finish their prayers. After a while the Chinese let them alone. I think they were a little afraid of them, even though they were armed and the Turks were not, not with guns, anyway. Not one single one of them went to a communist orientation lecture. They said they couldn't understand the language, but after a while, most of them had found a friend to help, who in return of friendship, would teach them English. We had informers among us, and we knew who they were. I still know. The Turks did not have one single informer.

"They didn't have any more to eat than we did, but they shared it. When I was so sick I thought I was going to die, Hakim brought me soup, and sat with me, and pulled me through it. I think he gave me courage; so many GIs just died because they gave up, but the Turkish soldiers in the camp didn't lose a single man. They looked after each other. They organized, and when one of them was sick, the others shared what little food they had with him until he was well again.

"I taught Hakim English, and he taught me Turkish. He studied it so well that he became a driver for an American officer in Turkey after the war. But I only remember one Turkish phrase. I have remembered it for nearly forty years. It is *Iyi arkadaşım*, my good friend."

A NOTE ABOUT THE AUTHOR

Mary Lee Settle lived in Turkey from 1972 to 1974. In 1989 she returned to that country. This is the story of what she discovered and rediscovered. She won the National Book Award for *Blood Tie* in 1978. The novel is set in Turkey. She is also the author of the Beulah Quintet. She lives in Charlottesville, Virginia.